SECRET POWER

To Ken,

From Fritz & da boys.

WANKER.

To Julia, Rose and Tom, with love.

SECRET POWER

NICKY HAGER

CRAIG
POTTON
PUBLISHING

Published by Craig Potton Publishing
Box 555, Nelson, New Zealand.

First published 1996

©Copyright 1996 Nicky Hager

ISBN 0 908802 35 8

CONTENTS

ACKNOWLEDGEMENTS

A large amount of painstaking research went into documenting the secret activities described in this book. I could never have done this without the help, in ways large and small, of many other people. When I look through my notes it is clear how much it has been a group effort. I hope these people will feel that the result has been worthwhile.

First, I want to acknowledge several dozen people who, by virtue of their positions within government organisations and elsewhere, cannot be named. Most of them would deserve special thanks, if they could be identified, for the information and comments they provided and for the trust they showed me by being prepared to help. Some of them will not agree with all that I have written and my conclusions; in these cases I appreciate all the more that they were still willing to contribute information in the public interest. My special thanks also to those people (whoever you are) who provided information anonymously.

Of the people I can name, thanks first to Owen Wilkes, who helped me get started on this book and, more generally, played a large part in raising public awareness around the world of the implications of electronic intelligence activities. Other researchers have helped me greatly with information, comments and encouragement: thanks to Duncan Campbell and Jeff Richelson in particular, who, over several years, have given a lot of useful guidance and helped me put my New Zealand research into an international context, and also to Peter Wills, Bill Robinson and Des Ball. I am also grateful to Bob White and the Centre for Peace Studies for their support. Thanks to the Ombudsmen and their staff, Leo Donnelly in particular, for all the time spent reviewing official information matters for me; and to librarians in general. I have enjoyed working with the editor Anna Rogers and the publishers Robbie Burton and Craig Potton. I have been lucky to have such friendly and supportive publishers.

The greatest thanks go to my friends, workmates and family. Over the years of research and then writing I have relied a lot on their encouragement and practical support, including help with fieldwork, library work, compiling information and commenting on drafts. In particular, I want to acknowledge (in alphabetical order): Jill Bagnall, Paul Bensemann, Gordon Campbell, John Carter, Jim Chapple, Karen Coulton, Mark Derby, Steve

Dixon, Alistair Duncan, Jenny Easton, Mike Ennis, Lyn Holland, Ann Hunt, Michael Kopp, Alison McCulloch, Kate McPherson, Ken Mansell, Claire Mortimer, Raymond Pelly, Llyn Richards, Mark Roach, Sian Robinson, Ron Smith, Erin Taylor, Kerry Taylor, Lisa Thompson, Warren Thomson, Lynette Thorstenson, Diana Unwin, Joy Vasbenter, Nick Wheeler, Tony Wills, Evin Wood and Julian Young. Special thanks to Kevin Hackwell, Christina Wells, Fergus Wheeler and all of my family.

There are others, too many to list, who helped with research, fieldwork, illustrations, production and distribution, passed on pieces of information and contacts, replied to my letters, put me up for the night and generally took an interest in the project. Like those people who cannot be named, please take this as grateful acknowledgement of your part in the book.

FOREWORDS

Once upon a time life was easy for the intelligence community.

Michael Joseph Savage made a mark in the sands of history with his 'where Britain stands we stand' declaration. It was only right that we saw the world through British eyes and, when Britain retreated, only sensible that we should go all the way with LBJ as an Australian Prime Minister (in whose memory a swimming pool in Melbourne was named) once declared. The Cold War kept us in line and on line.

In the mid-1980s we bucked the system. We may have been ahead of our time on matters nuclear, but we were out of step with what was called the 'Western Alliance'. It took a break with the United States and Britain to make the people of New Zealand aware that we were part of an international intelligence organisation which had its roots in a different world order and which could command compliance from us while withholding from us the benefits of others' intelligence.

Life at the time was full of unpleasant surprises. State-sponsored terrorism was a crime against humanity as long as it wasn't being practiced by the allies, when it was studiously ignored. In the national interest it became necessary to say 'ouch' and frown and bear certain reprisals of our intelligence partners. We even went the length of building a satellite station at Waihopai. But it was not until I read this book that I had any idea that we had been committed to an international integrated electronic network.

It was with some apprehension that I learned that Nicky Hager was researching the activity of our intelligence community. He has long been a pain in the establishment's neck. Unfortunately for the establishment, he is engaging, thorough, unthreatening, with a dangerously ingenuous appearance, and an astonishing number of people have told him things that I, as Prime Minister in charge of the intelligence services, was never told.

There are also many things with which I am familiar. I couldn't tell him which was which. Nor can I tell you. But it is an outrage that I and other ministers were told so little, and this raises the question of to whom those concerned saw themselves ultimately answerable.

It also raises the question as to why we persist with the old order of things. New Zealand doesn't have much in common with Major's Britain and probably less with Blair's Britain. Are we philosophically in tune with

Clinton's USA? Is he?

Does all of that prejudice our new orientation to Asia?

There will be two responses to this book. One will be to take the easy course of dumping on Hager. He is quite small and can easily be dumped on. The other will be to challenge the existing assumptions and to have a rational debate on security and intelligence. I have always enjoyed taking the easier course but we may have been the poorer for it.

David Lange
Prime Minister of New Zealand 1984-89

The world of signals intelligence is one that governments have traditionally tried to keep hidden from public view. The secrecy attached to it by the United Kingdom and its allies in the Second World War, particularly codebreaking operations, carried over into the Cold War. Whether their adversaries were attacking them with weapons or diplomatic strategies, the concern was the same — that revelations about methods and successes would lead an adversary to change codes and ciphers and deny the codebreaker the ability to read the foe's secret communications.

Another aspect of the Second World War that carried over into the Cold War era was the close co-operation between five countries — the United States, the United Kingdom, Canada, Australia and New Zealand — formalised with the UKUSA Security Agreement of 1948. Although the treaty has never been made public, it has become clear that it provided not only for a division of collection tasks and sharing of the product, but for common guidelines for the classification and protection of the intelligence collected as well as for personnel security.

But over the last 50 years, codebreaking has become far more difficult, and often impossible — due to the use of computer-based encryption. At the same time, the interception of unencrypted communications (for example, air-to-ground communications) and other electronic signals — particularly radar emanations and missile telemetry — has grown dramatically in importance. This expanded role for signals intelligence was made evident in the construction and operation of a vast network of ground stations spread across the world, aircraft equipped with intercept antenna patrolling the skies (and sometimes being shot down), and eventually the launch of eavesdropping satellites. This activity did not escape the notice of the Soviet Union, which also was busy establishing its own elaborate network. It also became very evident to outsider observers that signals intelligence was an important and very expensive part of the Cold War.

That signals intelligence became more noticeable did not, for many years, alter the attitudes of the authorities about the necessity for strict secrecy. In the United States the National Security Agency, established in 1952, was officially acknowledged only in 1957. For years, what were well known to be US operated signals intelligence stations have been officially described as facilities engaged in the research of 'electronic phenomena' or the 'rapid-relay of communications.' It took the US over 20 years after the Soviet Union obtained detailed information on a US signals intelligence satellite even to acknowledge the existence of such satellites. Other nations have been equally reticent — the very existence of Canada's Communications Security Establishment was first revealed by the media in 1975.

In recent years some of the UKUSA governments have been somewhat more forthcoming about signals intelligence sometimes with regard to historical events, sometimes with respect to organisational structure, and sometimes about some aspects of current operations. But secrecy is still intense (although no more than in other countries). What the public does know, it knows largely because of the efforts of industrious researchers who have collected and analysed obscure documents and media accounts, and interviewed present and former intelligence officers who can shed light on signals intelligence operations. These researchers have included Desmond Ball in Australia, James Bamford in the United States and Duncan Campbell in the United Kingdom.

Nicky Hager's *Secret Power* earns him a place in that select company. Indeed, he has produced the most detailed and up-to-date account in existence of the work of any signals intelligence agency. His exposé of the organisation and operations of New Zealand's Government Communications Security Bureau (GCSB) is a masterpiece of investigative reporting and provides a wealth of information.

The reader of Mr Hager's book will learn about not just New Zealand's signals intelligence activities, but those of its partners. Specifically, the reader will learn about the origins, the evolution, and internal structure of the GCSB; the Tangimoana and Waihopai ground stations and their operations; New Zealand's role in the UKUSA alliance, and some of the signals intelligence operations of the other UKUSA nations. *Secret Power* also serves as a fascinating case study of the role of a junior partner in an intelligence alliance.

Some, undoubtedly, will object to the unprecedented detail to be found in the book, taking the traditional view that secrecy is far more important than public understanding of how tax dollars are being spent on intelligence. Certainly, revelations that defeat the purpose of legitimate intelligence activities are unfortunate and waste those tax dollars. But the UKUSA governments and their intelligence services have been far too slow in declassifying information that no longer needs to be secret and far too willing to classify information that need not be restricted. A Canadian newspaper made the point rather dramatically a few years ago — after being denied access to a Canadian signals intelligence facility, the paper promptly purchased on the open market, and published, a satellite photograph of the facility, and its antenna system, first obtained by a Soviet spy satellite.

There are many individuals within the services who would prefer greater openness, but they frequently cannot overcome the intense opposition of those preaching the need for tight secrecy. The internal bureaucratic battle to get information declassified can be a long and intense one and those opposing disclosure have an advantage — often they are those in charge of security, who have developed a mindset which views any revelation as damaging. In the meantime, the public is kept in the dark. A free press, as manifested in books such as Mr Hager's, is a large step towards alleviating the problem.

Jeffrey T. Richelson
Alexandria, Virginia
May, 1996

Jeffrey Richelson is a leading authority on United States intelligence agencies and author of *America's Secret Eyes in the Sky*, and co-author of *The Ties That Bind*.

INTRODUCTION

The Government Communications Security Bureau (GCSB) is the most secret organisation in New Zealand. It is also by far the country's largest and most significant intelligence organisation, yet not one in 100 New Zealanders would even know its name. This book, which focuses on the GCSB but covers other New Zealand agencies involved in foreign intelligence work, aims to change that. Every chapter contains important information that has never before been published. Readers deserve some explanation of how the information has come to be published — and of why I believe that they should be not just curious or intrigued, but actively concerned about the activities of intelligence organisations.

I began research on the GCSB almost accidentally in mid-1984 when I went with friends to visit the recently discovered Tangimoana signals intelligence station, north of Wellington. (Signals intelligence, the work of the GCSB, involves spying electronically on others' communications. With so much human activity revolving around the use of telephone, telex, fax and e-mail, it is the most important type of spying in the world today.) When no one appeared from the buildings to tell us to go away, we wandered around noting down everything we could see: from the shapes of the aerials that surrounded us to the number plates of the cars in the station car park.

Much later, a trip to the Post Office provided the names of the cars' owners, and suddenly a window into the inner workings of the GCSB was thrown open. I had some spare time between projects so I went to a library and looked up the names in the index of the voluminous annual public service staff lists. There they were, listed in an obscure Ministry of Defence occupational class, together with 80 of their colleagues who had also been hidden there. By looking at the lists from earlier years I could see the growth of New Zealand radio interception activities over 30 years, including where they had been based before Tangimoana and their regular postings to

Singapore, Australia and elsewhere.

Two years passed before I had time to investigate further. Then it occurred to me that the rest of the GCSB staff were probably also hidden within the Defence lists. Although they were scattered anonymously through pages of ordinary Defence personnel, there was a ridiculously simple way to sort the military from the spies. Using the Ministry of Defence internal phone directory, I crossed out all the names of true Defence staff — leaving me with a virtually full list of the staff and their positions in the secret organisation.

It was these staff lists that allowed me to begin to understand what went on inside the GCSB. None of the sources for the lists was secret and since then I have pieced together information from a great many other sources. As with all research, each step forward suggested new ones. Much of the information in the book was obtained from interviews with more than 50 people who are or have been involved in intelligence and related fields in New Zealand and elsewhere. Because of the nature of their jobs, these interviews had to proceed on the condition that the people involved would not be identified. Some of the information arrived in unexpected ways. Other snippets turned up simply because New Zealand is a small place.

Other sources of information have included the Official Information Act, the National Archives, job advertisements, overseas researchers and publications and a lot of fieldwork. It has of course not been easy to research such closed organisations. Often days or weeks of work have gone into compiling the facts for one or two pages of final text. Rigid secrecy within intelligence agencies has meant that, even where inside sources were used, many 'insiders' could only contribute fragments of the story, and even the most informed sources still knew no more than 5-10% of the subjects covered. The straightforward way I have recorded the information belies the difficulties of gathering it.

The New Zealand intelligence organisations are so thoroughly a part of the United States system that I have been able to uncover new information about the workings of the entire international system. Chapters 2 and 3, for instance, contain the first description ever published of the American-British-Canadian-Australian-New Zealand system that targets most of the civilian communications in the world, including where the interception occurs, how it is done, its capabilities, how the staff operate the system and even the secret codenames. This information has significance for many countries far from New Zealand.

If this book contained only information that the intelligence authorities were prepared to make public, it would be very short and much of its content would be misleading. There are, however, various pieces of sensitive information about the GCSB that I have not included. For example, revealing some intelligence targets (both of New Zealand and allied agencies) would have damaged interests that most readers would agree are worth protecting, without adding substantially to an understanding of the organisation. But naming some of the targets in general terms will be no great surprise to the targets themselves. In the case of some other small and vulnerable nations, if they have not suspected that they are being intercepted, they should know.

Also, I have named senior staff, at the levels where such people in all government organisations can expect publicity, but have mentioned other staff only where it adds to an understanding of the organisations concerned. Detailed references to an individual do not mean that I obtained the information concerned from that individual. I have not spoken to or received information from any of the intelligence staff specifically described in this book.

In some places detailed information has been included primarily so that it will be harder for the intelligence authorities to claim that the main content of the book is unfounded. In other places a lot of detailed information has been left out, either because it is not relevant to the book's central themes or so that individuals who provided information cannot be identified.

I have thought hard about the new information published in this book and I am confident that it will help, not harm, the real defence and security of New Zealand. I say this because the predictable response of secretive institutions when they are exposed is to claim (as they will) that the security of the country has been imperilled. I believe it is vital to uncover important information that is being withheld from governments and the public and to prompt some very necessary change.

There is a difference between defence and security and individual opinions about defence and security. Publishing this book will not fit with some officials' political opinions about what is best for the defence and security of New Zealand, but that is quite a different matter from what actually matters for the protection and security of New Zealanders.

I would appreciate being contacted by readers who have information that adds to the information in the book or who have information on other subjects that should be made public.

All writers write from a particular perspective. I believe that spying and other intelligence activities are not, in themselves, necessarily good or bad. Issues of right and wrong arise in relation to who is being spied upon, who is given access to the intelligence and what they do with it. Few New Zealanders would object, for example, to intelligence activities aimed at protecting New Zealand from attacks such as the 1985 *Rainbow Warrior* bombing. But I am appalled that New Zealand provides very detailed intelligence about its small and vulnerable South Pacific neighbours to outside powers which are aggressively pursuing their own interests in the region.

Intelligence is not just neutral information; it can be powerful and dangerous. Intelligence gathering and military force are two sides of the same coin. Both are used by countries and groups within countries to advance their interests, often at the expense of others. To influence or defeat an opponent, knowledge can be more useful than military force.

The type of intelligence described in this book, signals intelligence, is the largest, most secret and most expensive source of secret intelligence in the world today. This eavesdropping on the communications of other countries has implications for power relations between countries in every part of the globe.

Too often, the signals intelligence alliance has involved New Zealand in international military and political issues and disputes which, if they knew about them, many New Zealanders would not support. The middle chapters of the book document New Zealand involvement in electronic spying operations against countries and territories including Russia, China, Vietnam, France, Japan, Argentina, Bougainville, East Timor, Vanuatu and all the other South Pacific states, usually directly on behalf of one of the intelligence allies. Some of these operations just appear pointless for New Zealand, others are for very dubious purposes.

These are also the chapters that describe how the spying is done, who does it and the common security regulations and technical systems which bind the alliance together. As you read it will become clear that virtually everything — the equipment, manuals, ways of operating, jargon, codes and so on — has been imported in entirety from the overseas allies to be used in New Zealand as part of the international system.

Although, superficially, the intelligence alliance provides New Zealand with a great deal of information, it appears that very little of it is important. Chapter 12 has precise details of the intelligence New Zealand receives from its four closest allies; then the final chapter quotes a range of senior officials and politicians who argue that this intelligence has served little or no useful purpose for New Zealand. The publicly claimed benefits of intelligence cooperation, such as that New Zealand receives vital economic intelligence and information on terrorism, do not stand up to close examination. Examples such as the *Rainbow Warrior* bombing show that agencies set up to serve alliance priorities repeatedly fail when they are needed close to home.

I have found no significant evidence of the intelligence alliance defending New Zealanders or of the intelligence it produces having an important influence on policy decisions. The implications of being a junior member of the alliance — which means New Zealand interests coming second to those of the larger allies — have probably had far more significance for government policy than has the actual intelligence collected and exchanged.

But there is ample evidence that the intelligence alliance has contributed to the destruction rained upon innocent people in wars since 1945, and that most often it has been assisting powerful interests at the expense of the vulnerable. In any account of the activities of the powerful it is hard to keep sight of what it all means for the ordinary people who, somewhere far below, suffer as a result. I believe the challenge for the thoughtful is to try keep these human results in mind. When nations compete, whether it be politically, militarily or economically, it is not the Josef Stalins, George Bushs or Saddam Husseins who are hurt or killed.

No criticism is intended of the majority of people who work for the intelligence organisations described in this book. Most of them sincerely believe they are acting in the best interests of their country; they are ordinary people who just happened to end up with a job in intelligence. Many have (or, if they knew what was going on, would have) the same concerns about the organisations as other citizens. Good people can work in organisations that do great harm.

Some senior officials, however, do deserve criticism, for an arrogance that leads them to believe they know better than the politicians and public they are supposed to serve. When this involves them in secretly pursuing policies contrary to what the public would support and without even the permission of the government, change is obviously overdue.

Numerous examples are given of officials withholding information from governments and the public — and, at times, actively deceiving them. The book shows, for example, that in the 1985-90 period, when the public and government were led to believe New Zealand was moving to greater independence in intelligence matters, a process of rapid integration into the alliance was actually occurring. Similarly, the much debated 1985 'cut' of United States intelligence to New Zealand did not occur. The government and the public were hearing only what it suited the officials to tell them.

Inadequate New Zealand control over the GCSB, the reasons for which are described in Chapter 13, means that the alliance partners have considerably more influence over New Zealand intelligence priorities and operations than do New Zealand governments. Chapter 13 also explains why new intelligence oversight legislation passed in 1996 did little to improve this situation — it actually shut the door on Parliament being able to find out for itself what New Zealand's spies are up to.

Researching and writing about intelligence activities has been a continuation of my work in helping to secure New Zealand's nuclear-free status. The vision behind the nuclear-free policy is that international politics must change and that small countries have a role in helping to lead the way. This applies equally to New Zealand's membership of the intelligence alliance, which stands in the way of New Zealand playing a positive role in world affairs. That role should be one of reducing international conflict, confronting injustice and protecting the environment. By leaving the alliance, New Zealand would have more integrity in its international relations and could, over time, set a much needed example for other nations. That is what the nuclear-free policy has done, but for the last decade the intelligence alliance has maintained its counter-influence over New Zealand politics because, to date, it has been impregnably secret.

New Zealand's intelligence ties also, I believe, work against participatory democracy, by encouraging a culture of secrecy and by replacing democratic processes with channels for foreign influence. The effect has been to increase the power of a highly paid group of government officials, reduce the influence of the government and Parliament and often entirely exclude the public from important issues.

During the time I have been involved with the nuclear-free issue I have often found myself pushing against this invisible current, a current which time and again leads governments to follow the wishes of the foreign allies against the majority wishes of the New Zealand public. This, alone, is enough justification for leaving the intelligence alliance. New Zealand policy cannot help being affected by the fact that the main intelligence allies have a 'big power' view of the world, quite different from that of most New Zealanders, and often favour violent solutions to international disputes. Two of them continue to be nuclear armed.

The research for this book was undertaken with the knowledge of the GCSB, who were offered an opportunity to discuss it with me. I wrote to the director, Ray Parker, three times offering to visit him to discuss my research. The first two times he did not even acknowledge the offer. The third time, when I asked why he was not replying, he replied tersely: 'I acknowledge your offer to visit the Bureau for the purpose of explaining the purpose of your research. I do not wish to avail myself of your offer.'

Over the last 10 years a lot has been heard in New Zealand about the dangers of 'bureaucratic capture', about senior officials controlling their ministers rather than the other way around. The area of government activity described in this book is the ultimate example of bureaucratic capture. Politicians, whom the public has presumed will be monitoring the intelligence organisations on their behalf, have been systematically denied the information required to do that job.

If a democratic society wants to control its secret agencies, it is essential that the public and politicians have the information and the will to do so. Providing information on these most secret state activities is the purpose of this book. Anyone who reads it will know a lot more about New Zealand intelligence activities and the international system of which they are part than all the members of Parliament, the Cabinet ministers and even the prime ministers who have supposedly been in charge. Then it is up to those readers to take this information and force long overdue restructuring and change.

CHAPTER ONE

1984

It was a grumpy Rob Muldoon who walked across from the Beehive building to the parliamentary chamber on Tuesday, 12 June 1984. After nine years as an increasingly embattled prime minister, his rule was disintegrating. That morning the Leader of the Opposition, David Lange, had announced his party's foreign policy: New Zealand would be made unconditionally nuclear free and the ANZUS Treaty would have to be renegotiated. Later that day two National Party MPs crossed the floor in Parliament to vote for a Labour Party-sponsored Nuclear Free New Zealand Bill, almost defeating the government. Two days later, blaming these anti-nuclear defectors, a visibly intoxicated Muldoon threw in the towel and called an early general election.

That Tuesday afternoon Muldoon was on his way to the 2.30 pm session of Parliament to read a prepared ministerial statement about a quite different subject: an obscure agency called the Government Communications Security Bureau (GCSB). The GCSB had been set up secretly under Muldoon seven years earlier and had been quietly growing in size throughout his reign.

Until just two months before Muldoon's statement the public had never even heard of the GCSB. Then peace researcher Owen Wilkes publicised the existence of a secret radio eavesdropping station run by the GCSB at Tangimoana Beach, 150 kilometres north of Wellington, revealing for the first time that New Zealand was involved in this type of intelligence collection. Muldoon was delivering the government's reply to the publicity.

The brief statement he read was, and remains, the most information the government has ever been prepared to release about the GCSB and the Tangimoana station. It acknowledged that the GCSB was involved in signals intelligence — intercepting the communications of governments, organisations and individuals in other countries — and said New Zealand had collected that type of intelligence since the Second World War. It noted that the GCSB liaised closely with Australia, Canada, the United Kingdom and the United States — the closest the government has ever come to talking about the secret five-nation signals intelligence alliance of which the GCSB is part. But much of the statement was designed to mislead.

It said that the Tangimoana station did not monitor 'New Zealand's friends in the South Pacific'. The big aerials at the station were right then monitoring nuclear-free Vanuatu, the Solomon Islands, Fiji and all New Zealand's other South Pacific neighbours — everyone in the South Pacific, in fact, except for the Western intelligence allies and their territories. Large quantities of telexes and Morse code messages sent by long-distance radio in the Pacific region were being recorded at Tangimoana and sent to the GCSB in Wellington for distribution to select public servants and to the four intelligence allies.

The statement also said that Tangimoana 'does not come under the direction of any Government, or external agency, other than the New Zealand Government'. In fact, the communications officers in a secure room within the station were regularly receiving directions from the overseas allies and sending them back intelligence collected on their behalf.

As soon as Muldoon sat down, the Leader of the Opposition stood up to respond. Lange, who five weeks later would be Prime Minister, thanked Muldoon for removing the cause of suspicion which had surrounded the Tangimoana facility: 'In particular, I am grateful that he has given an absolutely unqualified assurance, which I believe to be of paramount importance, that the facility is under the full control of the New Zealand Government'.

On that same Tuesday one of the GCSB's newest employees left for work from his home in Khandallah, overlooking Wellington Harbour. He had recently moved into a key position overseeing the GCSB's policy and planning. After the GCSB director, this would be the most influential position in determining the GCSB's direction through its most important period of growth.

Glen Singleton had already made an impression on his colleagues. He was always polite and sociable, but kept his opinions to himself. Privately, he told work friends that he did not much like the top people at the GCSB. The other directors at the GCSB, mostly ex-Air Force, had little in common with his tastes for antiques, paintings and good food.

Arriving at work, Singleton took the lift to the 14th floor of the Freyberg Building headquarters. He held his magnetic security pass up to the right spot on the heavy wooden doors and an unseen black box registered that he had arrived and automatically opened the door.

In 1984 this top floor contained the GCSB's communications centre, its 24-hour link to its overseas allies, the linguists who translated intercepted messages and some of the deputy directors. Singleton's office had been positioned next to the director's, with wide views across the harbour. Staff recall that 'he wandered in and out of the director's office whenever he wanted' and that he 'had the director's ear'.

Glen Singleton, an American intelligence officer, was Director of Policy and Plans at the GCSB from 1984 to 1987, without government knowledge (pictured arriving at work; note number plate).

One of the many things Lange did not know about the GCSB when he spoke in Parliament that afternoon, and would never know, even as Prime Minister, was that this new officer was not under the control of the New Zealand government at all. Paid in American dollars and living in a house rented for him by the local United States embassy, Singleton was an employee of an organisation called the National Security Agency (NSA).

The NSA is the United States' largest, most secret and probably most expensive intelligence organisation. It rings the world with intelligence stations, ships, submarines, aircraft and satellites that act as the 'platforms' for its global electronic spying operations. It has immense intelligence collecting capabilities. As a remarkable exposé, *The Puzzle Palace* by James Bamford, shows, the NSA is the big brother of all such intelligence organisations in

the Western world. Its intelligence links with four especially close allies —
Britain, Canada, Australia and New Zealand — are formalised in a highly
secret agreement called UKUSA (pronounced 'you-koo-za').

Glen Singleton, still in his early 30s, was on a three-year posting to the
GCSB. He had grown up and been educated in the city of Cleveland in
Ohio. After university study in international relations, he moved to Washington DC to work for the NSA. In late 1984, after settling in as a foreign
officer inside the GCSB, he was formally appointed as the GCSB's Deputy
Director of Policy and Plans. In this role he advised the GCSB director regularly, directed the work of other GCSB staff and showed overseas visitors
around the GCSB. He visited the United States embassy often, travelled to
the Defence Signals Directorate (DSD) in Melbourne for meetings and received special private communications from his Washington bosses. Between
1984 and 1987 he would help to make the plans for a period of dramatic
expansion of the GCSB's operations and capabilities. Later he would return
to the GCSB, having left the NSA, and move into another key role.

Having an American inside the GCSB serving as a foreign liaison officer
would be one thing; allowing an officer from another country to direct policy
and planning seems extraordinary.

During his first three years on the NSA posting Singleton hosted 50 or
more staff from the Wellington intelligence organisations to 4 July parties at
his home. But outside intelligence circles, not even the Prime Minister knew
of his role. As another former Prime Minister said about the GCSB: 'You
don't know what you don't know. The whole thing was a bit of an act of
faith.'

Nineteen eighty-four was a special year for the GCSB. The directors of the
five UKUSA agencies meet together once a year to plan and co-ordinate the
activities of the global intelligence alliance. The agencies take turns to host
the meeting; this year it was the GCSB.[1]

Throughout the early 1980s the GCSB had been expanding: more than
doubling its staff, opening the Tangimoana station and, most pleasing to the
director, establishing various new intelligence analysis sections that had given
the GCSB more to offer within the alliance.

Five years before, the organisation had been squeezed into a corner of
Defence headquarters. Now the flags of the five nations were out on display
to greet the UKUSA agency heads to the spacious new Freyberg Building
headquarters. After a special welcome for the overseas directors, they met in
the 14th floor conference room attached to the director's office, looking out

over the pine-clad Wellington hills and, in the foreground, the Stars and Stripes fluttering outside the nearby American embassy.

The most important visitor was Lieutenant-General Lincoln D. Faurer, head of the NSA. With him were Peter Marychurch, head of the British Government Communications Headquarters (GCHQ), Peter Hunt, head of the Canadian Communications Security Establishment (CSE), and Tim James, head of the Australian DSD.

Although what was discussed at this meeting is not known, the issues facing the intelligence alliance were clear. The agenda would have included plans for new computer and communications systems, which would help to integrate GCSB operations into the NSA-controlled network, and in particular preparations for a new, super-secret global intelligence system of which New Zealand would be an integral part. It would have been made clear that, as part of the new global system, the NSA required new signals intelligence stations in the South Pacific by the end of the decade to intercept satellite communications. Over the next three years, it would be the job of the GCSB Director, Colin Hanson, and his Australian counterpart to manoeuvre their governments towards approving such a project.

The meeting may also have discussed the nuclear-free issue, which was simmering away as Lange's new Labour government settled into office.

Only a few months later, on 27 February 1985, Lange met a United States State Department official, William Brown, across the dining table of the New Zealand consul general's residence in Los Angeles. It was a short and tense meeting.

The nuclear-free issue had come to head in New Zealand. Deciding to follow public opinion rather than the advice of its officials, the Labour government had refused entry to the American nuclear-capable warship, USS *Buchanan*, and now Lange was being read the list of retaliatory measures that would be imposed by the United States government. These included cutting many of the military ties between the two countries; in effect the ANZUS Treaty died that day. And, as part of the reprisals, according to the then Chief of Defence Staff, Sir Ewan Jamieson, 'the flow of information [from the United States], on which the New Zealand intelligence community was heavily dependent, was terminated'.[2]

All the journalists, commentators and 'well placed sources' were repeating the same message. As far as the public knew, all intelligence ties between New Zealand and the United States were severed.

This was completely untrue. While intelligence from military sources

February 1985 news of severed intelligence links was simply untrue.

was cut considerably, most of the intelligence flow from the United States continued uninterrupted. The United States government wanted other countries to see New Zealand punished for its nuclear-free policies, but the UKUSA alliance was too valuable to be interrupted by politics.

A few days before Lange's meeting in Los Angeles, the GCSB received a call from its liaison officer at the NSA's headquarters in Washington DC. Warren Tucker, who had moved into the position a few weeks before and would later become Director of Operations back at the GCSB, told the senior GCSB staff that the announcement was coming but reassured them that his position at the NSA was secure. While other New Zealand diplomatic staff in Washington were frozen out by their United States government contacts, Tucker was envied because his position was largely unaffected.

The communications centre (the 'commcen') back in the GCSB's Wellington headquarters was the first place where practical signs of the Los Angeles reprisals were noticed. Here mostly ex-Navy communications staff worked around the clock maintaining contact with the four sister agencies.

Every day, hundreds and hundreds of intelligence reports were spat out of the large sound-proofed printers, more reports than the small Wellington intelligence agencies even had time to read. In February 1985, the GCSB was receiving reports about the minute details of the Iran-Iraq War, Soviets in Afghanistan, a weekly list of all the Libyan students in Britain and a lot of other marginally interesting top secret reports. But there was nothing, among the screeds of reports on international terrorism, about the French DGSE agents who were right then on their way to New Zealand to become the first foreign terrorists in New Zealand's history: blowing up the Greenpeace ship *Rainbow Warrior*.

Most of the daily flood of overseas reports did not stop. But the communications staff noticed that the 'routing indicators', which show the origin and destination of documents within the UKUSA system, had been removed from incoming reports. While the public condemnation of New Zealand's nuclear-free policy by the United States government increased in pitch, it seems some strategist in Washington decided there should be no tangible evidence that United States intelligence reports were still arriving in Wellington. They did not want to take the risk that one of these documents might one day be held up in public as evidence that the New Zealand had got away with its nuclear-free policy.

Later, when the public debate had cooled, the usual routing indicators quietly reappeared on the overseas reports. While governments, journalists and the public around the world were led to believe that United States-New Zealand intelligence ties had been cut, inside the five-agency network it was mostly business as usual.

The United States military was unsentimental about its decades of alliance links with the New Zealand armed forces; military exercises, exchanges and other visible links were completely cut. But New Zealand's involvement in the UKUSA intelligence alliance, first alluded to in public by Muldoon only nine months before, was too useful to the overseas allies to be interrupted by a quarrel over nuclear ships.

CHAPTER TWO

HOOKED UP TO THE NETWORK
THE UKUSA SYSTEM

Ten years later, on Saturday, 15 January 1994, technicians in satellite earth stations around the Pacific were busy tuning their equipment to a new satellite. The first of the new generation of Intelsat 7 series satellites, it had been launched several weeks before, from the European Kourou air base in French Guyana, and then manoeuvred into position far out in space above the Equator at 174 degrees east, due north of New Zealand above Kiribati.

The 20 Intelsat (International Telecommunications Satellite Organisation) satellites that ring the world above the Equator carry most of the world's satellite-relayed international phone calls and messages such as faxes, e-mail and telexes. The new satellite, Intelsat 701, replaced the 10-year-old Intelsat 510 in the same position. The changeover occurred at 10 pm New Zealand time that summer evening.

At the GCSB's station at Waihopai, near Blenheim in the north of the South Island, the radio officer staff were just as busy that evening, setting their special equipment to intercept the communications which the technicians in legitimate satellite earth stations would send and receive via the new satellite. These specially trained radio officers, who learned their skills at the

26

Marlborough Express

The Waihopai station — part of a super-secret global system called ECHELON — automatically intercepts satellite communications for the foreign allies. The Labour government that approved the station was not told about these links.

Tangimoana station, usually work day shifts, but on 15 January 1994 they worked around the clock, tuning the station's receivers to the frequency bands the GCSB wanted to intercept, selecting the specific channels within each band that would yield the types of messages sought within the UKUSA network and then testing that the high-tech intelligence collection system was working smoothly. That satellite changeover was a very significant event for the Waihopai station and the GCSB. Although it would always be only a small component of the global network, this was the moment when the station came into its own.

There have been various guesses and hints over the years about what the Waihopai station was set up to monitor — 'sources' in one newspaper said foreign warship movements; a 'senior Telecom executive' told another newspaper it was most likely 'other countries' military communications' — but, outside a small group of intelligence staff, no one could do more than theorise. Waihopai was established specifically to target the international satellite traffic carried by Intelsat satellites in the Pacific region and its target in the mid-1990s is the Intelsat 701 that came into service in January 1994, and is the primary satellite for the Pacific region.

Intelsat satellites carry most of the satellite traffic of interest to intelligence organisations in the South Pacific: diplomatic communications between embassies and their home capitals, all manner of government and military communications, a wide range of business communications, communications of international organisations and political organisations and the personal communications of people living throughout the Pacific. The Intelsat 7 satellites can carry an immense number of communications simultaneously. Where the previous Intelsat 5s could carry 12,000 individual phone or fax circuits at once, the Intelsat 7s can carry 90,000. All 'written' messages are currently exploited by the GCSB. The other UKUSA agencies monitor phone calls as well.

The key to interception of satellite communications is powerful computers that search through these masses of messages for ones of interest. The intercept stations take in millions of messages intended for the legitimate earth stations served by the satellite and then use computers to search for pre-programmed addresses and keywords. In this way they select out manageable numbers (hundreds or thousands) of messages to be searched through and read by intelligence analysis staff.

Until the Intelsat 701 satellite replaced the older 5 series, all the communications intercepted at Waihopai could already be got from two existing UKUSA stations covering the Pacific. But, unlike their predecessors, this new generation of Intelsat 7s had more precise beams transmitting communications down to the southern hemisphere. The existing northern hemisphere-based stations were no longer able to pick up all the southern communications, which is why new stations were required.

Eleven months later, on 3 December 1994, the other old Intelsat satellite above the Pacific was replaced by Intelsat 703. Since then Waihopai and its sister station in Australia constructed at the same time have been the main source of southern hemisphere Pacific satellite communications for the UKUSA network.

Many people are vaguely aware that a lot of spying occurs, maybe even on them, but how do we judge if it is ubiquitous or not a worry at all? Is someone listening every time we pick up the telephone? Are all our Internet or fax messages being pored over continuously by shadowy figures somewhere in a windowless building? There is almost never any solid information with which to judge what is realistic concern and what is silly paranoia.

What follows explains as precisely as possible — and for the first time in public — how the worldwide system works, just how immense and powerful it is and what it can and cannot do. The electronic spies are not ubiquitous, but the paranoia is not unfounded.

The global system has a highly secret codename — ECHELON. It is by far the most significant system of which the GCSB is a part, and many of the GCSB's daily operations are based around it. The intelligence agencies will be shocked to see it named and described for the first time in print. Each station in the ECHELON network has computers that automatically search through the millions of intercepted messages for ones containing pre-programmed keywords or fax, telex and e-mail addresses. For the frequencies and channels selected at a station, every word of every message is automatically searched (they do not need your specific telephone number or Internet address on the list).

All the different computers in the network are known, within the UKUSA agencies, as the ECHELON Dictionaries. Computers that can search for keywords have existed since at least the 1970s, but the ECHELON system has been designed to interconnect all these computers and allow the stations to function as components of an integrated whole. Before this, the UKUSA allies did intelligence collection operations for each other, but each agency usually processed and analysed the intercept from its own stations. Mostly, finished reports rather than raw intercept were exchanged.

Under the ECHELON system, a particular station's Dictionary computer contains not only its parent agency's chosen keywords, but also a list for each of the other four agencies. For example, the Waihopai computer has separate search lists for the NSA, GCHQ, DSD and CSE in addition to its own. So each station collects all the telephone calls, faxes, telexes, Internet messages and other electronic communications that its computers have been pre-programmed to select for all the allies and automatically sends this intelligence to them. This means that the New Zealand stations are used by the overseas agencies for their automatic collecting — while New Zealand does not even know what is being intercepted from the New Zealand sites for the allies. In return, New Zealand gets tightly controlled access to a few parts of the system.

When analysts at the agency headquarters in Washington, Ottawa, Cheltenham and Canberra look through the mass of intercepted satellite communications produced by this system, it is only in the technical data recorded at the top of each intercept that they can see whether it was intercepted at Waihopai or at one of the other stations in the network. Likewise, GCSB staff talk of the other agencies' stations merely as the various 'satellite links' into the integrated system. The GCSB computers, the stations, the headquarters operations and, indeed, the GCSB itself function almost entirely as components of this integrated system.

In addition to satellite communications, the ECHELON system covers a range of other interception activities, described later. All these operations involve collection of *communications intelligence*,[1] as opposed to other types of signals intelligence such as electronic intelligence, which is about the technical characteristics of other countries' radar and weapon systems.

Interception of international satellite communications began in the early 1970s, only a few years after the first civilian communications satellites were launched. At this time the Intelsat satellites, located over the Atlantic, Pacific and Indian Oceans, simply beamed all their messages down to the entire hemisphere within their view.

Throughout the 1970s only two stations were required to monitor all the Intelsat communications in the world: a GCHQ station in the south-west of England had two dishes, one each for the Atlantic and Indian Ocean Intelsats, and an NSA station in the western United States had a single dish covering the Pacific Intelsat.

One of two dishes at a British spy station in Cornwall that between them intercepted all Atlantic and Indian Ocean satellite phone and telex until the early 1980s.

The English station is at Morwenstow, at the edge of high cliffs above the sea at Sharpnose Point in Cornwall. Opened in 1972-73, shortly after the introduction of new Intelsat 4 satellites, the Morwenstow station was a joint British-American venture, set up using United States-supplied computers and communications equipment, and was located only 110 kilometres from the legitimate British Telecom satellite station at Goonhilly to the south. In the 1970s the Goonhilly dishes were inclined identically towards the same Atlantic and Indian Ocean satellites.[2]

The Pacific Intelsat satellite was targeted by an NSA station built on a high basalt tableland inside the 100,000-hectare United States Army Yakima Firing Centre, in Washington State in the north-west United States, 200 kilometres south-west of Seattle. Also established in the early 1970s, the Yakima Research Station initially consisted of a long operations building and the single large dish. In 1982, a visiting journalist noted that the dish was pointing west, out above the Pacific to the third of the three Intelsat positions.[3]

Yakima is located between the Saddle Mountains and Rattlesnake Hills, in a desert of canyons, dunes and sheer rock cliffs, where the only vegetation is grass. The Army leases the land to ranchers who herd their cattle in the shadow of the dishes. When visited in mid-1995 the Yakima station had five dish antennae, three facing westwards over the Pacific Ocean and two, including the original large 1970s dish, facing eastwards. Besides the original operations building there were several newer buildings, the largest of them two-storey, concrete and windowless.

Two of the west-facing dishes are targeted on the main Pacific Intelsat satellites; the Yakima station has been monitoring Pacific Intelsat communications for the NSA ever since it opened. The orientation of the two east-facing dishes suggests that they may be targeted on the Atlantic Intelsats, intercepting communications relayed towards North and South America. One or both may provide the link between the station and the NSA headquarters in Washington. The fifth dish at the station is smaller than the rest and faces to the west. Given its size and orientation, it appears to be the UKUSA site for monitoring the Inmarsat-2 satellite that provides mobile satellite communications in the Pacific Ocean area. If so, this is the station that would, for example, have been monitoring Greenpeace communications during the nuclear testing protests in the waters around Moruroa Atoll in 1995.

The GCSB has had important links with the Yakima station since 1981, when the GCSB took over a special, highly secret area of intelligence analysis for the UKUSA network (see Chapter 6). Telexes intercepted using Yakima's single dish were first sorted by the Yakima computers, and then subjects allocated to New Zealand were sent to the GCSB for analysis. The Yakima station had been using Dictionary-type computers for this searching work for many years before the full ECHELON system was operating.

Between them, the Morwenstow and Yakima stations covered all Intelsat interception during the 1970s. But a new generation of Intelsat satellites launched from the late 1970s required a new configuration of spy stations. The Intelsat 4A and 5 series satellites differed from earlier ones in that they did not transmit only to the whole of the side of the world within their view;

they now also had 'east and west hemispheric' beams that transmitted separately.[4] For example, Intelsat 510, which operated above the Pacific until its replacement in December 1994, had one 'global' beam covering the whole region, but all the other transmissions went either to the east or to the west Pacific. Yakima was not within the 'footprint' of any hemispheric beams covering Australasia, South East Asia and East Asia, making interception of these signals difficult or impossible.

These changes to Intelsat design meant that the UKUSA alliance required at least two new stations to maintain its global coverage. Again the GCHQ provided one and the NSA one. A new NSA station on the east coast of the United States would cover Atlantic Intelsat traffic beamed down towards North and South America (Morwenstow covered the eastern Atlantic), and a GCHQ station in Hong Kong would cover both the western hemisphere of the Pacific Intelsats and the eastern hemisphere of the Indian Ocean Intelsats.

The site chosen for the new NSA station was hidden in the forested South Fork Valley in the mountains of West Virginia, about 250 kilometres south-west from Washington DC, on the edge of the George Washington National Forest, near the small settlement of Sugar Grove. The site had been used in the 1950s and early 1960s for a failed attempt to spy on Russian radio communications and radars by means of reflections from the moon. The current satellite interception station was developed during the late 1970s, when a collection of new satellite dishes (from 10 to 45 metres in diameter) and the new windowless Raymond E. Linn Operations Building were constructed. It also incorporated a two-storey underground operations building already at the site. It started full operations about 1980.[5]

Like Morwenstow and Yakima, Sugar Grove is only 100 kilometres from an international satellite communications earth station, making it easy to intercept any 'spot' beams directed down to the legitimate stations. In this case it is the Etam earth station, the main link in the United States with the Intelsat satellites above the Atlantic Ocean.

The other new station, in Hong Kong, was constructed by the GCHQ also in the late 1970s. The station, which has since been dismantled, was perched above the sea on the south side of Hong Kong Island, across Stanley Bay from the British Stanley Fort military base and right next to high-rise apartments and luxury housing. In crowded Hong Kong the station's anonymity was assured simply because there are so many satellite dishes scattered over the island. What helped to give away this one was the sign, on the entrance to an exclusive housing enclave across the bay, saying that taking photographs is strictly forbidden. When one of the Indian guards on the gate was asked why it was forbidden to take photos of a housing area, he pointed across the bay and said in serious tones, 'Communications facility — very, very secret'.

The Hong Kong station had several satellite dishes and buildings, including a large windowless concrete building (similar to the ones at Yakima and Sugar Grove) and a collection of administration and operations buildings running down the hill into the base from the gates. Intelsat communications intercepted at the station were seen regularly by GCSB operations staff in Wellington.[6]

When visited in August 1994, the station fitted the requirements of the Intelsat monitoring network. It had one dish pointing up east towards the Pacific Intelsats, another towards the Indian Ocean Intelsats and a third, for the station's own communications, pointing up to a United States Defence Satellite Communications System satellite above the Pacific. Other dishes had perhaps already been removed. Dismantling of the station began in 1994 — to ensure it was removed well before the 1997 changeover to Chinese control of Hong Kong — and the station's staff left in November that year. News reports said that the antennae and equipment were being shipped to the DSD-run Shoal Bay station in Northern Australia, where they would be used for intercepting Chinese communications.

It is not known how the Hong Kong station has been replaced in the global network. One of the Australian DSD stations — either Geraldton or Shoal Bay — may have taken over some of its work, or it is possible that another north-east Asian UKUSA station moved into the role. For example, there were developments at the NSA's Misawa station in northern Japan in the 1980s that would fit well with the need for expanded Intelsat monitoring.[7]

Throughout the 1980s a series of new dishes was also installed at the Morwenstow station, to keep up with expansion of the Intelsat network. In 1980 it still required only the two original dishes, but by the early 1990s it had nine satellite dishes: two inclined towards the two main Indian Ocean Intelsats, three towards Atlantic Ocean Intelsats, three towards positions above Europe or the Middle East and one dish covered by a radome.

The Morwenstow, Yakima, Sugar Grove and Hong Kong stations were able to provide worldwide interception of the international communications carried by Intelsat throughout the 1980s. The arrangement within the UKUSA alliance was that, while the NSA and GCHQ ran the four stations, each of the five allies (including the GCSB) had responsibility for analysing some particular types of the traffic intercepted at these stations.

Then, in the late 1980s, another phase of development occurred. It may have been prompted by approaching closure of the Hong Kong station, but a more likely explanation is that, as we have seen, technological advances in the target Intelsat satellites again required expansion of the network.

Two UKUSA countries were available to provide southern hemisphere coverage: Australia and New Zealand. One of the new southern hemisphere stations would be the GCSB's Waihopai station and the other would be at Geraldton in West Australia. (Both stations are described in detail later.) The new stations were operating by 1994 when the new Intelsat 7s began to be introduced. Waihopai had opened in 1989, with a single dish, initially covering one of the older generation of Intelsat satellites.

The positioning of the Geraldton station on Australia's extreme west coast was clearly to allow it to cover the Indian Ocean Intelsats (they all lie within 60 degrees of the station, which allows good reception). Geraldton

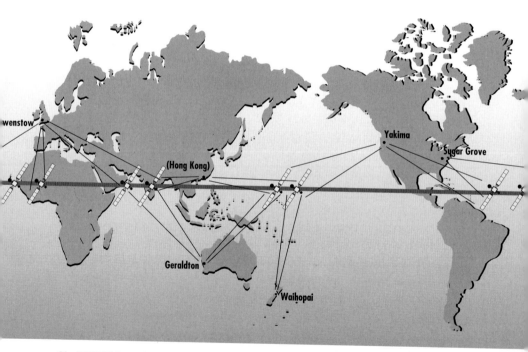

Six UKUSA stations target the Intelsat satellites used to relay most satellite phone calls, internet, e-mail, faxes and telexes around the world. They are part of a network of secret stations and spy satellites which, between them, intercept most of the communications on the planet.

opened in 1993, with four dishes, covering the two main Indian Ocean Intelsats (at 60 degrees and 63 degrees) and possibly a new Asia-Pacific Intelsat introduced in 1992. It also covers the second of the two Pacific Intelsats, Intelsat 703.

The logic of the system suggests that, at the same time as the Waihopai and Geraldton stations were added to the network, a seventh, as yet undiscovered, station may have been installed in the South Atlantic. This station, probably located on Ascension Island, would complete the 1990s network by intercepting the Atlantic Intelsats' southern hemisphere communications.[8]

New GCSB operations staff attend training sessions that cover the ECHELON system, showing how the GCSB fits into the system and including maps showing the network of UKUSA stations around the world. The sessions include briefings on the Intelsat and the maritime Inmarsat satellites — their locations, how they work, what kinds of communications they carry and the technical aspects of their vulnerability to spying. This is because these are primary targets for the UKUSA alliance in the Pacific.

But the interception of communications relayed by Intelsat and Inmarsat is only one component of the global spying network co-ordinated by the ECHELON system. Other elements include: radio listening posts, including the GCSB's Tangimoana station; interception stations targeted on other types of communications satellites; overhead signals intelligence collectors (spy satellites) like those controlled from the Pine Gap facility in Australia; and secret facilities that tap directly into land-based telecommunications networks.

What Waihopai, Morwenstow and the other stations do for satellite communications, another whole network of intercept stations like Tangimoana, developed since the 1940s, does for radio.

There are several dozen radio interception stations run by the UKUSA allies and located throughout the world. Many developed in the early years of the Cold War and, before satellite communications became widespread in the 1980s, were the main ground signals intelligence stations targeting Soviet communications. Some stations were also used against regional targets. In the Pacific, for example, ones with New Zealand staff were used to target groups and governments opposed by Britain and the United States through a series of conflicts and wars in South East Asia.

A recent new radio interception station is the Australian DSD station near Bamaga in northern Queensland, at the tip of Cape York. It was set up in 1988 particularly to monitor radio communications associated with the

The controversial Pine Gap base in central Australia is a major ground station for United States electronic spy satellites. It has kept expanding after the Cold War; today there are 12 'golf balls'. It plays a key role in United States military strategies.

conflict between Papua New Guinea and the secessionist movement in Bougainville.[9] GCSB staff are also aware of Australian intercept staff posted in the early 1990s to the recently opened Tindal Air Force base in northern Australia, suggesting that an even newer — as yet undisclosed — DSD intercept station may have been established there.

Most of this network of stations target long-range high frequency (HF) radio. A powerful HF radio transmitter can transmit right around the world, which is why HF radio has been a major means of international communications and is still widely used by military forces and by ships and aircraft. Other stations target short-range communications — very high frequency and ultra high frequency radio (VHF and UHF) — which, among other things, are used extensively for tactical military communications within a country.

There is a wide variety of these radio interception operations. Some are very large, with hundreds of staff; others are small — a few staff hidden inside a foreign embassy bristling with radio aerials on the roof; others (like the Bamaga station) are unstaffed, with the signals automatically relayed to other stations. Because of the peculiarities of radio waves, sometimes stations far from the target can pick up communications that closer ones cannot.

Each station in this network — including the GCSB's Tangimoana station — has a Dictionary computer like those in the satellite intercept stations. These search and select from the communications intercepted, in particular radio telexes, which are still widely used, and make these available to the UKUSA allies through the ECHELON system.

The UKUSA network of HF stations in the Pacific includes the GCSB's Tangimoana station (and before it one at Waiouru), five or more DSD stations in Australia, a CSE station in British Columbia, and NSA stations in Hawaii, Alaska, California, Japan, Guam, Kwajalein and the Philippines. The NSA is currently contracting its network of overseas HF stations as part of post-Cold War rationalisation. This contraction process includes, in Britain, the closure of the major Chicksands and Edzell stations.

The next component of the ECHELON system covers interception of a range of satellite communications not carried by Intelsat. In addition to the six or so UKUSA stations targeting Intelsat satellites, there are another five or more stations targeting Russian and other regional communications satellites. These stations are located in Britain, Australia, Canada, Germany and Japan. All of these stations are part of the ECHELON Dictionary system. It appears that the GCHQ's Morwenstow station, as well as monitoring Intelsat, also targets some regional communications satellites.

United States spy satellites, designed to intercept communications from orbit above the earth, are also likely to be connected into the ECHELON system. These satellites either move in orbits that criss-cross the earth or, like the Intelsats, sit above the Equator in geostationary orbit. They have antennae that can scoop up very large quantities of radio communications from the areas below.

The main ground stations for these satellites, where they feed back the information they have gathered into the global network, are Pine Gap, run by the CIA near Alice Springs in central Australia, and the NSA-directed Menwith Hill and Bad Aibling stations, in England and Germany respectively.[10] These satellites can intercept microwave trunk lines and short-range communications such as military radios and walkie-talkies. Both of these transmit only line of sight and so, unlike HF radio, cannot be intercepted from faraway ground stations.

The final element of the ECHELON system are facilities that tap directly into land-based telecommunications systems, completing a near total coverage of the world's communications. Besides satellite and radio, the other main method of transmitting large quantities of public, business and government communications is a combination of undersea cables across the oceans and microwave networks over land. Heavy cables, laid across the seabed between countries, account for a large proportion of the world's international communications. After they emerge from the water and join land-based microwave networks, they are very vulnerable to interception.

The microwave networks are made up of chains of microwave towers relaying messages from hilltop to hilltop (always in line of sight) across the countryside. These networks shunt large quantities of communications across a country. Intercepting them gives access to international undersea communications (once they surface) and to international communication trunk lines across continents. They are also an obvious target for large-scale interception of domestic communications.

Because the facilities required to intercept radio and satellite communications — large aerials and dishes — are difficult to hide for too long, that network is reasonably well documented. But all that is required to intercept land-based communication networks is a building situated along the microwave route or a hidden cable running underground from the legitimate network. For this reason the worldwide network of facilities to intercept these communications is still mostly undocumented.

Microwave communications are intercepted in two ways: by ground stations, located near to and tapping into the microwave routes, and by satellites. Because of the curvature of the earth, a signals intelligence satellite out in space can even be directly in the line of a microwave transmission. Although it sounds technically very difficult, microwave interception from space by United States spy satellites does occur.[11]

A 1994 exposé of the Canadian UKUSA agency called *Spyworld*,[12] co-authored by a previous staff member, Mike Frost, gave the first insights into how much microwave interception is done. It described UKUSA 'embassy collection' operations, where sophisticated receivers and processors are secretly transported to their countries' overseas embassies in diplomatic bags and used to monitor all manner of communications in the foreign capitals.

Since most countries' microwave networks converge on the capital city, embassy buildings are an ideal site for microwave interception. Protected by diplomatic privilege, embassies allow the interception to occur from right within the target country.[13] Frost said the operations particularly target microwave communications, but also other communications including car telephones and short-range radio transmissions.

According to Frost, Canadian embassy collection began in 1971 following pressure from the NSA. The NSA provided the equipment (on indefinite loan), trained the staff, told them what types of transmissions to look for on particular frequencies and at particular times of day and gave them a search list of NSA keywords. All the intelligence collected was sent to the NSA for analysis. The Canadian embassy collection was requested by the NSA to fill gaps in the United States and British embassy collection operations, which were still occurring in many capitals around the world when Frost left the CSE in 1990.

Separate sources in Australia have revealed that the DSD also engages in embassy collection. Leaks in the 1980s described installation of 'extraordinarily sophisticated intercept equipment, known as Reprieve' in Australia's High Commission in Port Moresby, Papua New Guinea and in the embassies in Indonesia and Thailand. The operations are said to take a whole room of the embassy buildings and to be able to listen to local telephone calls at will.[14] There is good reason to assume that these operations, too, were prompted by and supported with equipment and technical advice from the NSA and GCHQ.

Of course, when the microwave route is across one of the UKUSA countries' territory it is much easier to arrange interception. For example, it is likely that there is a GCHQ operation intercepting, and feeding through Dictionary computers, all the trans-Atlantic undersea cable communications that come ashore in Cornwall.

There are also definitely United States and possibly Canadian facilities for this type of interception. By far the most important of these is the NSA-directed Menwith Hill station in Britain. With its 22 satellite terminals and over 2 hectares of buildings, Menwith Hill is undoubtedly the largest station in the UKUSA network. In 1992 some 1200 United States personnel were based there.[15] British researcher Duncan Campbell has described how Menwith Hill taps directly into the British Telecom microwave network, which has actually been designed with several major microwave links converging on an isolated tower connected underground into the station.[16] The station also intercepts satellite and radio communications and is a ground station for the electronic eavesdropping satellites. Each of Menwith Hill's

Canada's Leitrim station, just south of Ottawa, appears to be used to intercept Latin American satellites.

powerful interception and processing systems presumably has its own Dictionary computers connected into the ECHELON system.

Menwith Hill, sitting in northern England, several thousand kilometres from the Persian Gulf, was awarded the NSA's Station of the Year prize for 1991 following its role in the Gulf War. It is a station which affects people throughout the world.

In the early 1980s James Bamford uncovered some information about a worldwide NSA computer system codenamed Platform which, he wrote, 'will tie together fifty-two separate computer systems used throughout the world. Focal point, or "host environment", for the massive network will be the NSA headquarters at Fort Meade. Among those included in Platform will be the British SIGINT organisation, GCHQ.'[17]

There is little doubt that Platform is the system that links all the major UKUSA station computers in the ECHELON system. Because it involves computer-to-computer communications, the GCSB and perhaps DSD were only able to be integrated into the system in the 1990s when the intelligence and military organisations in the two countries changed over to new computer-based communications systems.

The worldwide developments, of which construction of the Waihopai station was part, were co-ordinated by the NSA as Project P415. Although most of the details remained hidden, the existence of this highly secret project targeting civilian communications was publicised in August 1988 in an article by Duncan Campbell. He described how the UKUSA countries were 'soon to embark on a massive, billion-dollar expansion of their global electronic surveillance system', with 'new stations and monitoring centres ... to be built around the world and a chain of new satellites launched'.

The satellite interception stations reported to be involved in P415 included the NSA's Menwith Hill station, the GCHQ's Morwenstow and Hong Kong stations and the Waihopai and Geraldton stations in the South Pacific. Other countries involved, presumably via the NSA, were said to be Japan, West Germany and, surprisingly, the People's Republic of China.

'Both new and existing surveillance systems are highly computerised,' Campbell explained. 'They rely on near total interception of international commercial and satellite communications in order to locate the telephone and other target messages of target individuals....'[18]

There were two components to the P415 development, the first being the new stations required to maintain worldwide interception. More striking, though, was the expansion of the NSA's ECHELON system, which now links all the Dictionary computers of all the participating countries.

The ECHELON system has created an awesome spying capacity for the United States, allowing it to monitor continuously most of the world's communications. It is an important component of its power and influence in the post-Cold War world order, and advances in computer processing technology continue to increase this capacity.

The NSA pushed for the creation of the system and has the supreme position within it. It has subsidised the allies by providing the sophisticated computer programmes used in the system, it undertakes the bulk of the interception operations and, in return, it can be assumed to have full access to all the allies' capabilities.

Since the ECHELON system was extended to cover New Zealand in the late 1980s, the GCSB's Waihopai and Tangimoana stations — and indeed all the British, Canadian and Australian stations too — can be seen as elements of a United States system and as serving that system. The GCSB stations provide some information for New Zealand government agencies, but the primary logic of these stations is as parts of the global network.

On 2 December 1987, when Prime Minister David Lange announced plans to build the Waihopai station, he issued a press statement explaining that the station would provide greater independence in intelligence matters: 'For years there has been concern about our dependence on others for intelligence — being hooked up to the network of others and all that implies. This government is committed to standing on its own two feet.'

Lange believed the statement. Even as Prime Minister, no one had told him about the ECHELON Dictionary system and the way that the Waihopai station would fit into it. The government was not being told the truth by officials about New Zealand's most important intelligence facility and was not being told at all about ECHELON, New Zealand's most important tie into the United States intelligence system. The Waihopai station could hardly have been more 'hooked up to the network of others', and to all that is implied by that connection.

CHAPTER THREE

THE POWER OF THE DICTIONARY
INSIDE ECHELON

The GCSB's analysts work in a long, open plan room on the 14th floor of the Freyberg Building. Their boss, called K, is the same Glen Singleton who first came to the GCSB on posting from the NSA. On any day, some of the analysts are reading intercepted Japanese diplomatic cables, some are sorting through personal and government telexes from South Pacific countries, others are checking French communications and so on.

The strange feeling of reading other people's private communications has long worn off and the contents are generally routine. Some members of the KE section studiously plough their way through translations of the longest established — but also a notoriously boring — area of the GCSB's work: intercept from Russian fishing boats.

The radio telexes, from fishing trawlers back to their Russian companies, report their catch sizes and the types of fish: hoki for the trawlers around the South Island, southern blue whiting from further south and orange roughy from the Chatham Rise. Telegram-style Morse code messages from a Russian base in Antarctica say that Vladimir will be returning to Russia early, on 15 March, and that the last of the tractor parts have finally arrived.

Hardly earth-shattering national security information, but it constitutes the GCSB's part of the UKUSA alliance's reduced, but still considerable, preoccupation with monitoring all things Russian.

Geoff Holmes, who is one of these Russian analysts, is fairly typical of the intelligence analysis staff. After he left Otago University in 1983 with a BA (Hons) in Russian language, he ended up with a salesman job while he took further part-time Russian courses. In January 1986 he noticed a job advertised at the Ministry of Defence involving report writing and research and requiring 'oral and written foreign language ability'. The people, who turned out to be part of something called the Government Communications Security Bureau, sounded particularly interested in his Russian training. They flew him to Wellington for two days of interviews and personality, psychological and language tests. He was offered a job, still without being told precisely what the work was about, and, after waiting some months for his SIS clearance, he joined the K2 Russian analysis cell in July of that year.

The Waihopai Dictionary computer reads everything intercepted — government faxes, diplomatic cables, environmentalists' e-mail, even birthday messages — searching for pre-programmed keywords. Each overseas agency has a separate search list in the Waihopai Dictionary and is automatically sent all messages containing its keywords.

His first experience of the UKUSA alliance was its security 'indoctrination' (they really use this word). The indoctrination was done by GCSB security officer Don Allan, and consisted of a strict lecture about never, for the rest of his life, talking about his job with anyone except other indoctrinated people. GCSB workers are forbidden to say anything about their work, even to their partners.

The indoctrination concluded with Holmes signing the two-page indoctrination form, which refers to New Zealand laws for punishing infringements (in the Crimes Act) but which originates primarily in UKUSA regulations. Equivalent forms must be signed by staff throughout the UKUSA alliance.

By 1994 Holmes had been seven years at the GCSB as a Russian linguist, including training courses overseas and a two-year stint as acting head of the

Russian language cell while his boss was on a posting to the Canadian UKUSA agency. The stories of the GCSB's other analysts are similar – most are language graduates who end up in the intelligence world by chance after seeing an advertisement. Mostly they arrive soon after graduating, faced with the need to find a job that fits their language degrees. But usually they do not stay long, once they find out what the job actually involves.

One of the main inducements to stay in the job is the possibility of overseas travel and postings to the other UKUSA agencies. In addition to a comprehensive structure of joint procedures, regulations and systems, an important device for integrating a small agency like the GCSB into the UKUSA alliance is developing personal links between staff in the different agencies. Indoctrinated GCSB staff cannot discuss their work with their families and friends, but they can talk with foreign agency staff. These personal links are developed in the GCSB through overseas training courses, postings and staff exchanges, regular UKUSA visitors, meetings and intelligence conferences and recruiting staff from the other agencies.

In the middle of 1994 Holmes got his first overseas posting — and a prestigious one at that. He is currently living in Ellicott City, a satellite city of Washington DC, on a three-year posting to the centre of the UKUSA alliance, the enormous NSA headquarters at Fort George G. Meade. This posting was the first one ever by a GCSB analyst to the NSA. Before he left Wellington his daily work, like that of all the analysts, revolved entirely around that most striking manifestation of GCSB's links with the NSA: the ECHELON Dictionary system.

Each morning the signals intelligence analysts in Wellington log on at their computer terminals and enter the Dictionary system, just as their equivalents do in Washington, Ottawa, Cheltenham and Canberra. What follows is a precise description of how the system works, the first time it has been publicly described.

After entering their security passwords, the analysts reach a directory that lists the different categories of intercept available, each with a four-digit code; 4066, for instance, might be the Russian fishing trawlers, 5535 Japanese diplomatic traffic in the South Pacific, 4959 communications from South Pacific countries and so on. They type in the code for the category they want to use first that day. As soon as they make a selection, a 'search result' appears, stating the number of documents which have been found fitting that category.

The day's work then begins, reading through screen after screen of intercepted telexes and other types of messages. If a message appears worth reporting on, the analyst can select it from the rest and work on it out of the Dictionary system. He or she then translates the message — either in its entirety or as a summary called a 'gist' — and writes it into the standard format of all intelligence reports produced anywhere within the UKUSA network.

This is the 'front end' of the Dictionary system, using a commercially available computer programme (called BRS Search). It extracts the different categories of intercepted messages (known just as 'intercept') from the large GCSB computer data base of intercept from the New Zealand stations and overseas agencies. Before anything goes into this data base, the actual searching and selection of intercepted messages has already occurred — in the Dictionary computers at the New Zealand and overseas stations.

All the text messages (written communications such telexes, faxes, e-mail) intercepted at the Waihopai station are fed into these computers. This is an enormous mass of material — literally all the business, government and personal messages that the station catches. The computers automatically

GCSB analysts received raw intelligence, codenamed GERANIUM, from the GCHQ's Hong Kong station until its closure in 1995. The hill behind the station, until 1991, was a radio interception site which New Zealanders helped to operate (see Chapter 5).

search through everything as it arrives at the station.

This is the work of the Dictionary programme. It reads every word and number in every single incoming message and picks out all the ones containing target keywords and numbers. Thousands of simultaneous messages are read in 'real time' as they pour into the station, hour after hour, day after day, as the computer finds intelligence needles in the telecommunications haystack. It is not known whether telephone conversations intercepted by the station are processed in the same way. The GCSB does not routinely analyse telephone communications but this does not mean it is not collecting them for the other agencies.

Mike Frost's exposé of Canadian 'embassy collection' operations revealed that the NSA has computers called Oratory that can 'listen' to telephone calls and recognise when keywords are spoken. Just as we can recognise words spoken in all the different tones and accents we encounter, so, too, can these computers. Telephone calls containing keywords are automatically extracted from the masses of other calls and recorded digitally on magnetic tapes to be listened to by analysts back in the agency headquarters.

The implications of this capability are immense. The UKUSA agencies can use machines to search through all the telephone calls in the world, just as they do for written messages. Since they have this equipment to use in embassy collection, they will certainly use it in all the stations throughout the ECHELON network, including, in all probability, the GCSB stations. Anyone who makes international telephone calls needs to be aware of this capability. It has nothing to do with whether someone is deliberately tapping your telephone, simply whether you say a keyword or combination of keywords that is of interest to one of the UKUSA agencies.[1]

All the messages intercepted at the two GCSB stations are connected by Telecom line to the Information Centre in the Wellington headquarters, sent there in unbreakable UKUSA codes. From the 'Infocen', they are transmitted by fibre optic cable down to the GCSB data base computers on the 12th floor. These computers are connected back up to computer terminals used by the operations staff who study and process the intercept on the 14th floor.

A highly organised system has been developed to co-ordinate this process of selection within the different Dictionary computers and between the different agencies in the ECHELON system. This system, which controls what is being searched for by each station and who can have access to it, is organised as follows.

The individual station's Dictionary computers do not simply have a long list of keywords to search for. And they do not send all the product into some huge data base into which participating agencies can dip as they wish. It is much more controlled than this.

The search lists are organised into the same categories, referred to by four-digit numbers, that the analysts use. Each agency decides its own categories according to its responsibilities for producing intelligence for the network; for the GCSB this means South Pacific governments, Japanese diplomatic and so on. The agency then works out about 10 to 50 keywords to use to select for this category. The keywords include such things as names of people, ships, organisations, countries and subjects. They also include the known telex and fax numbers and Internet addresses of the individuals, businesses, organisations and government offices they want to target. These are generally written as part of the message text and so are easily recognised by the Dictionary computers.

The agencies also specify combinations of these to help sift out communications of interest. For example, they might search for diplomatic cables containing both the words 'Suva' and 'aid', or cables containing the word 'Suva' but *not* the word 'consul' (to avoid the masses of routine consular communications). It is these sets of words and numbers (and combinations of them), under a particular category, that are placed in the Dictionary computers.

The whole system, devised by the NSA, has been adopted completely by the GCSB, which has separate ECHELON Dictionary computers for the Waihopai and Tangimoana stations. Because they are intercepting such massive quantities of communications and having to process them all in real time, each of these computers has the capacity for only a certain number of the categories.

Both stations have several GCSB categories, since the GCSB has primary responsibility within the network for reporting on the South Pacific, which these stations help to cover. But they also have various categories containing sets of keywords for each of the other UKUSA agencies. Likewise, some GCSB categories are in the Dictionaries of some of the other agencies' stations. As a GCSB worker explained, 'it all works as one system'.

The Dictionary computers search through all the incoming messages and, whenever they encounter one with any of the agencies' keywords, they select it. At the same time the computer automatically notes such technical details as the time and place of interception on the piece of intercept so that analysts reading it, in whichever agency it is going to, know where it came from and what it is.

Finally the computer writes the four-digit code (for the category with the keywords in that message) at the bottom of the text of the message. This is important. It means that when all the intercepted messages end up together in the data base at the GCSB or another agency, the messages on a particular subject can be located again. Later, when the analyst using the Dictionary system selects the four-digit code for the category he or she wants, the computer simply searches through all the messages in the data base for the ones that have been tagged with that number.[2]

Something like 2000 individual messages are selected out by the ECHELON system for the GCSB each week, coming from the stations in New Zealand and overseas. Over the week the 2000 messages go into the Freyberg Building computer data bases. Each piece of intercept is numbered as it is placed in the data base (so that the analysts can know they had looked through them up to document number 824 yesterday and start at number 825 today).[3]

This system is very effective for controlling which agencies can get what from the global network. Each agency requests to have 'numbers' placed on the Dictionaries of particular stations run by the other agencies. Over time, they also regularly ask that the combination of keywords and numbers for that number be amended to improve or refocus the selection of messages extracted by the computer.

But each agency gets the intelligence out of the ECHELON system only from its own numbers. It does not have any access to the raw intelligence coming out of the system to the other agencies. New Zealand does not even know what communications its station has intercepted and sent to the allies unless a GCSB keyword happens to be in the intercepted message as well. In this case the GCSB analysts also receive a copy of the intercept and can see the other agencies' numbers recorded (along with the GCSB's one) at the bottom.

The analysts in Holmes' section mostly target telex numbers through the Dictionary system. For example, the Japanese diplomatic traffic comes largely from searches for the telex numbers of the targeted diplomatic posts (which are written as part of the telex text). A French military search would be based on some important telex numbers, plus keywords such as 'Mororoa' and 'nucléaires'. South Pacific nation search lists would have many names of political personalities and organisations.

The best set of keywords for each subject category is worked out over time, in part by experimentation. Staff in the GCSB's SIGINT Collection Unit also identify key telex numbers for targeting on particular subjects. The staff sometimes trial a particular set of keywords for a period and, if they find they are getting too much 'junk', they can change some words to get a different selection of traffic.

(If it is all starting to sound like an impersonal processing job, remember that these messages, the 'junk' and the interesting ones, are the supposedly private communications of individuals and organisations throughout the Pacific.)

One person in the C unit has the job of Dictionary Manager. This role dates from the second half of 1988 when Ann Wiseman was moved to the section and sent to the NSA for a few months of special training for this job — at the same time, according to Duncan Campbell's information on Project P415, as staff from other signals intelligence agencies around the world were also getting specialised training at the NSA on the ECHELON system.

Wiseman had previously been doing South Pacific reporting in the GCSB's K3 cell. One of the few non-graduate analysts, she had originally been in the British Army, and then emigrated to New Zealand and got a job in Army signals before joining the GCSB in August 1987.[4] After she returned from the NSA her job was to liaise with the GCSB analysts about what types of telexes were of most interest and to select keywords that covered those subjects. At that time there was a computer searching through the radio telexes intercepted at Tangimoana and those containing the keywords went to the analysis cells. A year later, when the Waihopai station was opened and a new computer-based communications system introduced to link the GCSB to its allies, the full ECHELON Dictionary system came into operation.

The Dictionary Manager administers the sets of keywords in the two GCSB Dictionary computers, adding, amending and deleting as required. This is the person who adds the new ship name to the keyword list in the four-digit Russian ship intercept category, deletes a keyword from another because it is not triggering interesting messages, or adds a 'but not *****' to another category because it has been receiving too many irrelevant messages and a lot of them contain that word.[5]

Each station in the ECHELON network has enough space in its Dictionary computers only for a certain number of categories (and older stations such as Yakima have quite a limited capacity). Also, some stations are better able to pick up certain classes of intelligence because of their locations. The station that can intercept a message from Hong Kong to an organisation operating in the Solomon Islands may not be able to intercept the organisation's reply from the Solomon Islands back to Hong Kong.

There is, therefore, continuous liaison and co-ordination between the

The Yakima station collects intelligence for the American NSA and, since the early 1980s, the GCSB has been allocated the job of analysing some of this for the alliance. Yakima is the main United States site for intercepting Pacific satellites.

UKUSA allies about how best to deploy the overall system. The GCSB station Dictionaries are not necessarily set to search first for GCSB target subjects; if, for example, experience shows Waihopai and Tangimoana are not getting much on two of the GCSB's numbered categories, they may take these numbers off the Dictionary and free up the space for numbers from the other agencies that are more productive.

There are examples of this at the Waihopai station. Staff there do not know what specific messages are being intercepted, but they do know that traffic analysis has shown that the station does not get much of the French intelligence analysed in the GCSB's KP section. But it is very good, for example, at picking up Papua New Guinea communications for the Australian agency, the DSD.

The French communications required for the GCSB are mostly intercepted at other UKUSA stations (particularly Yakima). Papua New Guinea communications, to assist Australia in its questionable policies towards that nation and neighbouring independence movements in West Papua and Bougainville, are intercepted at Waihopai.

Inside the five UKUSA agencies, the staff using the ECHELON system are encouraged to approach their work as a collaborative effort between the allies. Each of the five agencies has clearly defined areas about which it produces finished intelligence reports for the alliance. The etiquette is that if your keywords are producing interesting material in another agency's area of work, you leave it to their analysts to write it up as a finished report (although you would check that they received a copy of the intercepted message).

Although a considerable part of the GCSB's intelligence production is primarily to serve the UKUSA alliance, New Zealand does not, by any means, have access to the whole ECHELON network — and the access it does have is strictly controlled. As a GCSB officer explained: 'The agencies can all apply for numbers on each other's Dictionaries. The hardest to deal with are the Americans.... [there are] more hoops to jump through, unless it is in their interest in which case they'll do it for you.'

There is only one agency which, by virtue of its size and role within the alliance, will have access to the full potential of the ECHELON system: the agency that set it up — the NSA. The GCSB has no access at all to most components of the ECHELON system. It has limited access even to the areas to which it contributes, notably the civilian satellite communications.

The existence and capabilities of the ECHELON Dictionary system, and New Zealand participation in it, are among the GCSB's greatest secrets. In fact there has only ever been one public reference to the Dictionary system anywhere in the world. This was in 1991 when a former British GCHQ official spoke anonymously to Granada Television's *World in Action* about abuses of power by the GCHQ. He told the programme about an anonymous red brick building at 8 Palmer Street in London where the GCHQ secretly intercepts every telex that passes into, out of or through London, feeding them into powerful computers with a programme known as 'Dictionary'.

He explained that the operation is staffed by carefully vetted British Telecom people: 'It's nothing to do with national security. It's because it's not legal to take every single telex. And they take everything: the embassies, all the business deals, even the birthday greetings, they take everything. They feed it into the Dictionary.'[6]

What the programme did not reveal is that Dictionary is not just a British system; it is UKUSA-wide.

The only known public reference to the ECHELON system was made in relation to the Menwith Hill station. In July 1988, a United States news-

51

paper, the Cleveland *Plain Dealer*, published a story about electronic monitoring of the phone calls of a Republican senator, Strom Thurmond. The alleged monitoring had occurred at Menwith Hill.

Behind this story, a congressional investigation was occurring after allegations of corruption and misspending had been made to a congressman by a former computer specialist at the station, Margaret Newsham. As an employee of the Lockheed Space and Missiles Corporation, she had worked at Menwith as a contract employee. She is said to have told congress staff that, while at Menwith, she was able to listen through earphones to telephone calls being monitored. After leaving the base, she was, until the mid-1980s, software manager for more than a dozen VAX computers at Menwith Hill which operate as part of the ECHELON system.[7] When investigators subpoenaed witnesses and sought access to plans and manuals for the ECHELON system, they found that there were no formal controls over who could be targeted; junior staff were able to feed in target names to be searched for by the computers without any check on their authority to do so.[8]

None of this is surprising and it is likely to be insignificant compared with official abuse of the system. The capabilities of the ECHELON system are so great, and the secrecy surrounding it makes it so impervious to democratic oversight, that the temptation to use it for questionable projects seems irresistible.

The Newsham information concerned the ECHELON system as it was in the early 1980s, when it probably included only United States (and possibly British) stations. By the 1990s, when New Zealand, Australia, Canada and a number of non-UKUSA nations have been integrated into it and new facilities have became operational, the upgraded and expanded ECHELON system will have an even greater capability. Advances in computer technology alone will have multiplied its capacity.

In June 1992 a group of current 'highly placed intelligence operatives' from the British GCHQ spoke to the *Observer*: 'We feel we can no longer remain silent regarding that which we regard to be gross malpractice and negligence within the establishment in which we operate.' They gave as examples GCHQ interception of three charitable organisations, including Amnesty International and Christian Aid. As the *Observer* reported:

> "At any time GCHQ is able to home in on their communications for a routine target request," the GCHQ source said. In the case of phone taps the procedure is known as Mantis. With telexes this is called Mayfly. By keying in a code relating to Third World aid, the source was able to demonstrate telex "fixes" on the three organisations.

"It is then possible to key in a triggerword which enables us to home in on the telex communications whenever that word appears," he said. "And we can read a pre-determined number of characters either side of the keyword."[9]

Without actually naming it, this was a fairly precise description of how the ECHELON Dictionary system works. Note that it was being used for telephone calls. Again, what was not revealed in the publicity was that this is a UKUSA-wide system. The design of the ECHELON system means that the interception of these organisations could have occurred anywhere in the network, at any station where the GCHQ had requested that the four-digit code covering Third World aid be placed.

Examples of questionable use of the intelligence system by some agencies does not imply that a small agency like the GCSB does the same. But within the integrated system it does not need to to be co-operating in whatever is being done. Interception projects by any of the other agencies can be using a GCSB station, with the messages extracted according to the other agency's keywords, and (apart from the general subject) the GCSB staff would not even know what their station was providing.

It is not known what four-digit categories have been placed on the Dictionary computers at Waihopai and Tangimoana for the other agencies. Only a handful of GCSB staff (and certainly no politicians) will know. But, as the most junior ally in the network, New Zealand is in no position to refuse a request. The contents of this secret list are an

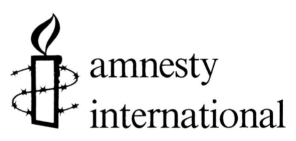

The British GCHQ routinely uses the ECHELON Dictionary system to spy on groups such as Amnesty International.

important element of New Zealand foreign policy, determining who New Zealand helps the United States and the other allies to spy on.

Other worrying cases of misuse of the intelligence services in Britain have come to light. In the mid-1980s, GCHQ staff revealed anonymously that international arms dealers and prospective arms buyers were being targeted by the GCHQ. According to Duncan Campbell:

These sources say that 'anything of value indicating a potential arms deal' — especially contracts being negotiated by other countries — is immediately passed on to an authorised official of the Defence Sales Organisation of the Ministry of

Defence. But the same is not true of GCHQ intelligence concerning, say, civil engineering contracts or other British manufactured goods. Only opportunities for private arms sales are given priority in British intelligence 'targeting'.[10]

The aim of the GCHQ work was not to control or monitor the activities of the arms traders, but to give British arms manufacturers tip-offs about where they might get a sale and how to beat their competitors.

In a further misuse of the GCHQ, a former intelligence employee revealed that Prime Minister Margaret Thatcher had personally ordered interception of the Lonrho company, owners of *Observer* newspaper, after that newspaper published a series of articles in 1989 exposing events surrounding a multi-billion dollar British arms deal with Saudi Arabia. The newspaper said the deal had been pushed strongly by Mrs Thatcher, and it was alleged that massive bribes were made to middlemen, including her son, Mark, who was said to have received a £10 million commission.

The former employee of the British Joint Intelligence Committee, Robin Robison, broke his indoctrination oaths and told the *Observer* that, as part of his job, which involved sorting intelligence reports from the British intelligence agencies, he personally forwarded GCHQ transcripts of intercepted communications about Lonrho to Mrs Thatcher's office.[11]

Since the introduction of the ECHELON Dictionary system, if the arms dealers' communications (or the communications of Amnesty International as it worked to expose some of the human effects of this trade) happened to be routed via the Pacific satellite being monitored by the GCSB, then New Zealand could have assisted its allies in this abuse of power.

Mike Frost, co-author of the CSE exposé, wrote about a similar incident involving Margaret Thatcher. He said that in February 1983 the CSE received a special request from the GCHQ to conduct a short interception operation in central London. They were briefed that Thatcher suspected two of her ministers were not 'on side' and wanted them spied. The CSE agreed and Frost's boss travelled to London to conduct the operation from inside the Canadian High Commission building. The GCHQ provided the frequencies to look for and paid all the costs. His boss simply handed over all the tapes to the GCHQ at the end of the operation. 'I don't know if she got what she was looking for,' he later told Frost, 'but some of it was very interesting.'[12]

Why did the GCHQ ask Canadians to do the job? Deniability. If questions had ever been asked, it could 'honestly' have been said that the GCHQ had conducted no such interception. It appears that this sort of favour is often done between the UKUSA agencies to avoid political accountability in the country wanting some illegal or sensitive interception done.

Frost had been involved in some highly questionable operations within his own country. In 1975, for example, he was instructed to intercept the then Prime Minister's wife, Margaret Trudeau, on behalf of the Royal Canadian Mounted Police Security Service. For several weeks he monitored her car phone from the CSE headquarters, for no better reason than that the Security Service wanted information about whether she was 'buying and using pot'.[13] He was also aware of an analysis section at the CSE dealing purely with the 'French Problem', apparently indicating that communications concerning Canadian Quebec separatists were being intercepted.

Like the British examples, Frost's stories will be only the tip of the iceberg. There is no evidence of a UKUSA code of ethics or of a tradition of respect for Parliament or civil liberties in their home countries. The opposite seems to be true: that anything goes as long as you do not get caught. Secrecy not only permits but encourages questionable operations.

These are the organisations with which the GCSB is most closely linked, on which it models itself and to which it owes numerous favours for training, equipment and intelligence supplied.

Three observations need to be made about the immense spying capability provided by the ECHELON system.

The first is that the magnitude of the global network is a product of decades of intense Cold War activity. Yet with the end of the Cold War it has not been demobilised and budgets have not been significantly cut. Indeed the network has grown in power and reach. Yet the public justifications, for example that 'economic intelligence is now more important', do not even begin to explain why this huge spying system should be maintained. In the early 1980s Cold War rhetoric was extreme and global war was seriously discussed and planned for. In the 1990s, the threat of global war has all but disappeared and none of the allies faces the remotest serious military threat.

The second point about the ECHELON capabilities is that large parts of the system, while hiding behind the Cold War for their justification, were never primarily about the Cold War at all. The UKUSA alliance did mount massive operations against the Soviet Union and other 'communists', but other elements of the worldwide system, such as the interception of Intelsat communications, microwave networks and many regional satellites, were not aimed primarily at the Russians, the Iraqis or the North Koreans. Then, and now, they are targeting groups which do not pose any physical threat to the UKUSA allies at all. But they are ideal to use against political opponents, economic competitors, countries where the allies may want to gain some advantage (especially access to cheap resources) and administrations (like Nicaragua's Sandinista government) which do not fit an American-dominated world order.

The third observation is that telecommunications organisations — including New Zealand telephone companies — are not blameless in all of this. These companies, to which people pay their monthly bills believing that the phone calls they make and the faxes they send are secure, should be well aware of the wholesale interception of 'private' communications that has been occurring for decades. Yet they neither invest in encryption technology nor insist that organisations such as the Washington-based Intelsat Corporation provide encryption. They do not let their customers know that their international communications are open to continuous interception. Wittingly or unwittingly, this lack of action assists large-scale spying against the individuals, businesses and government and private organisations that innocently entrust their communications to these companies.

ECHELON is a staggeringly comprehensive and highly secret global spying system, over which the smaller allies have virtually no control but to which they contribute fully. Around the world there are networks of spy stations and spy satellites which can intercept communications anywhere on the planet. New Zealand is part of that network. In the chapters that follow its role is revealed publicly for the first time.

CHAPTER FOUR

FIGHTING THE COLD WAR
THE ROLE OF UKUSA

In the late 1940s the United States and Britain signed one of the most significant and influential international agreements of the last 50 years: the UKUSA agreement. Just as the Bretton Woods Conference of 1944 shaped international trade, so this agreement has shaped and dominated Western signals intelligence operations throughout the post-war period. Like Bretton Woods, the UKUSA agreement between a victorious United States and a depleted Britain placed the former firmly in the dominant role.

The UKUSA agreement served to establish a post-war alliance between the United States, Britain, Canada, Australia and New Zealand for covertly intercepting and analysing radio communications from countries all around the world. It built into a permanent force a worldwide electronic spy system that the American and British authorities believed had been a crucial element of their victory in the Second World War.

In the 1990s, radio officers with earphones have largely given way to satellite interception and the immense computer capabilities of the ECHELON system, but UKUSA is still the basis of it all. It is New Zealand's deepest, strongest and most valued alliance tie to the United States, Britain and Australia.

How did New Zealand, small and remote from the world's major power

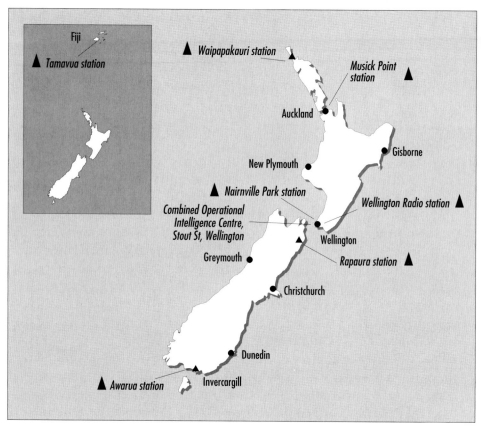

New Zealand Second World War signals intelligence facilities: seven secret New Zealand-run radio interception stations operated during the Second World War.

conflicts, come to be one of five members of the closest and most powerful intelligence alliance in the Western world? For the most part it was an accident of history.

The UKUSA alliance grew directly out of relationships developed during the Second World War, when urgency and necessity led to rapid integration of United States and Commonwealth intelligence operations. Not only was New Zealand part of the Commonwealth, and so, inevitably, part of British military plans, but it was also the only time that New Zealand has been seriously threatened. Submarine nets were being constructed across harbour entrances, large guns were being built around the coasts, the whole population and economy were mobilised towards the war effort. Tens of thousands of American troops passed through and were based in New Zealand during those years and the large numbers of New Zealanders fighting overseas operated as part of Allied military forces. There was a compelling logic to united effort and co-operation with larger, stronger allies.

The secret component of this co-operation, New Zealand's Second World War intelligence organisation, was mostly constructed very rapidly in 1941 and 1942 when, after attacking Pearl Harbor in December 1941, the Japanese military was expanding into the Pacific at an alarming rate. A network of signals intelligence stations was constructed to help counter this threat and operated as part of the British-American intelligence system. The seven New Zealand stations and the Wellington intelligence headquarters (which were linked to Allied analysis centres in Australia) are documented for the first time in Appendix D.[1]

The United States-Commonwealth wartime intelligence co-operation was formalised in the 1943 BRUSA agreement, just as the Pacific War was finally turning. Island by island, the massive American military forces were destroying Japanese military strongholds and pushing back Japan's area of military control. Modern-day supporters of New Zealand participation in an American-led military alliance frequently refer to the experiences of the Second World War to explain the value of such involvement. But the 1940s is arguably the last time that the alliance with northern hemisphere Western powers was strongly in New Zealand's interests. Within two years of the BRUSA agreement atomic bombs had been dropped on Hiroshima and Nagasaki and the war was over. The intelligence alliance born of wartime co-operation was transferred almost immediately to a new, quite different, Cold War, which was rapidly developing into a nuclear confrontation.

Immediately after the war there had been rapid demobilisation: most service people, including nearly all of the intelligence staff, returned to civilian life, coastal defences were dismantled, the Wellington intelligence centre was disbanded and the New Zealand-run signals intelligence stations were either returned to the Post and Telegraph Department or closed. However, within months of the Japanese surrender, the five Anglo-Saxon Allied nations began rebuilding their intelligence capabilities.

Throughout 1946 secret discussions were looking at the arrangements for ongoing intelligence co-operation. During that year Britain had meetings with the three predominantly white-skinned, English-speaking Commonwealth allies (Canada, Australia and New Zealand, but no African or Asian colonies) dividing up the world into geographical areas of responsibility. The meetings related to three main types of intelligence: signals intelligence, joint military intelligence and naval intelligence.[2] In essence, the *British/Allied* arrangements of the Second World War were converted into post-war *Commonwealth* arrangements, with signals intelligence (SIGINT) effectively coming under the control of a British-American alliance.

In April-May 1946 a Commonwealth Prime Ministers' meeting (Walter Nash represented New Zealand) was held in London to discuss how Commonwealth defence could be shared to relieve the economically exhausted Britain. It was at this conference that the concept of dividing the world into regional responsibilities was agreed. Australia's Ben Chifley told the meeting that they had in mind intelligence organisations based in Melbourne, covering the Pacific area, staffed by both Australians and New Zealanders.

Then the following month, June 1946, the London Conference on Post-War Commonwealth SIGINT Organisation worked out arrangements that incorporated New Zealand into the new Commonwealth SIGINT Organisation (CSO), headed by the GCHQ and with spheres of cryptographic influence shared between Britain, Canada, Australia and New Zealand.[3] An Australian SIGINT Centre, to be known publicly as Defence Signals Bureau, would be established and assigned an operational area of 'Ceylon, Malaysia, Hong Kong, New Zealand, Australia and all areas within this perimeter'. It was also agreed that 'Australian, New Zealand and United Kingdom personnel would be equally eligible for appointment to posts in the Centre', that New Zealand would provide an intercept and radio direction-finding (D/F) station, that the Melbourne centre would control the overseas intercept and D/F stations in its area of operations and that it would be 'responsible for the dissemination of signal intelligence to all Ministries, Departments and Command Headquarters (whether British, Australian or New Zealand) within the area'.[4]

Defence House in Stout Street, Wellington, contained New Zealand's intelligence headquarters during and after the Second World War. Today it houses the Directorate of Defence Intelligence and Security Intelligence Service.

Australia responded quickly to the Commonwealth plans. The DSB began operating in Melbourne in 1946,[5] as did the Joint Intelligence Bureau, the sister organisation of the JIBs in Ottawa and London formed the same year.

Prime Minister Peter Fraser agreed that New Zealand did not need its own separate signals intelligence organisation or Joint Intelligence Bureau. He believed that New Zealand should fit into the Australian structures, with small numbers of New Zealand staff posted to the DSB and JIB in Melbourne.[6] (In fact, New Zealanders were posted to the DSB but New Zealand established its own JIB in Wellington in 1949. The arrangement with the DSB, later called the DSD, lasted for the next 30 years.)

In the summer of 1946-47 the Director of the GCHQ, Sir Edward Travis, who had chaired the London SIGINT conference, visited Australia and New Zealand to finalise plans for the Commonwealth SIGINT Organisation, which was finalised later that year.[7] On 12 November 1947 an Australian Cabinet Committee, made up of only the Prime Minister and Minister of Defence, formally approved Australian participation.[8] New Zealand approval would have been given at this time too, preparing the way for establishment soon after of the UKUSA alliance.

It is very clear what the British believed the alliance was needed for. A May 1948 British Joint Intelligence Committee paper called 'Sigint Intelligence Requirements — 1948' contains a list, in priority order, of all the targets for British signals intelligence.[9] Of the 52 subjects on the list, 45 concern the Soviet Union, including all those ranked priority I, II or III.

The remarkable thing about the UKUSA agreement, given its significance, is that it has largely succeeded in remaining invisible. A wall of secrecy erected in the 1940s has kept nearly everything about it hidden from the citizens of the member countries. The contents of the agreement are competely secret, the membership is officially secret, the name itself is never officially acknowledged. Even the date of the agreement has been unclear. Until recently most writing referred to it as a 1947 agreement but the correct date is 1948.[10] Some bare details such as the name and membership have leaked out, but none of the governments involved is prepared even to acknowledge its existence.

All writing about the UKUSA agreement to date has incorrectly described it as a five-nation agreement, but individuals who have read it say that it is definitely signed only by the United States and Britain. Like BRUSA before it, UKUSA is a two-country agreement which, in practice, covers more than two countries. It forms the basis of the five-nation alliance — but with the United States and Britain the dominant partners from the start.[11]

Although, strictly speaking, New Zealand is not a formal party to UKUSA, the agreement has been the basis of New Zealand's most secret alliance links since the late 1940s and is the foundation upon which the GCSB has been built. The explanation for this lies in the protocols included in UKUSA, which provided for Britain's three Anglo-Saxon Commonwealth partners to participate in signals intelligence arrangements with the two actual signatories — provided that they agreed to observe all the agreement's regulations and procedures. Although Fraser presumably agreed to New Zealand's involvement, a New Zealand National Archives search of confidential Cabinet papers from 1947 and 1948 turned up no documents at all concerning New Zealand's intelligence relations. Whoever made the decision, they clearly decreed that no record of it be placed on the files.[12]

New Zealand's status within the new alliance was summed up in the signing of the protocols, where Australia signed on New Zealand's behalf — and the 'Australian' official who held the pen was in fact a British officer who had been seconded to Australia to head its new post-war signals intelligence organisation. Thus the signature for New Zealand on the UKUSA agreement is Commander J.E. (Teddy) Poulden, from the GCHQ, who had been appointed Director of the Melbourne-based Defence Signals Bureau (DSB) on 1 April 1947.[13]

The UKUSA agreement, formally called the UK-USA Security Agreement, therefore consists of two main signatories, of which the United States is clearly the dominant partner, and three junior partners, of which New Zealand, by virtue of size, is clearly the least dominant. In the decade from 1938 to 1948 New Zealand signals intelligence went from being a link in a colonial chain, to being a sub-unit in a British-American system and, finally, to being a junior partner in an American- and British-led alliance.[14]

New Zealand's most enduring and significant intelligence links (and, in particular, its choice of primary allies) have never been a subject of public discussion since they were cemented in the late 1940s. Nevertheless, New Zealand intelligence staff clearly understand the UKUSA agreement to be the basis of the five-country system within which signals intelligence — always referred to as SIGINT — operations occur each day.

By the beginning of 1947, even before the UKUSA agreement was signed, many of the details of the post-war intelligence alliance had been decided and from that time on New Zealand intelligence planning was shaped by these. One of the first moves, in 1946-47, was the inception of plans for a permanent New Zealand signals intelligence station, as had been recommended at the London conference. Similar developments were occurring in

Royal New Zealand Navy Museum

New Zealand's post-war eavesdropping station, called NR1, operated in complete secrecy for 33 years in the central North Island. A former officer says, 'There was no significant New Zealand input into priorities or targets.' (NR2 pictured.)

Australia; in 1946 the DSB's Pearce station was opened in Perth, in February 1947 it was followed by a station at Cabarlah and, in 1949-50, GCHQ/DSB operations started in both Hong Kong and Singapore.[15]

Although no intelligence files on this period have ever been released to National Archives — they are regarded as too current — seemingly routine administrative correspondence from the late 1940s reveals the next stage in the development of signals intelligence in New Zealand.

In January 1947 the Navy Department began negotiations with the War Assets Realisation Board to purchase a Second World War radio receiving station just south of Waiouru which the Air Force had closed down the year before. (It was only 400 metres away from another receiving station run by the Navy (NR2);[16] there would be no need for two stations in peacetime.) The closed station, situated in swampy country that ensured good radio reception, was bought by the Navy for £5,000 and the following year New Zealand's post-war signals intelligence station, referred to only by the name NR1 (for Navy Receiver 1), began operations.[17] After it changed to intelligence work, NR1 altered little on the outside except for the addition in 1949 of 'unclimbable' security fences and in 1950 of bars on all windows.

That is the end of the information available from Defence files. The description of what went on inside the station has to rely mostly on inside sources. They show that nearly every aspect of its operations over the next 34 years centred on working within and serving the UKUSA alliance.

Throughout the 1950s, 1960s and 1970s, NR1 — New Zealand's most secret facility — operated in clear view of State Highway One, as it runs through rolling hill country in the Central North Island. The country's only signals intelligence station aroused little curiosity as it was located, together with the Navy's main radio receiving station, NR2, amidst hectares of aerials. (The Irirangi station, south of Waiouru, should not be confused with the Navy transmitting station situated directly across the highway from Waiouru township.)

For 30 years the staff of NR1 worked in shifts searching through the airwaves for target transmissions, tapping away at typewriters to record the intercepted messages and sending reports off to the UKUSA allies. These radio intercept officers, communications officers, technicians and clerical staff were totally separate from the Navy staff in NR2.

If a visitor entered the long wooden building, he or she would initially get no further than the entrance area or the offices and mess room leading off it. To get to the operations area, it was necessary to go through a security door and be escorted along the building past the technicians' workshop. In the operations area was the array of radio receiving, cipher and teleprinter equipment that were the heart of the station. And this equipment was constantly being updated, to keep up with the communications 'technology race'.[18]

It was a dismal place to work, isolated on the bleak volcanic plateau, surrounded by screens and thick steel bars across all the windows. The all-male, ex-Navy staff initially stayed in cabins belonging to the Navy radio station.[19] Later they lived in the Waiouru Army camp in rented houses or, for the single men, in a special hostel in Camp Road. A van drove them to and from the station, 10 kilometres south of the Army camp. The main form of socialising was drinks at the local Returned Services Association club. One of the staff described his colleagues as intelligent and eccentric, with a fondness for heavy drinking.

When the first staff arrived at the new station early in 1949, there were only about a dozen radio officers and a couple of technicians, all uniformed military personnel. (It was not until the mid-1950s that all NR1 workers were civilians.) In the early years the staff were being trained, but they still worked tiring eight-hour Navy shifts around the clock. Unlike the strictly run operation across the paddocks, however, the early staff recall the intelligence station as being more like a pirate ship. At this stage NR1 was run by the Navy (overseen by an inter-service committee).

NR1 staff from those times emphasise the central role Britain played in helping to establish the organisation. During its first decade of operations the station was under the control of an officer sent from the British signals intelligence establishment. A second British officer was in charge of technical training. (Although UKUSA was a United States-led alliance, the British GCHQ was more closely involved in all aspects of support for the Waiouru station throughout its existence.) A senior New Zealand radio officer says that from about the 1960s Australia tended to follow the United States in its structures while New Zealand followed Britain. This is seen, for example, in the wholly civilian staff at the GCSB (like the GCHQ) whereas a large proportion of the staff working in the DSD headquarters are uniformed military officers (as at the NSA).

In the mid-1950s the head of the station, the Station Radio Officer (SRO), was H.E. Stutton, recorded in Navy records as 'on loan from Admiralty'.[20] The GCSB, typically, denies that there were ever foreign staff at NR1, but a top secret 1956 document found in the British national archives confirms that Stutton was a senior British signals intelligence officer.[21] He ran the station from sometime before 1955 until 1959, with a New Zealander, Jim Timlin, as his deputy. During those years, besides setting up equipment and procedures, he built up the staff numbers to the roughly 40 level at which they would remain for the next two decades. For some of that 1955-59 period Timlin disappears from the records while he was 'being groomed for the boss's job' in Britain inside the GCHQ. He took over as SRO on 1 July 1959, with Wally Brendon as his deputy.

Before this, shortly after the war, New Zealand military staff began to be posted to the Melbourne-based DSB to work in the posts New Zealand had agreed to fill there (as a substitute for setting up a separate signals intelligence organisation of its own). These were not signals intelligence specialists, but rather military officers filling analysis, communications and administrative roles. These postings have continued up to the present.

The GCSB has refused to release the staff numbers for NR1, a decision which was upheld by the Ombudsman, who argued that this information would harm the security or defence of New Zealand.[22] In fact, all the staff numbers are already public information. One need only look at annual gov-

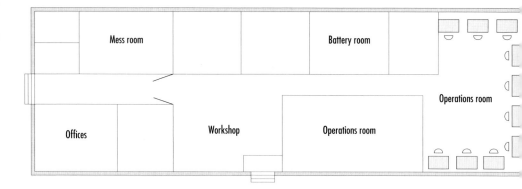

Waiouru NR1 station: target instructions arrived from Melbourne and all the intelligence gathered was sent overseas for analysis.

ernment civilian staff records available on the shelves of many libraries to track the growth of the Waiouru operation. The station's most sensitive workers, the radio officers, appear in the Defence lists as the 'Radio Officers Occupational Class'. Obviously no one thought they needed further disguising. In addition there were about half a dozen technicians at NR1 and a smaller number of administrative staff.

The first two signals intelligence workers to appear in these civilian staff lists are Timlin and Brendon, both of whom left the Navy to become civilian workers on 9 November 1951. Working together, and as good friends, these two would between them run New Zealand signals intelligence operations for the next 30 years. Timlin, who is no longer alive, was greatly respected by his staff and was regarded as brilliant. A colleague described Timlin and Brendon as: 'the last really working for New Zealand .... Now they're more interested in money, but in my day I felt they were really working for New Zealand.'

Timlin, Brendon and the other senior staff were mostly about the same age. They had gone through the war years in their teens and, by the time they helped set up NR1, were in their 20s. Many spent their entire working lives within the signals intelligence world, finally retiring in the 1980s and 1990s.

During the 1950s the station's work mainly involved intercepting Morse code messages and transcribing them into text. All the directions on when and what to monitor came from the DSB in Melbourne. According to NR1 staff, Melbourne acted as the 'controlling centre' for the Pacific-South East Asia region and it, in turn, came under the GCHQ's influence. Within the worldwide network, the NR1 station was referred to as NZC-331.

The shift supervisor did all the external communications (via a highly encrypted telex link), receiving instructions from Melbourne and sending back the raw data collected. In the early years only two or three radio receiver positions were operated at once, meaning that only two or three different targets could be intercepted at one time. This number grew to five or six positions from 1955 when the station was fully operational (it takes four or five radio officers at a station for each position to maintain eight-hour shifts and allow for time off). Some were doing interception tasks, others were analysts searching for and identifying new transmissions as possible future targets. It was a high-pressure job. The officers worked their shifts without any meal or tea breaks and as a shift ended the next worker would slide into position, putting his headphone in as the other pulled his out.

The intercept work was very specialised. Workers say it was important to understand the targets, including the type of communications gear and procedures being used, and also to know the subject so that they could work out gaps in the intercept, but they were not very concerned with the content of messages. The function of the station was interception, not analysis. A major target was ships in the Pacific and the information from this work made sense only when all the information was put together in the United States.

Since the NR1 station functioned as an intercept site for the Melbourne organisation, it can be assumed that at different times it monitored targets from South East Asia across the Pacific and south to Antarctica. Those targets would have been determined by the UKUSA priorities (i.e. mostly British and American) passed on to the Melbourne control centre and by technical decisions about which station would allow the best reception. One of the NR1 officers confirmed this, saying that 'a lot of what we collected did not concern New Zealand. There was no significant input into priorities or targets.'

He said that, as in all Western intelligence organisations during these decades, the primary preoccupation was Communism — which means the Soviet Union, China, independence movements and all manner of more or less socialist oriented organisations. Also, whenever there were possible revolutions or other disruptions in the region — whether Communist or not — they would be targeted.

By the 1960s Morse code was being used less, as communications technology provided equipment that could transmit messages faster and more securely. The developments went through several stages. First, some targets moved to a kind of automated Morse code, where the message was punched on a 'perforator' as holes in a paper tape; later came teleprinter type machines. For some sensitive Soviet transmissions, sophisticated equipment detected and filtered out messages disguised by rapid switching between frequencies. The NR1 officers were impressed by the advanced technology made available by the American and British agencies, repeatedly finding that technological developments applied to signals intelligence would not even be heard of in the commercial world until years later. To keep up with the technological changes, the assistant head of the station, Wally Brendon, went to Britain from 1963 to 1965 for training within the GCHQ and then returned to Waiouru to train his radio officer colleagues in the new skills he had acquired.[23]

It took until 1955 for the fledgling Waiouru operation to be made a permanent and ongoing organisation. The New Zealand Combined Signals Organisation (NZCSO) was established on 15 February of that year, formalising the New Zealand arm of the UKUSA network. Until the formation of the GCSB on 1 September 1977, the NZCSO was responsible for all New Zealand signals intelligence and for the running of the NR1 station.[24] The formation of the NZCSO was the result of a report prepared for the New Zealand government by a Mr Burrough, an officer from the British signals intelligence establishment. Britain wanted New Zealand to form the organisation, in the same way that it pressed for the formation of the New Zealand Special Air Service (SAS), which was also established in 1955, and the New Zealand SIS, which was established the following year. Burrough's report spelt out in detail how New Zealand would contribute to the UKUSA alliance over the following decades.

The NZCSO staff comprised all the radio officers, technicians and administrative staff at the Waiouru station; there was no separate head office until the formation of the GCSB. Instead the NZCSO was overseen by a single Distribution Officer, posted inside Defence Headquarters in Wellington.[25] In practice, the Distribution Officers, who were military officers posted to the position for three-year terms, had much less influence than the bosses at the station 250 kilometres away: Timlin and Brendon.[26] The Stout Street office, which initially contained just the Distribution Officer and his assistant, was in effect a high security mail room. The Distribution Officer took around by hand top secret signals intelligence reports received from the overseas organisations. According to two of the recipients, this intelligence had a very limited circulation (mainly Chiefs of Staff and intelligence directors) and was, in any case, of little use to New Zealand. The intelligence included 'very raw decrypted messages, rather than reports. You had to try to make something of it yourself.' It also included summaries of war situations in which the UKUSA allies were interested.

From about 1966, as the Vietnam War intensified, the volume of overseas signals intelligence reports arriving increased dramatically. In 1966 there was one NZCSO radio officer based in the Defence Headquarters communications centre to help receive signals intelligence materials; by 1968 three staff were being forced to work long hours to clear the volume of traffic flooding in. By 1971, five NZCSO staff were required for this work.[27] By 1973 the Distribution Officer had a staff of 10, including six radio officers and three clerical staff. That year Brendon moved to Wellington to act as Assistant Distribution Officer and later became the Distribution Officer.

All the NZCSO staff were treated administratively as Defence staff and are therefore visible on the staff lists. All three services provided assistance at times (maintenance, technical, operational or administrative). On occasions Army, Navy or Air Force intelligence staff were posted overseas, including the Melbourne postings and as communications intercept officers on Navy ships. Also, the Director of Defence Communications, a position held at one time by the current GCSB Director, Ray Parker, was responsible for policy and for planning 'for the provision of communications facilities in support of the NZCSO'.[28]

Another important recommendation adopted from the Burrough Report was that New Zealand provide trained intercept officers to work in overseas UKUSA stations. A 1965 reference notes that 'the report provided, inter alia, for the contribution by New Zealand of 13 trained civilian personnel to serve overseas in Australia and Singapore'.[29]

The plan involved nine postings in Singapore, three in Melbourne and one training position at HMAS *Harman* in Canberra. The Melbourne postings, within the DSD's headquarters, involved 'traffic analysis' of intercept from the DSD and NZCSO stations. One radio officer explained that his work at Melbourne had 'nothing to do with the content of the messages but [was about] managing interception ... working out when a station is transmitting, how it varies its frequencies and so on'.

From 1955 until early 1974 New Zealand signals intelligence officers were regularly posted to a secret interception station on Singapore Island run by the British and Australians. During their three-year postings they were engaged in interception operations targeted on various South East Asian

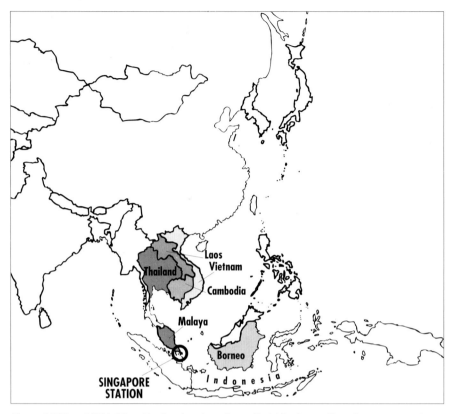

From 1955 to 1974, New Zealanders in a large British-Australian intercept station on Singapore Island spied on communications from all these countries, assisting Britain and the United States during a series of conflicts.

countries. The intelligence they helped to collect was used to locate and identify groups of people during a number of conflicts for targeting by Army operations and bombing raids.

Singapore had been a base for British signals intelligence since the 1930s, with the Far Eastern Combined Bureau (FECB) acting as a regional centre for electronic intercept and codebreaking. The FECB had to be moved abruptly in early 1942 when the Japanese military overran the island, but by 1946 signals intelligence operations had resumed in Singapore against the new enemy, the Soviet Union. The British 800 Special Intelligence Company, commanded by a Major Gibson, was located at Yio Chu Kang camp and had in 1946 embarked on training its new personnel in Russian language.[30]

According to a 1973 Australian Cabinet paper, Britain maintained a

SIGINT facility in Singapore as part of the combined Commonwealth Signals Organisation from approximately 1949 until 1971. In October 1950, the Australian government gave approval for Australian Army personnel to be sent there as 'integrated members' of the station. From then until 1971, when the British withdrew, it was a joint British-Australian Army operation controlled operationally by the DSD, Melbourne.[31] A GCHQ officer who worked at the station is emphatic that it was a GCHQ station, with all the organisation coming from Britain and the Australians and New Zealanders there as guests. The DSD 'operational control' would have been regional co-ordination only.

Four years after Australians started working at the station, the Burrough Report recommended that New Zealand supply staff too. Although the NR1 staff resisted the idea that they were only a 'training station', the other UKUSA allies viewed the station largely as a source of trained staff for overseas operations.

In 1955 there were only 16 civilian radio interception staff at NR1 but by 1961 this had grown to 38, and through into the 1970s it remained at a steady level of about 40 staff.[32] As the numbers of available staff increased, so, too, did the contribution to the Singapore station. The first staff went in 1955 and, by 1966, 10 out of 37 NZCSO radio officers were 'seconded' to the station.[33] Until 1973 there were 10 staff at the station on three-year postings,[34] which meant that most of the NZCSO staff had at least one posting there.

The staff numbers may sound small — New Zealand, after all, had several hundred soldiers permanently based in Singapore until the late 1980s — but signals intelligence operations are disproportionately influential. A quite small covert interception operation can have more effect in a conflict than large numbers of regular troops. (The staff of all New Zealand's intelligence organisations combined totals less than 500; the military, by comparison, numbers over 10,000.)

The types of interception duties at the Singapore station are shown in a diagram drawn by a New Zealand officer who worked at the station in 1966, which found its way accidentally into the unclassified archives of the State Services Commission. The diagram shows that the radio officers in Singapore were engaged in radio direction-finding interception (unlike the Waiouru station) for helping to identify the location of target transmitters, interception of Morse code transmissions, interception of a range of non-Morse transmissions (voice and teleprinter), message handling and distribution duties within the station, cipher duties and typing messages into the teleprinters for transmision to the UKUSA agencies.[35]

By 1966 the station in Singapore (and the one at Waiouru except for direction finding) were equipped to intercept all these different types of radio communications. During the period that New Zealanders were based there, the Singapore station targeted a series of areas of conflict. According to a radio officer at the station, these included: 'Communist' groups in Malaya during the Emergency in the mid-1950s, Thailand (Siam) in the early 1960s, Borneo/Indonesia in the mid-1960s; and Vietnam throughout the 1960s and into the 1970s. During this period the Soviet Union was said to not be a major target for the station. (Other stations were better sited and had staff trained in Russian Morse code.) The Singapore station was very large, so it can be assumed that all these countries, and others such as Laos and Cambodia, were targeted continously throughout this period. In the conflicts listed above New Zealand and Australia were also fighting along-

In Vietnam the most powerful nation on earth fought one of the least powerful: signals intelligence was New Zealand's secret contribution to the war.

side Britain and the United States in the countries concerned.

In 1966-67, when there were only about five radio officers per shift at Waiouru, the Singapore station had about 50 per shift.[36] This gives some insight into the power of the station, where 50 different target transmissions could be monitored simultaneously. Fifty staff per shift suggests a total radio officer staff of over 200. The British staff were civilian radio officers like the New Zealanders, while the Australian staff were Army personnel. The radio officer numbers were reduced to about 150 after July 1971 when it became an Australian-run station.[37]

For the first 20 years, the Singapore station (known as CK2) was located near the middle of Singapore Island at Chai Keng, 8 kilometres along Serangoon Road from the central business area. In 1971 the station (now called KR2) was moved to a much larger complex at Kranji on the northern side of the island beside the Johore Strait.[38]

Because of the stringently enforced 'need to know' rules governing access to information in a signals intelligence station, most or all staff have little idea of how or where the intelligence they are collecting is finally used. For this reason, the story of one Australian Army radio officer working at the Singapore station during the Vietnam War is particularly interesting.

The officer had been conscripted into the Army and, owing to his Quaker beliefs,

As people marched at home, here in Dunedin, the Singapore station identified targets inside Vietnam, Laos and Cambodia for US Air Force bombing strikes.

had opted for non-combat duties. Eventually he found himself working in the large Singapore station, handling intercepted messages sent on the Second World War radios used by the Vietnamese, between different military units fighting the United States and allied troops.

After a while in the job, he realised that names of locations within Vietnam and Laos which he had decoded were appearing in the newspapers a few days later as targets of the American B52 bombing strikes. As time passed, he concluded that signals intelligence from the station was being passed to the United States military to help target its saturation bombing.

An NR1 intercept officer agreed Singapore intelligence was probably used for B52 bombing: 'Yes, that would be standard stuff. They probably used their direction-finding equipment for [B52 targeting] as well.' By 1968 the targeting of all B52 strikes was being conducted from the intelligence centre located inside the United States military headquarters building in Saigon. An analyst working there on locating Laos and Vietnam targets in 1967-68 has described how signals intelligence identifying Vietnamese forces was the favoured information source for targeting. The bombing was so intense that he faced a recurring problem: 'there weren't always enough significant B-52 targets to go around and sometimes we had trouble meeting our daily quota'.[39] Signals intelligence collected at the Singapore station indicating Vietnamese positions would have been used to help fill these deadly quotas. (A year later secret United States B52 bombing raids were weakening Cambodia and providing propaganda for Pol Pot's takeover of the country. There is no reason to assume that the Singapore station was not assisting this operation as well.)

As we have seen, Australia took over the Singapore station in July 1971 after Britain's 1967 decision to withdraw its forces from east of Suez. But in February 1973, in the midst of news about the end of the Vietnam War, the existence of the previously secret 'electronic intelligence unit' in Singapore suddenly hit the news headlines. Gough Whitlam, Australia's newly elected Labour Prime Minister, had disclosed the information in an off-the-record briefing to journalists in Canberra to help explain decisions concerning withdrawal of troops from Singapore.

The first newspaper to publicise the slip had breached an edict issued by the previous Menzies government prohibiting publication of material relating to intelligence operations, but the story was out and was seen as very embarrassing for the supposedly non-aligned Singapore government, which had turned a blind eye to the operation.[40] Within a couple of days of the 15 February briefing, the news was that the Singapore station was being withdrawn.[41]

In fact it took until February 1974, presumably the date when the station closed, before the last of the New Zealand staff at the Singapore station had left. About 70 of the Australian Army staff moved to the new DSD Shoal Bay station in Darwin which was completed in 1974. The New Zealand Assistant Station Radio Officer at the station, I.C. Alford, who had arrived only a year before, was transferred directly from Singapore to a new posting in Melbourne.[42]

By 1973, 10 NZCSO officers were posted to Singapore and three to Australia. After the closure of the Singapore station, the overseas contribution was shifted entirely across the Tasman to Australia, with 13 postings there from 1974. Some of these staff worked in the DSD's Melbourne headquarters and some worked in DSD radio interception stations.

New Zealanders and Australians could still be engaged in communications interception in Singapore today if the operation had not accidentally been exposed in 1973. The Australia New Zealand Military Intelligence Staff (ANZMIS) unit, which photographs shipping in the Straits of Malacca from an American embassy launch, has managed to continue operating quietly in Singapore with the tacit approval of the Singapore government.

The electronic spying operations from the Singapore station were a secret contribution by New Zealand to the various South East Asian conflicts during this period. This meant taking sides — the wrong side according to an increasing number of New Zealanders — with the major powers that were participating in and fuelling these conflicts. The suppression of opposition in Malaya and Thailand, the destabilisation of the government in Indonesia and the destruction rained upon Vietnam, Laos and probably Cambodia were all assisted by these intelligence activities.

For the first 30 years of the post-war alliance, the New Zealand signals intelligence staff at Waiouru and overseas had served the UKUSA network. While governments formally approved the activities, there was no significant New Zealand input into priorities or direction.[43] The New Zealand Combined Signals Organisation was part of a tithe which a handful of officials and politicians agreed, in secret but willingly, to pay for membership of the United States-British alliance. In 1977, when the NZCSO was expanded into the Government Communications Security Bureau, the range of contributions to the UKUSA network increased considerably, but the terms remained substantially the same.

CHAPTER FIVE

THE GCSB, ANZUS AND A NUCLEAR-FREE NEW ZEALAND

Muldoon's approval of the formation of the Government Communications Security Bureau in March 1977 was entirely consistent with the direction in which he was steering his new government. In just 16 months as Prime Minister he had ditched the 1972-75 Labour government's more independent foreign policy and was doing all he could to strengthen the military alliance with the United States. The first ever ANZUS exercise held in New Zealand took place in February 1976 and, later that year, New Zealand troops were part of the biggest ANZUS exercise held in Australia. In all areas of foreign and defence activity, the United States alliance, presented in terms of a reinvigorated 1951 ANZUS Treaty, was becoming more dominant.

Soon after the 1975 election Muldoon opened New Zealand ports to United States nuclear warships. 'To bar them from visiting our harbours,' he said, 'is incompatible with membership of the ANZUS alliance and puts impossible restraints on our allies.' The first nuclear warship, the cruiser USS *Truxtun*, visited Wellington in August 1976. No nuclear warships had visited since early in the Vietnam War, yet a second nuclear cruiser, the USS *Long Beach*, visited Auckland only five weeks later. Both warships entered the harbours with protest yachts crossing their bows, the first actions of what would become a huge public campaign for a nuclear-free New Zealand.

During 1977 Muldoon pushed through unpopular amendments to the Security Intelligence Service (SIS) Act, including legalising electronic bugging of New Zealanders. This is the context in which planning for the GCSB was occurring.

The main promoter of the GCSB was Group Captain Colin Hanson, New Zealand's Director of Defence Intelligence (DDI) in the mid-1970s.

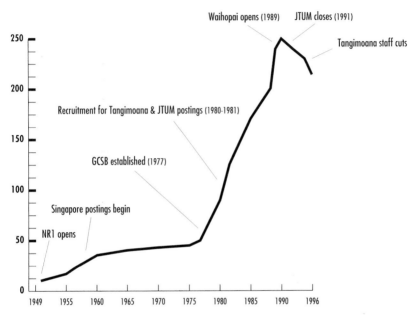

Signals intelligence staff numbers 1949-1996

Signals intelligence operations expanded rapidly after the GCSB formed in 1977.

Hanson had worked in defence intelligence since 1962 and now, as DDI, it was his job to 'formulate policy and maintain general supervision of the operation and development of the intelligence resources of the Ministry of Defence'.[1] These resources included the NZCSO.

In co-operation with the UKUSA allies, Hanson began planning to expand the NZCSO into an organisation equivalent to the other four UKUSA agencies.[2] This meant an organisation separate from the Ministry of Defence with the dual tasks of signals intelligence and communications security, that is, trying to keep New Zealand government communications secure. The signals intelligence role envisaged for the new organisation would not, like the NZCSO, be merely collecting raw intercept for the other agencies.

The recommendation to establish the GCSB came from the New Zealand Intelligence Council (NZIC), whose meetings occurred infrequently and were generally dull. The GCSB proposal will have been brought there by the Secretary of Defence, John Robertson, who went on to be Secretary of Justice when the Official Information Act was passed in 1982. (Later he was Chief Ombudsman, responsible for intelligence matters, when I was seeking material for this book under the Official Information Act.)

Muldoon approved the NZIC recommendation on 15 March 1977 although, as with the UKUSA decision 30 years earlier, no record of the decision was placed on the Cabinet records. The first public sign of the GCSB was a small advertisement for a director in May 1977. A month later Hanson was given the job and travelled overseas to the other UKUSA agencies making plans for his new organisation. The bureau officially came into existence on 1 September 1977. An internal letter written by Robertson in April 1977 noted that the director would 'take under his control the present combined signals organisation', which then had 55 staff, and that nine new positions were being requested to start staffing the bureau[3] — an initial staff of 64.

The GCSB began operating in the renewed Cold War of the late 1970s. All the intelligence activities during its early years were oriented to serving the alliance — and, in particular, to supporting the United States' and Britain's preoccupation with Communism. Key targets of the new organisation would be the Soviet Union and China, plus any other enemies of their UKUSA allies such as Argentina (in the Falklands War) and Japan (in economic competition with the United States).

Hanson's first task was getting the genuine communications security operations underway. One of his first appointments was Squadron Leader Eric Morgon, picked from among his former Air Force colleagues, who became the Assistant Director for Communications Security Policy (including a two-year posting at the NSA as a new GCSB communications system was established in the early 1980s).[4]

Then, in early 1978, several engineers and technicians were appointed to a new Technical Security section (S Section).[5] Technical security (TECSEC) means using high-tech equipment to search for electronic bugs in offices and buildings — in this case, 'sweeping' New Zealand government offices, high commissions and embassies. After training, with British help, these staff were divided into inspection teams and began their continuous schedule of TECSEC inspections around the world.

Later in 1978 the GCSB began moving into a totally new area of operations — a change of greater significance than any other development in New

Zealand signals intelligence during the preceding 40 years. Until 1979 the NZCSO and GCSB were almost exclusively *collection* agencies for the UKUSA network. But then the GCSB moved from collecting to producing intelligence, that is, not only sending off raw intercept to be analysed elsewhere but actually processing this into intelligence reports.

Signals intelligence is produced through a series of stages: planning collection, collection at the station, selecting specific target messages, codebreaking, translation and analysis/report writing. Within a few years the GCSB was doing all of this. Until now, it has managed to keep secret the extent of its move into signals intelligence production.

Again the British GCHQ was involved. The first GCSB director in charge of signals intelligence operations (the Deputy Director of Operations) was recruited directly from the GCHQ. Jim Blackford arrived in 1978 to oversee the expansion of signals intelligence activities in New Zealand. Later, still as a British citizen, he was the first 'New Zealand' liaison officer inside the American agency, the NSA.

The next sign of the GCSB's new role came with the appointment, in 1979, of a retired Army captain, John Brandon, to the new position of Executive Officer Signals Intelligence (later, Assistant Director SIGINT). Brandon had a reliable background. He was raised in an intelligence family, his father's name having featured on a controversial list of suspected SIS agents made public just before the 1977 amendment to the SIS Act made publication of agents' names illegal. He himself was a Vietnam War veteran.

During 1979 Brandon oversaw the establishment of the GCSB's first intelligence analysis cell, called K2, targeted on Soviet intelligence. Clive Comrey, a Russian linguist from the British signals intelligence system, was brought in to head the new cell.

To prepare for his job, Brandon received training in Washington, learning the correct UKUSA procedures for feeding signals intelligence reports into the

RUSS 233 RUSSIAN LITERATURE 2
A passes: K S Frykberg. A W Gale.
Other passes: B J Cresswell A M G McPherson, S N Tapsell.

RUSS 310 RUSSIAN LANGUAGE
A passes: B L McArthur. C S McGhie. R J Scott.
Other passes: A Blades. J A Brandon. M L Greenwood.

RUSS 332 THE NOVEL
A pass: B L McArthur
Other pass: J A Hogan

RUSS 334 SPECIAL TOPIC
Pass: J A HOGAN.

John Brandon, in charge of the GCSB's new analysis sections, studied Russian in work time at Victoria University.

After outgrowing its previous offices, the GCSB moved into its current Freyberg Building headquarters in Aitken Street, opposite Parliament, in 1982.

network, and then, to cement the orientation of the analysis section, he spent the following three years trekking up the hill in work time to learn Russian language at Wellington's Victoria University.

The next cell created, in response to the wishes of the UKUSA allies, was aimed at Japanese targets. Later, in 1983, a third cell was set up to cover French activities in the South Pacific, especially France's nuclear weapon testing programme. In 1984, another major intelligence production development began with staff being trained in preparation for setting up a codebreaking section.

Hanson initially located his fledgling GCSB empire in the same offices as the Directorate of Defence Intelligence (DDI), where he had already been working as director. The two intelligence organisations somewhat uncomfortably shared a locked-off section on the first floor of the Stout Street Defence headquarters building. Here, in a cramped back corner of the building (overlooking McGinnity Street), the first technicians and analysts established themselves. Meanwhile upstairs, on the third floor, the GCSB communications officers within the Defence communications centre continued handling signals intelligence as it passed in and out of the country. This centre, run by Air Force staff, is called the Defence Communications Unit (DCU), a name the GCSB later borrowed for the 'Defence Communications Unit (Tangimoana)' in an attempt to disguise its real function.

While he was at Stout Street, Hanson's most important visitor, on 24-26 November 1980, was undoubtedly fellow signals intelligence director Admiral Bobby Inman, head of the NSA. Inman was on a tour of UKUSA Pacific signals intelligence sites, including the DSD, one classified location (almost certainly in Thailand), the giant GCHQ/DSD station in Hong Kong and New Zealand.[6] Besides his formal briefing and discussions with the GCSB, Inman had dinner with Defence Secretary Denis McLean, Intelligence Council chairman Gerald Hensley and SIS director Paul Molineaux. The American later described his visit to Wellington as being 'at one of the NSA's listening posts'.[7] About a year after Inman's visit the first GCSB officer was posted to the position of New Zealand Liaison Officer (Washington) within the NSA.

During 1982, when the GCSB moved into its current offices on the top floors of the Freyberg Building, three important events occurred: the Falklands War, the opening, at Tangimoana, of a replacement for the NR1 station and the starting of a second secret intercept operation involving the GCSB in Melbourne.

It would have been inconceivable for the GCSB not to help in every way it could during the Falklands War. Britain had been involved in New Zealand signals intelligence at every stage of its history, mostly recently helping in the establishment of the GCSB. Its contribution was referred to in *The Ties That Bind* by Jeffrey Richelson and Des Ball, the most comprehensive book to date on the UKUSA alliance. Its two-page section on the GCSB reflects the lack of information available about the organisation at that time, but does note that: 'During the Falklands/Malvinas War in April-May 1982, the Irirangi station was able to monitor Argentine naval traffic in the South Pacific, thus providing intelligence which was used by Britain to form a clearer and more comprehensive picture of the Argentine Navy's Order of Battle and its deployments'.[8]

This report has been confirmed from within the GCSB. The NR1 station at Waiouru was not equipped for direction finding but it was used to monitor Argentinian military radio transmissions according to instructions provided from Britain. As one GCSB worker said: 'It's no secret that New Zealand could hear things in the Falklands War [owing to atmospheric conditions] which could not be heard in Argentina or Britain'.

In fact they tried to keep it secret. After *The Ties That Bind* was published, the claim about New Zealand signals intelligence involvement in the war was officially denied by New Zealand's Chief of Defence Staff. Sir Ewan Jamieson, later a vocal opponent of the nuclear-free policy, put out a press release that read: 'Air Marshal Jamieson...categorically denied that the [HMNZS Irirangi] station had monitored Argentine naval traffic during the Falklands conflict and passed intelligence material to Britain. The station has no intercept capability, he said.'[9] It is quite true that the Irirangi Navy station had not been intercepting Argentina. As Jamieson knew, the interception was occurring a couple of minutes' walk across the paddocks at the GCSB's NR1 station.

Shortly after the April-June 1982 Falklands War the staff began leaving

Associated Press

Despite official denials, the GCSB helped Britain during the Falklands War and has continued intercepting the Argentinian Navy for it up to the present.

NR1 to start up the GCSB's new station at Tangimoana Beach in the Manawatu. The Tangimoana station took over monitoring of Argentinian naval communications — 'to provide support for the Brits' — and is still targeting them for Britain in the mid-1990s.

When the station was officially opened on 18 August, the only person at the small ceremony, besides the intelligence staff, was Prime Minister Robert

Muldoon. The ceremony consisted of a short, formal speech by Muldoon in the operations centre, followed by a tour of the station and refreshments in the administration building.

Preparation for the new station had begun in 1979. In January that year Keith Smith, a former Air Force Squadron Leader who had worked with Hanson at Defence Headquarters, was appointed Deputy Director of Engineering. Over the following three years Smith oversaw design and construction of the new station.

At the same time there was a rapid period of recruiting of the increased number of radio officers, technicians and communications officers needed to run the station and for overseas postings — double the staff at Waiouru. The advertisements for the new intercept staff asked for experience in high frequency radio, especially Morse and teleprinter operations. They also showed that by mid-1979 the site for the new station had been chosen: the advertisements specified initial appointments at Waiouru 'prior to transfer to the Ohakea area'.

The new site was chosen partly because it was near to the Ohakea Air Force base, which would help to service and disguise the operation, and partly because the low, sandhill country was well suited to radio reception. The location was 150 kilometres north of Wellington in the middle of an isolated government land development farm, screened from roads by pine plantations, near the small beach settlement of Tangimoana.

The development of Tangimoana station was not occurring in isolation from the UKUSA allies. A top secret internal Australian intelligence report from 1974 explained the developments of which the new Tangimoana station was part. It described the network of high frequency direction-finding (HFDF) stations used by the UKUSA allies for ocean surveillance:

Australian participation (through DSD) in a combined HFDF network began in 1973 with the activation of a DF facility at the [Australian Air Force] station at Pearce, WA. This Australian DF facility is linked with collaborating US, British and Canadian agencies in a world-wide DF network....

The combined network has continued to expand this year with the opening of a small US-British facility at Diego Garcia in August and of a British station at Masirah (Oman) in October.... (The DSD-controlled station at Hong Kong currently participates on the net in a limited way and for Chinese targets only.)

The combined HFDF network makes a considerable contribution to surveillance of the Soviet naval presence in the Indian Ocean, and, by a consolidation of data, enables patterns of activity and changes in these patterns to be detected.[10]

Soon after this report was written, Australia began to expand its HFDF capability. In 1975 new antenna equipment, built by the British Plessey company for GCHQ and other users, was installed at the new DSD station outside Darwin. In 1978 the same equipment was installed at the DSD Pearce station in Perth and, in 1980, at the DSD Cabarlah station. Two years later it was precisely this same Plessey system that was brought into operation at Tangimoana, completing the Australasian arm of the worldwide network.

The HFDF network had not been very useful during the Falklands War but was highly effective against its primary target, the Soviet Navy. According-

Researcher Owen Wilkes discovered the then secret Tangimoana station in 1983 when he went on holiday nearby.

ing to a senior British intelligence officer in the early 1980s, a combination of ocean surveillance satellites, HFDF, undersea listening systems and very secret interception of compressed radio transmissions from Soviet submarines provided Britain and the United States with a continuous world plot of all Soviet naval deployments. Tangimoana's interception targets had a strong anti-Soviet emphasis. Russian research ships, Antarctic bases and fishing boats were targeted by the station and the intercept sent overseas.

The NR1 station remained secret for over 30 years, but it took less than two after its opening for Tangimoana to be on the front pages of the country's newspapers. It was very bad luck for the GCSB that peace researcher Owen Wilkes, recently returned from Scandinavia, was holidaying on a friend's farm only a short drive from the station in 1983. After years of research into intelligence issues in Europe, Wilkes was probably the only person in New Zealand who could have recognised the distinctive signals intelligence aerials as being something different from the normal radio facilities providing communications for the nearby Air Force base. Wilkes quietly studied the station and collected local information about its construction. Then, in April 1984, a special feature in *Peacelink* magazine released the story. (Recalling the story a decade later, one of the Tangimoana staff described it as 'an excellent article' and commented on the extent to which Wilkes 'got it right'.) This publicity led directly to Muldoon's admission in Parliament two months later about the existence and role of the intelligence station and the GCSB.

Another important new interception operation also began in the 1980s, but this story did not get out. It took nearly a decade to find it.

One of the mysteries during the research for this book was trying to figure out why New Zealand intercept officers from the Tangimoana station were regularly posted to Melbourne. Descriptions of Australian signals intelligence operations, which are quite well documented, contained no mention of any radio interception facilities there. Yet as the numbers of radio officers posted there grew it seemed that there must be some secret station in or near Melbourne.

Posting of New Zealand radio officer staff to Australia had begun in the mid-1950s, at the same time as the Singapore postings began, and when the Singapore station was exposed and then closed, New Zealand maintained its contribution by increasing the Melbourne contingent to 14.[11] For the rest of the 1970s, at least 10 radio officers were always on rotation to the DSD.[12] Then, as Tangimoana was opened, the number of postings to Melbourne (and other DSD stations, including Perth) was raised to 20-30. This meant that, even with its much larger staff, a significant proportion of the radio officers at Tangimoana were on three-year rotation to Australia at all times.

By plotting on a street map the houses of the New Zealand radio officers present in Melbourne each year, a striking pattern emerged: without exception, the dots on the map were clumped together in the sprawling suburbs of south-east Melbourne. If there was a secret station, which seemed the only logical explanation for the increased numbers, it was probably on this eastern side of the city.

Fieldwork failed to solve the mystery; there were no tell-tale aerial fields on that side of Melbourne. It was a wild goose chase and increasingly it seemed there was not even a goose. But then in 1991, after more than 30 years, nearly all the postings to Melbourne stopped. This was the clue needed.

A brief article in an Australian Air Force magazine later that year referred to the closing down of a DSD operation in Melbourne called the Joint Telecommunications Unit Melbourne (JTUM) in mid-February 1991[13] — just around the time that the New Zealand staff came home. A question in the Australian Senate revealed that JTUM was established at Victoria Barracks, then the home of the DSD, in 1982 — the same year as the jump in GCSB radio officer numbers in Melbourne occurred.[14]

For 10 years (1981-91) large numbers of GCSB staff spied on China and Russia from the second storey of the JTUM building in Melbourne. The bosses were Australians and the intelligence mostly went to the United States.

The solution to the mystery was much stranger than expected. JTUM was the secret facility where GCSB staff were working, but the reason there were no aerials to be found in Melbourne was that it was connected by satellite to a radio interception station at Chung Hom Kok on the south side of Hong Kong Island, over 7000 kilometres away. In 1982 the GCHQ's previous Little Sai Wan station on Hong Kong Island had been shifted to Chung Hom Kok and arrangements made for it to be operated remotely from Australia. Britain paid for the move.[15] From then on New Zealand and Australian intercept officers worked in shifts around the clock operating the Hong Kong spy base from a building in Melbourne. The presence of GCSB staff on posting from Tangimoana in the JTUM operation has since been confirmed by various GCSB staff. One described it as a 'British set-up operated from Australia'.

JTUM was located next to the DSD headquarters building in the grounds of the Australian Department of Defence's Victoria Barracks in St Kilda Road, Melbourne (the south-east Melbourne hypothesis had proved to be completely wrong). The grey stone two-storey, 30- by 20-metre building was erected in 1980-81 especially for this operation. It stands back from St Kilda

Road next to Wadey Street. The unit began initial operations on 1 July 1981.

New Zealand provided most of the staff in the early years; one of the GCSB staff estimated that 90 percent of the intercept officers were New Zealanders. Later the proportion was about half. This involved about 10 GCSB intercept staff on each of the three shifts a day, working in the operations centre on the windowless second storey. The GCSB had recruited and trained dozens of new staff in the late 1970s in preparation for contributing to JTUM. Some of the GCSB staff were sent directly from New Zealand and others moved to the new unit from postings at the DSD's Pearce station outside Perth.

One of the New Zealand JTUM staff explained that the GCSB staff were entirely integrated into an Australian operation: 'Australians were in charge of what we did, while most of the [intercepted information] went back to the NSA'. The heads of the unit were all Australians, even when GCSB was supplying most of the staff. For example, the commanding officer in JTUM's last years was an Australian Air Force officer, Brett Biddington. New Zealand had no say in what the unit did.

The GCSB staff working at JTUM were overseen administratively by a GCSB officer called the Government Communications Liaison Officer Melbourne (GCLOM), who had an office in the DSD building next door. Through most of the 1980s this officer was John Orchard, a long-time radio officer from NR1. In addition there were senior supervising staff on posting

Chinese and Russian military communications were intercepted in Hong Kong and then relayed by satellite to this dish on the outskirts of Melbourne.

from Tangimoana, including Trevor O'Reilly Nugent and Vince McQuillan.

The JTUM building was connected to the Hong Kong station by a special satellite link established for the purpose. A satellite dish in the neighbouring Hong Kong satellite interception station sent the intercepted radio signals via satellite to a facility near Darwin. The signals were then relayed by a second satellite to Melbourne. United States military communications satellites provided the link. In Melbourne the signals were received by the Project Sparrow satellite terminal across the city in the Simpson Barracks at Watsonia and relayed directly from there to JTUM by microwave. The large Watsonia dish was officially declared operational on 1 July 1981 — the same day that JTUM secretly began operations. Publicity about the new dish described it as providing a secure channel for communicating very large quantities of data;[16] a large capacity would be required to bring all the signals picked up by the aerials halfway around the world to the intercept staff.

The radio listening aerials were located on the top of the hill on Chung Hom Kok peninsula, behind where the satellite interception station was sited. Both stations were located within the same heavily fenced area overlooking Stanley Bay, allowing the communications link to be shared.[17]

So, who was being spied on by the JTUM/Hong Kong operation? Communists, of course. The primary targets of this station right through the 1980s were China and Russia. Of these, the long-term target of GCHQ stations in Hong Kong has been China. The first post-war signals intelligence station in Hong Kong targeted on China had opened in 1949, the year that the Communist government came to power. Also within its range were various other Asian nations from Korea to South East Asia, which were also targeted. For example, the GCHQ had used the station to provide secret assistance to the United States during the Vietnam War — although Britain 'stayed out of the war'.

When the new Labour government of 1984 asked what JTUM was doing, it was told that it was 'studying the Chinese Order of Battle'. The types of Chinese intelligence of interest are shown in the 1974 Australian intelligence report quoted earlier. It contains a list of subjects where signals intelligence was said to have been 'especially useful and often unique'. The first two items were: Chinese nuclear, advanced weapon and space testing activities; and Chinese military activities in the Paracel Islands (in the South China Sea) and related military deployments. It noted that when the Director of the Joint Intelligence Organisation visited Washington that year, 'senior NSA officials made a convincing case concerning the value of the Hong

Kong operation'.[18]

By 1981, when New Zealanders became involved through JTUM, the China spying continued but the operation was also 'now very much involved in monitoring Soviet naval movements down east Asia from the major naval bases at Vladivostok and Petropavlovsk-Kamchatka to Cam Ranh Bay in Vietnam'.[19] One of the New Zealand JTUM staff says that China and Russia were indeed the chief targets throughout the 1980s and into the 1990s, and that the station also targeted every other country of interest within that region.

By the time JTUM ceased operations, it 'had transferred the final parts of its operational mission progressively to a sister agency in the US'[20] — in other words, to the NSA. Although for historical reasons Hong Kong station was a GCHQ operation, the GCSB officer quoted above confirmed that the intelligence was being collected primarily for the NSA. By the 1980s the NSA was undoubtedly the dominant influence over the GCSB.

The United States intelligence organisations may have valued the Chinese intelligence, but its value for Australia, according to Australian intelligence staff, is questionable: 'Although access to the advanced technology entailed in [the operation] has proved highly satisfying to the DSD, the actual intelligence product is often arcane and of little value to Australia. As one intelligence analyst put it, "It's fun if you want to know if the screws on Chinese rockets have right or left-hand threads".'[21]

The aerials and equipment in Hong Kong were removed after JTUM closed. According to GCSB staff, this was to ensure that a station obviously targeted on China was gone well before any political problems relating to the Chinese takeover of Hong Kong. The GCSB staff in Melbourne stayed on there for a while after it closed. When they returned to New Zealand, the GCSB had no need for that number of radio officers so they were redeployed in headquarters units and retrained for new duties.

Spying on China and Russia from a foreign base, and under the control of a foreign government, could not have been further from what the official statements were claiming to be the purposes of the GCSB. The JTUM-Hong Kong operation is the most blatant example of New Zealand assisting in intelligence collection entirely to serve the UKUSA allies. If the end of British control of Hong Kong had not been looming, it is likely that the operation would still be going on.

A large proportion of the GCSB's intercept officers had postings to JTUM during the 1980s, representing, in terms of intercept staff numbers, over a third of the GCSB's intelligence collection during that decade. Add to this the GCSB's other Russian intelligence activities and it is clear that spying on distant Communist countries for the United States alliance was receiving most of the GCSB's resources right into the 1990s.

Not long after this quintessentially Cold War operation began in Melbourne, a small but significant event occurred at the GCSB. It was a sign of things to come.

In the last week of May 1982, the United States nuclear cruiser *USS Truxtun* made its third and last visit to Wellington. It was greeted by protest boats at the harbour mouth, union strikes within the port and public protest marches, rallies and church vigils on shore. Visits by nuclear weapon capable and nuclear-powered warships — *Truxtun* was both — were by now highly controversial and provocative events in New Zealand. The public was polarised on the issue and local and national politicians opposed to the visit were publicly refusing to attend any official functions arranged for the ships' crews.

It was against this background that the staff of the GCSB went on their first and only outing together. The American embassy issued an invitation to the entire GCSB staff to have a special private tour, during work time, of the controversial ship. Most went, ferried out to the warship at its explosives and dangerous goods anchorage in the middle of the harbour and, directors leading the way, were shown around by a United States Navy officer.

The *Truxtun* was the second to last United States nuclear warship to enter Wellington Harbour before the Labour government banned them. The nuclear-free policy, like all popular issues, had more significance to the public than just the immediate goal (in this case banning nuclear warship visits). For many people the anti-nuclear issue was an expression of disenchantment with Cold War attitudes and confrontations. It symbolised both a wish to distance New Zealand from big power politics and a greater independence in world affairs.

The GCSB visit to the *Truxtun*, and the predominantly anti-Communist orientation of its secret work, showed how far apart the public and secret worlds had become. This divergence of public and official opinion had been occurring since the Vietnam War but it had accelerated since 1977 and had culminated in the nuclear-free policy, which even conservative National Party politicians have not dared to change. Cocooned in secrecy and a creature of the alliance, the GCSB was not changing with the times.

By the time Muldoon made his June 1984 statement, acknowledging the GCSB's involvement in signals intelligence, the nuclear-free policy and the American alliance were on a collision course. During the next year the

In the midst of public protests against the USS Truxtun*'s May 1983 visit, the American embassy invited the GCSB staff for a private tour of the controversial nuclear cruiser. The intelligence agencies were increasingly out of tune with New Zealand opinion.*

nuclear-free policy came in and ANZUS went out. The only thing that allowed the hidden intelligence alliance to continue was the fact that it was so secret. Secrecy has been its main protection over the decade since, but the divergence between the public and secret worlds has continued. Since its junior role in UKUSA makes it impractical for New Zealand to go its own way within the alliance, sooner or later the decision whether to leave it will have to be faced.

By 1996, after perestroika and glasnost, the Cold War orientation of the GCSB has decreased — but only after and following reorientation of priorities by the overseas allies. This change of direction does not make the growing capabilities of the GCSB and UKUSA alliance more benign. The GCSB still operates as the alliance dictates, but in a sense it is marking time, trying to justify its existence by producing and trading tit-bits of economic and diplomatic intelligence. Marking time until the next Vietnam or Falklands, when it will be ready and willing to serve the alliance once more.

Chapter Six

Behind Closed Doors
What Happens Inside the GCSB

A minute's walk from Parliament in central Wellington, down a small side street, stands a very ordinary government office block set back from the road between the National Library and the National Archives. This is the Freyberg Building where, above nine storeys of military and other government offices, the headquarters of the Government Communications Security Bureau is located.

Looking up at the building you can see the tell-tale security curtains on the 10th to 14th floors. You can also see cooling units on the 11th and 12th floors, giving away the location of some computers. If you visit after dark you can see that the lights stay on all night in the corner of the top floor, the site of the 24-hour communications centre.

That is not much information. But those two paragraphs have probably told you more about what is inside New Zealand's largest intelligence organisation than you could find in the neighbouring National Library or National Archives, the two great repositories of information about New Zealand.

Like all the UKUSA intelligence organisations, the GCSB goes to a lot of effort to ensure that the public has no idea what goes on beyond those curtained windows. The following chapters provide a rare glimpse inside

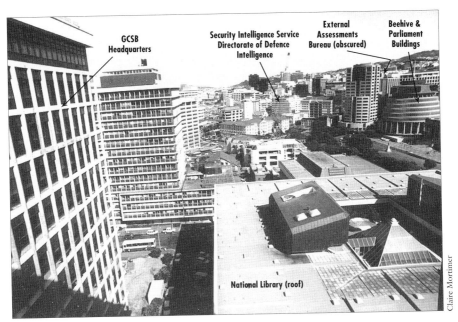

All New Zealand's intelligence agencies are within a few minutes' walk of each other in central Wellington. The GCSB is by far the largest, most secretive and least known of them.

this intelligence organisation to see exactly who works there and what they are doing in the unlabelled offices that line each corridor. Anyone who reads what follows will know more about the internal structure and workings of the GCSB than most of the people who work there.

The GCSB is New Zealand's largest intelligence organisation, twice the size of the Security Intelligence Service (SIS) and with an annual budget of about $20 million. It is directed from the Freyberg Building headquarters and has two interception stations: one at Tangimoana for intercepting other countries' radio communications and one at Waihopai for intercepting satellite communications.

While the SIS conducts intelligence operations within New Zealand (it is the equivalent of the British MI5 and Australian ASIO), the GCSB spies on other countries. In late 1977, controversial new legislation widening the powers of the SIS went through Parliament in almost the same month as the GCSB was established. While the SIS achieved national notoriety, the GCSB began with and retains almost total anonymity.

The few New Zealanders who have heard of the GCSB (whether they could remember its name correctly is another matter) know it for its intelligence *collection* activities: the stations at Tangimoana and Waihopai. The organisation's biggest secret is its significant intelligence *production* capability: turning raw intercepted messages into more useable intelligence reports. It is these sections of the organisation that lie at the heart of the intelligence operations. The complex systems and procedures within which they work show the nature of the GCSB's foreign links. The organisation is not large — but it has no need to be. Its spying capability relies not on staff numbers but on high-tech equipment, computer power and assistance from the UKUSA allies.

One of the striking discoveries made while researching the GCSB headquarters was uncovering details of a UKUSA-wide operation targeting Japanese diplomatic communications. Not only are these one of the GCSB's principal targets, but all the UKUSA agencies have sections established specifically for this Japanese work.

In 1981 the NSA pushed the GCSB to join a UKUSA-wide operation spying on Japanese diplomatic communications.

Japan allows over a dozen United States signals intelligence bases to be located on its territory, the NSA Far East headquarters is located in Tokyo and Japan is reported to be a third party to the UKUSA agreement, including extensive US-Japan intelligence co-operation,[1] yet Japan is itself a major target of UKUSA operations.

The Japanese diplomatic intelligence produced by the five agencies is referred to in alliance shorthand as 'JAD intelligence' ('JA' for Japan, 'D' for diplomatic). Special traffic designators at the top of reports containing intercepted Japanese embassy cables begin JAD-, followed by several numbers indicating which specific embassy communications link has been intercepted.

At the GCSB, this JAD analysis occurs in the KE section. The work began in 1981 when a Japanese linguist called Peter Ashen, an Australian Royal Air Force officer from the DSD, shifted to the GCSB to establish what was then called the K3 cell. The KE section's JAD work is oriented entirely to UKUSA co-operation. Co-ordinated by the NSA, but with all five agencies participating, it involves analysis of communications intercepted from all the key Japanese diplomatic posts around the world.

Japanese embassies use different ciphers for communications of different sensitivity, with anything regarded as sensitive supposed to be sent in one-time ciphers which are impossible to break.[2] Getting these communications would require other types of covert spy operations directed at embassy buildings and their staff. But there are other types of embassy communications, sent in lower grade ciphers, which the UKUSA agencies can and do intercept.

The communications being targeted and analysed at the GCSB are routine diplomatic business (visas, cultural events and so on) and large quantities of regular diplomatic reporting about all sorts of subjects and events in the country where the embassy is located. They are communications not regarded as highly sensitive; the Japanese realise they may be intercepted. Apparently little of this is new information; what it provides, if anything, is a Japanese perspective on foreign policy and trade subjects and commentaries on the countries concerned. The Japanese diplomats are said to write reports about everything.

The UKUSA stations monitor nearly every Japanese diplomatic post in the world; and specific links are divided up between the five agencies. The GCSB has been allocated the links between certain Japanese embassies in the Pacific and Tokyo, providing information particularly about trade, aid, fisheries and meetings of regional organisations. These are mostly telex messages.

This is a worldwide division of *analysis*. Wherever the actual interception happens to occur, the five agencies share out the work of producing finished intelligence reports. It has occupied about a third of the GCSB's analysts since 1981. Until New Zealand opened the Waihopai station, which was capable of satellite interception, this country could not intercept Japanese embassy communications, most of which are transmitted by satellite.

From 1981 to 1989, all the Japanese diplomatic intercepts analysed at the GCSB came from overseas interception stations, including from the NSA's Yakima station. The raw intercept would arrive through the GCSB communications centre, still in Japanese codes, and be passed to a staff member who decoded it, using special codebreaking programmes developed for the purpose.[3]

In the 1990s JAD communications are intercepted at the GCSB's satellite interception station at Waihopai and through its sister stations in the ECHELON network. Some of this interception may even occur at the NSA's Misawa satellite interception station, which is located in Japan. Once the intercept arrives at the headquarters, the GCSB analysts sort for messages of interest, translate them and write them into the standard formats of UKUSA reports for sending back into the global network. Because the intelligence reports produced in KE show that Japanese diplomatic codes have been broken, they are all classified as TOP SECRET UMBRA, the highest of the three main special signals intelligence classifications.

The NSA provides computer programmes it has developed to break the Japanese codes, and even recommended which computer the GCSB should buy to do the decoding. The GCSB simply contributes analysts to the NSA project and gets access to some of the product. The GCSB analysts are more likely to understand the South Pacific and the subjects being discussed in the Japanese messages, and so ensure a higher standard of intelligence reporting.

The huge investment of resources throughout the UKUSA system in JAD intelligence is surprising, considering the less secret types of traffic being netted. One argument used within the GCSB for this work is that, although most of the communications are very routine, every once in a while a Japanese official may slip up and send more sensitive information in the lower-grade codes.

Perhaps the biggest intelligence coup to make it into GCSB folklore occurred in the early 1980s. A Japanese diplomat accidentally sent out information, about how high Japan was prepared to go on a particular commodity price, in plain diplomatic code (rather than the high-level codes usually used in such cases). It was a big boast for some time afterwards about how much money the GCSB had saved New Zealand.

Yet, despite the mystique surrounding this kind of secret intelligence work, such achievements are few and far between. I heard this same, lone success story still being told by GCSB staff in the early 1990s. By then the word was that that one piece of information had saved New Zealand enough money to pay for the Tangimoana station (which was completed in 1982). The story refers to a New Zealand producer board (which would have access to the signals intelligence information) negotiating a price for meat exports with a Japanese purchasing organisation.

In the mid-1990s Japanese diplomatic intelligence remains a priority for the Waihopai station and GCSB analysts (the newest Japanese linguist was appointed in early 1996) — and Australia too. It was clearly intelligence reports based on these low sensitivity Japanese communications that were the subject of a front-page story, headlined 'Japanese secrets tapped in Canberra', in the *Sydney Morning Herald* in May 1995. The newspaper reported that copies of Japanese cables were being regularly seen by staff in various sections of the Department of Foreign Affairs and Trade, where they arrived in a special locked bag. A senior diplomat was quoted as saying: 'It's funny to read an embassy's account of a visit you have made to their mission and their interpretations of your conversations'.[4] There was no evidence in the story that sensitive Japanese communications were involved. The intercepted

Japan Information & Cultural Centre

Foreign Minister Don McKinnon chats with Japanese Prime Minister Miyazawa while the GCSB spies on his ambassadors. Is it in New Zealand's interests to be spying on neighbours and trading partners on behalf of old northern hemisphere allies?

cables may have given insights into how the Japanese diplomats saw the issues at the meetings, but the highly expensive, TOP SECRET UMBRA intelligence was still only telling the Australians about things like meetings they had already been at.

This information about the Japanese interception, and many other GCSB spying operations, came to light during investigation of the work of the GCSB's Operations Division, which includes all the important parts of the GCSB headquarters' intelligence work, the interception operations at the Tangimoana and Waihopai stations and the signals intelligence operations conducted for the GCSB by the New Zealand Defence Force.

It is here that the raw intelligence from the GCSB station Dictionary computers and from other parts of the ECHELON system is decrypted, translated, studied, written into finished intelligence reports — such as the JAD ones — and disseminated to New Zealand and overseas users. For example, the Dictionary computer at Waihopai may pick out the text of a fax (sent uncoded) from the Kiribati Prime Minister's office to a political ally. If it looks interesting, it will be translated into English, written into a report by an analyst in the KP section and distributed to all UKUSA intelligence organisations with an interest in Kiribati.

The Director of Operations until mid-1996 was Warren Tucker, who joined the GCSB in 1982. This Director, who is called O, oversees all the operations through the two station officers-in-charge and the managers of units called K, C and L.

The Operations Division includes the two stations, the SIGINT Production K Unit, the SIGINT Collection C Unit and the Customer Support L Unit. Altogether the Operations Division has about 120 staff — about 60 percent of the GCSB's staff.

The division dates from 1978 when the first Deputy Director of Operations (DDO), Jim Blackford, was recruited from the GCHQ. In 1982 he was replaced by Larry Lynch, who filled this position until 1989 (apart from a brief period as the GCSB representative at the NSA in 1984) when Tucker took over.

The K Unit is central to the GCSB's intelligence production role. There are two intelligence analysis sections, KE and KP. Here analysts, like Geoff Holmes, translate intercepted messages into English and write the information into reports which are then distributed through the UKUSA network. There is also a small KH section, where cryptanalysts (codebreakers) use computers to try to break some of the codes that are used to protect target communications.

The Manager SIGINT Production, called K, is Glen Singleton. This is the job he ended up in after he left the NSA and became a GCSB employee. Part of his work as an NSA officer had been checking the quality of intelligence reports produced by the GCSB for the alliance. Now he is directly in charge of the GCSB's report production. He had returned to New Zealand after leaving the NSA and been given a four-year contract as a consultant in the Policy and Plans Division (starting in February 1990). Later he was transferred, still as a consultant, to the Operations Division in mid-1992. He applied for and received New Zealand citizenship during this period.

The important position of K has previously been held by John Brandon, Bas Keane, Brian Gore and Ian Brownlie.

The development of the K Unit began in the late 1970s when John Brandon (now Director of Information Systems Security) was appointed as Executive Officer (SIGINT). From 1980 he oversaw the creation of the three K sections: the K2 Russian cell, the K3 Japanese cell and the K4 French cell (these were later restructured into KE and KP).

According to GCSB staff, each of the three cells was established at the suggestion of the UKUSA allies. Staff from the time say that there was specific pressure for these developments from the NSA and GCHQ. Clearly the areas of analysis — Russian, Japanese and French (and later South Pacific) — would have been established in exactly the opposite order had New Zealand interests been the basis of the structure. As one GCSB worker explained, 'There is a careful carve-up of areas of responsibilities between the agencies: areas, subjects, languages. It certainly wasn't New Zealand deciding what was necessary for New Zealand.'

Development of the Russian and Japanese cells was part of a co-ordinated allocation of responsibilities between the UKUSA allies. The smaller allies were being asked to do segments of the analysis for global interception projects. Thus both the Australian DSD and Canadian CSE also have sections for Russian and Japanese analysis (as, of course, do the large United States and British agencies). In the 1980s, for example, the DSD had three analysis cells — Russian, Japanese and Indonesian — in one division and a separate division for its Chinese operations.

The CSE produces signals intelligence reports from interception of Russian ships in the North Pacific, the GCSB from the South Pacific and the DSD from South East Asia and some of the Indian Ocean. Similarly, the GCSB produces reports of intercepted Japanese diplomatic communications from the South Pacific and perhaps a few other areas, while the DSD covers South East Asia and elsewhere and the CSE covers Latin America.

The GCSB's French nuclear testing analysis also appears to have been part of a UKUSA division of work. While the DSD focuses on the Chinese nuclear programme for the alliance, the GCSB has covered the French tests.

The K2 Russian cell was the first to be set up, in 1980. Clive Comrey, the British signals intelligence officer brought to New Zealand to set up the cell, was joined by Barry O'Shea, a Russian linguist posted from the DSD. He was the first of a succession of Russian analysts on two-year postings from the DSD, all or most of them Australian naval officers. The K3 Japanese cell was established a year later, followed by the K4 French cell, which was set up in 1983 staffed by two New Zealanders.[5] The DSD has no French analysis; all work relating to French in the South Pacific is allocated to the GCSB. Between them, these three cells accounted for all the GCSB's intelligence production for more than a decade. Although these cells no longer exist in this form, virtually all the areas of intelligence analysis now described were transferred to the KE and KP cells that replaced them in 1992.

The work of the K2 cell was analysing all the Russian language intercept from the GCSB's Tangimoana station and its predecessor at Waiouru. In the absence of better Russian targets to offer the UKUSA network, most of this work focused on Russian fishing vessels in the South Pacific. K2 also served as the alliance's source of information about the South Pacific region for a United States computer data base that tracks *all* Russian naval and commercial vessels.

Tangimoana intercepts Russian Morse code and radio telex messages being sent back to the fishing companies on the Russian Pacific coast, which give details of the ships' positions, personnel matters, catch sizes and the types of fish. The K2 reports produced from this intercept were sent overseas and were also given to the New Zealand fisheries authorities. The best reason that could be given inside the GCSB for why Russian fishing fleets (and not those of any other countries) were monitored was said to be that 'We don't trust the Russians, so we'll just watch them anywhere they are near us.'

Some of this information was recorded on a large lockable fisheries chart on the wall in K2, where the positions of the ships were plotted to assist the

Greenpeace/Morgan

Radio messages from Russia's Leningradskya base (pictured), and all other Russian Antarctic bases, are targeted by the GCSB as part of the UKUSA preoccupation with spying on Russia.

analysts' report writing, for example, indicating when a trawler left the fishing grounds for port. The intelligence collecting was definitely not to check whether the fishing boats were doing covert spy work, as alarmist media stories sometimes suggested. The cell also took a close interest in the occasional Russian research vessels in the South Pacific and any other Russian activities in the South Pacific (such as the Russian fishing negotiations in Kiribati in the mid-1980s).

The other area covered by K2 was Antarctica, mainly the communications from the Russian bases but some other (non-UKUSA) countries' bases too when they were intercepted. The Russian messages were described by an analyst as 'utterly unimportant personal messages, and messages about movements of staff and equipment and maintenance matters'. The rationalisation within the GCSB was that 'the Russians are trying to move into Antarctica'. The Russian cell analysts do not analyse intercepted Russian diplomatic communications.

There was, and still is, close co-operation between the GCSB, DSD and CSE on this Russian monitoring. The CSE was noted as 'getting good Russian traffic'; for example, from its Masset station on the Pacific coast (at the north end of the Queen Charlotte Islands). K2 also saw a lot of reports from the DSD's Harman station near Canberra. The K2 reports — which did not involve codebreaking — were usually classified as SECRET SPOKE or SECRET MORAY, not the more secret TOP SECRET UMBRA.

Russia remains an important GCSB target in the 1990s, as it has been for the New Zealand Security Intelligence Service. The SIS has spied on Russian diplomats and other Russian people in New Zealand throughout its existence, for example, at least until recently, regularly watching Russian diplomatic cars from secret observation houses in Messines Road, Lancaster Street and beside the Kelburn Viaduct in Wellington and dispatching observation cars to tail them around the city.

The main work of the K4 cell was reporting on the French nuclear testing programme in French Polynesia. Starting in 1983, the French linguists analysed all the French radio messages intercepted by the Tangimoana station. In particular, the K4 staff handled long-distance radio links between Paris, Tahiti, Noumea and the nuclear testing site at Moruroa. Later they also received intercepted satellite communications.

The K4 cell, and the KP section that succeeded it, have also covered other types of French military communications from the South Pacific. For example, when the cell first started it did a lot of analysis of French police and military radio communications in New Caledonia (tensions between the indigenous Kanak people and French were high during that period). Needless to say, the information was not supplied to the Kanaks, who are seeking an end to French colonial rule. Movements of French naval vessels were also monitored.

But by far the main interest has been the nuclear testing programme at Moruroa and Fangataufa. Most of the work of the cell has focused on military communications that could give an indication of an upcoming test. For example, the movement of aircraft carrying stores to and from Moruroa in preparation for tests has been monitored closely for this purpose. Also, as a nuclear test approached, tell-tale patterns in the messages sent from French Polynesia could be seen, even though the actual messages, which were in unbreakable codes, could not be read.

New Zealand's spying on the French nuclear programme began in the late 1960s or early 1970s (the first nuclear test above Moruroa was on 2 July 1966). Communications between France and the nuclear testing centre on Moruroa were monitored by the NR1 station and Joint Intelligence Bureau (later External Intelligence Bureau) staff in Wellington produced intelligence reports for the Western allies on the nuclear programme.

Greenpeace

French telexes to and from Moruroa were intercepted by New Zealand and supplied to the nuclear-armed UKUSA allies.

Collecting information about French testing has been one of the main arguments used by the intelligence bureaucrats to justify the GCSB to New Zealand politicians. This was certainly the case in the 1970s when the government agreed that it be established (interest in nuclear testing was strong in those years) and this justification has been used in explanation ever since.

In July 1991 France conducted what people soon after believed would be its last nuclear test in the Pacific. A moratorium on testing was announced on 8 April 1992 and the analysts were directed onto other subjects. In 1995-96, with the resumption of nuclear testing at Moruroa, GCSB targeting of French nuclear testing communications was increased and the analysts in the KP section temporarily focused on this work again.

British Prime Minister John Major refused to condemn France's 1995 nuclear testing. The British GCHQ worked closely with the GCSB monitoring the tests, but the purpose was not to stop them.

British High Commission

Most New Zealanders would probably think it is a good thing to collect intelligence about what the French are doing at Moruroa. After 25 years of public campaigning on the issue, there is almost unanimous public hostility towards the testing. But the GCSB's interest is not what it might initially seem. The United States and British UKUSA allies, as fellow nuclear powers, have far more in common with the French nuclear establishment than with the New Zealand people opposing it.[6] While the GCSB can use its French operations to sell itself to New Zealand politicians, most of its intelligence collection in this area is destined for the American and British military establishments, which want to find out as much as they can about French nuclear weapon development. This is why the NSA has allowed GCSB keywords relating to French nuclear testing to be placed in the Dictionary computers at the Yakima station. French communications intercepted there are written into reports by GCSB analysts and then disseminated to the UKUSA allies. The United States and Britain are said to use the GCSB's predictions about the timing of future Pacific explosions to direct their own intelligence collection about French nuclear testing. The GCSB has also given both New Zealand intelligence staff and the allies detailed information from intercepted French official reports about the French testing programme.

From 1975 — when international pressure forced nuclear tests underground — to 1991, there is no evidence that the aim of this intelligence collection was to stop the tests. With little New Zealand government action beyond the ritual diplomatic protest made after each test, no one expected the French to stop testing, regardless of whether or not New Zealand was collecting intelligence about them.

It is known by GCSB intelligence staff that the British GCHQ is the main other agency targeting French communications concerning its nuclear programme and that it is most interested in the GCSB French nuclear reporting. Again, this was not because it wanted to stop them. In 1995, at the height of international opposition to French nuclear testing, Britain was conspicuous by its silence and British Prime Minister John Major refused to criticise the tests. 'I know the responsibility of being a nuclear power,' he said, when in New Zealand for the CHOGM meeting in November 1995. 'I understand the difficulties facing the President of France. I am not prepared to condemn him for discharging those responsibilities.'[7]

About 1986 the scope of the K3 cell was extended to cover reporting on South Pacific countries as well as Japanese diplomatic communications. Later, in 1990, this South Pacific reporting was moved into K4 since it was seen to fit better with the K4's reporting on French activities in the South Pacific. Later chapters document wholesale spying on all the South Pacific countries.

The South Pacific analysis at the GCSB initially involved a wide range of radio (mainly telex) communications which had been intercepted by Tangimoana. These included communications of the South Pacific governments, other political figures, companies and the small military and police forces. For example, after the coups in 1987 a lot of attention was directed at Fiji and, at the same time, the Prime Minister of Vanuatu, Walter Lini. Lini's political opponent, Barak Sope, and a number of other influential Vanuatu people were also being monitored.

This monitoring included very detailed information about the internal situations in the South Pacific countries. In 1987, for example, there was intensive interception of communications from and concerning the Rotuma people who were pushing for independence from Fiji. There was sufficient interest in the issue for Tangimoana staff even to tape intercepted radio telephone messages from the island (which were in English) and send them to Wellington for analysis.[8] The vast majority of all traffic has, however, been telex, and transcribed Morse code.

From 1987-88 the radio telexes intercepted at Tangimoana were sorted by computer according to specified keywords and telex numbers. This allowed the telexes that were more likely to be of interest to be selected out of the large quantities of intercepted messages. Even when the messages themselves were not interesting, information could be gleaned about who key people were communicating with by reading the telex numbers at the beginning of the messages.

When Waihopai began operations the targets for all three cells remained much the same, but a wider range of communications was available.

The K analysts work in a long office along the southern side of the 14th floor of the Freyberg Building. Their large desks have plenty of room for dictionaries and other reference publications to assist their work. Sitting at computer work stations, they call up the intercepted communications from the Dictionary system and then prepare translations and finished reports.

The section leader looks through the mass of intercepted messages, decides which are worth translating and writing into reports and allocates the day's work to the other analysts. They are supposed to produce reports from any intercepted messages that look interesting for New Zealand and accord with known interests of the other UKUSA countries. The New Zealand subjects are determined by liaison with the Wellington intelligence organisations. Clear criteria guiding what to produce for the overseas agencies are communicated agency to agency.

The analysts produce reports using special UKUSA jargon, formats and procedures that standardise the product produced anywhere in the network. There are three specific types of reports produced: reports, gists and summaries (described in Chapter 12). For any category of intelligence produced, such as Russian fishing trawlers, the K analysts can look up lists showing the agencies, stations, intelligence organisations and even individual intelligence officers around the world that automatically get a copy of reports on that subject. (These systems are also described in Chapter 12.)

Once the report is completed in the correct format and with the correct UKUSA directions indicating who should receive it, it is checked out by the senior K staff and sent straight to the GCSB communications staff for transmission through the UKUSA network.

The K analysts spend some of their time reading periodicals and keeping themselves up to date about the issues on which they are reporting. This reading matter includes South Pacific and South East Asian periodicals, External Assessments Bureau (EAB) publications and foreign affairs ministry cables. They also get to see the reports produced by analysts working on similar subjects in the other four agencies, and the internal newsletters of the analysis sections in the NSA and GCHQ. Such sources, together with New Zealand Intelligence Briefing Memoranda on each country in the South Pacific and piles of dictionaries, provide the analysts with the references they need. For example, they may want to check if they have the correct spelling of a name or location or have understood the details of the particular situations on which they are reporting.

Security regulations require the publications, manuals, work notes and so on used in the analysts' daily work to be put away in locked cupboards, the office safe or in the large 14th-floor vault each night (depending on how sensitive they are). Staff are told that, during a fire or earthquake alarm, they are supposed to clear everything away before leaving. This is a regulation which, in a real emergency, they have no doubt they will ignore.

The intercepted traffic does not stop, and so the K analysts have to cover Christmas and other holiday breaks during the year. During periods of crisis the analysts are expected to work long hours to provide rapid reporting for the New Zealand and overseas intelligence users. Also, although the K sections have their designated main areas of work, the analysts pride themselves on being able to handle any other languages that may, from time to time, need to be translated (and the GCSB management encourages them to do further study).

Even since South Pacific reporting was introduced the GCSB has had no specific Polynesian linguists, but in 1993 one person boasted of being able to translate Fijian and Nauruan and another was au fait with the Pidgin language used in Melanesia. Ann Colman, who was in KE until 1993, was sent to university by the GCSB to study Chinese language for the occasions when Chinese intercept turned up (she had already done a small amount of Chinese at university).

Analysts describe the job as very routine. There is a high staff turnover because graduates expect an interesting job — although the secretive GCSB provides few details before they get there — and quickly find themselves doing what is generally a repetitive processing job. Far from reporting on momentous secrets, most of the job is translating mundane administrative messages which the countries concerned have judged do not warrant high-level codes. As one analyst said, 'It was like being on an assembly line, you

Ministry of External Relations and Trade

Prime Minister Jim Bolger, pictured here at the South Pacific Forum, told Parliament that the GCSB does not monitor the communications of 'New Zealand's friends in the South Pacific'. In fact it spies continuously on most of these countries, including the Prime Ministers, and passes on the intelligence to the outside powers which are its intelligence allies.

put in your bit and then it went on to someone else. There was no sense of influencing the job. You just reported what was put on your desk.'

In 1992, as part of a major reorganisation of the whole Operations Division, the three analysis cells were reorganised into the current two sections.

KP covers political, military and economic intelligence from the GCSB's area of the South Pacific, particularly the governments, companies and regional and international organisations in Fiji, Vanuatu, Noumea, Tahiti and the small South Pacific states; and French nuclear testing, military and gendarme activities and ship and aircraft movements in the region.

KE covers Russian and Japanese fishing activities, Japanese diplomatic communications in the South Pacific, economic intelligence about countries in the wider Pacific region and Antarctica.

The section heads in 1996 are Geoff Sanderson (KP) and Kay Flanagan (KE). The former joined the GCSB in the late 1980s as Japanese linguist in the K3 cell. Kay Flanagan joined the K Unit at a similar time, as a language graduate from Victoria University (including Russian language). She may have had an overseas posting in 1992, but by 1994 was back as a GCSB customer relations officer, located inside the Directorate of Defence Intelligence at Defence Headquarters. Both have held their current positions since 1995. The position of KE had previously been held by two other former students of the Victoria University Russian Department: Alistair Macklin and Grant Fletcher.

The 'P' in KP stands for Pacific and the 'E' in KE for economics. The main significance of the reorganisation was that the GCSB, like all post-Cold War intelligence organisations intent on ensuring their survival, wanted to create the impression of having a strong new focus on economic intelligence. There were a few real changes in this direction. For example, KE analyst Joy Larkin expanded her linguistic skills to include Iranian so that there could be some reporting of trade-related intercept and, for the first time, some keywords like 'beef' were added to the Dictionary search lists to see what would come out.

But the reorganisation was primarily just a repackaging of the old alliance roles to fit the new justification. KE simply took over K3's Japanese diplomatic reporting responsibilities and K2's Russian fishing trawler and Antarctic reporting responsibilities — while using the Japanese linguists to expand to reporting on Japanese fishing trawlers as well. This is, in a sense, all economic intelligence, but the choice of targets was mainly a continuation of past duties.

Before these changes, the GCSB analysis already included a component of economic-related intelligence. The GCSB analysts might, for example, pick up diplomatic reporting about a large Japanese aid project in one of the countries in the region, knowledge that could help New Zealand companies to win contracts. Although the analysts feel that work like this is more useful than some of the other areas they cover, the value of such intelligence to a country like New Zealand is highly overstated (the importance of economic intelligence is looked at in Chapter 14).

The K analysts have a high level of contact with the overseas agencies, including overseas staff training, postings and exchanges. In the early 1990s the GCSB began conducting its own training courses for the K analysts, teaching them the special procedures and regulations governing the production of signals intelligence reports for the UKUSA network. It is at these courses where the analysts are told about the UKUSA agreement, which is described by the senior staff as the 'foundation stone' of all the arrangements with the 'partner' agencies.

Until then, right through the 1980s, all new analysts attended a two- to four-week reporting officers' training course at the DSD in Melbourne.[9]

There they found that if their own organisation tended to be obsessed with things Russian, the DSD was 'totally paranoid about Indonesia'. As part of the course the trainees were presented with scenarios by the DSD trainers and then had to practise report writing within those scenarios — and apparently the recurrent theme was the risk of Australia being invaded by Indonesia. The DSD's Indonesian analysis section, called CN3, was larger than both the Russian and Japanese sections. The GCSB staff also noticed immediately that, unlike their headquarters, which has almost entirely civilian staff, the DSD includes large numbers of uniformed military staff. The CN3 'Indon' section included a lot of military personnel (particularly naval),[10] Indonesian linguists who are posted to DSD stations to translate intercepted messages.

Also, for a short period around 1986-87 a number of GCSB graduate K and L staff were sent on 12-month training courses at the DSD, which involved being rotated for three-month blocks to different areas of the DSD, including analysis and cryptanalysis. The cost of this training meant it did not last long.

Since 1988 GCSB K analysts have been sent to Canada on postings, partly as a result of tensions caused by the New Zealand-United States nuclear warship dispute. Senior GCSB staff say that the introduction of these postings was part of a deliberate building up of links between the GCSB and CSE. They say that the CSE senior staff feel sympathetic towards the GCSB because they see the DSD trying to dominate the New Zealand organisation in the same way that the NSA in the United States causes problems for them.

The first person posted to the CSE was Ian Brownlie, head analyst in the K2 cell. Brownlie finished 10 years of full-time study in Russian language at the end of 1983 and then joined the GCSB in January 1984. He left for Ottawa in early 1988, and worked in the Russian section at CSE headquarters. He has since moved to an analyst position at the External Assessments Bureau, where his area of responsibility is Russia and the other states of the former Soviet Union.

When Brownlie returned in late 1990, another analyst left on a two-year posting. This time it was Ann Colman from the Japanese K3 cell. Daughter of a former Labour minister, she had joined the GCSB in November 1983 two years after completing a degree in Japanese language at Canterbury University in Christchurch. She returned from Canada in 1992 to be head of the KP section, but did not settle back into the GCSB. She returned to Ottawa, this time to work for the CSE. Canadian government records show that, during 1993, she was awarded a $50,555 contract by the CSE for 'military' research.[11] Her and Brownlie's postings — in Russian and

Japanese diplomatic reporting — show the common analysis areas between the GCSB and CSE.

Since 1990 there has also been a K analyst posting to the DSD. The first of these was a Japanese language graduate, Inge Little, who, after settling into a job in K3, was posted for two years to the DSD. Geoff Holmes' three-year posting to the NSA headquarters in 1994 was also a first. The SIS and EAB both also have staff exchanges with their sister intelligence agencies in Australia.[12]

The training and posting of GCSB analysts (and other GCSB staff) inside the sister agencies is regarded, by the workers themselves, as status and a perk of the job. For the UKUSA agencies it serves a wider purpose, reinforcing for the staff the sense of working as part of a joint alliance effort. These contacts are a concrete example of the intertwined operations of the UKUSA agencies.

The GCSB's cryptanalysts or codebreakers who work in the KH section have received special training in using sophisticated mathematics and computer programmes to try to break other countries' codes. They search for similarities between yesterday's and today's coded messages that might give away the code.

The GCSB introduces the new trainees to the world of codebreaking by advising them to read two of the greatest exposés of signals intelligence: James Bamford's *The Puzzle Palace* and David Kahn's *The Code Breakers*.[13] These books document how much codebreaking achievements have contributed to the power of signals intelligence organisations. Since many of the most sought-after communications are sent in code, the UKUSA agencies (particularly the NSA and GCHQ) have invested immense resources in trying to break the codes.

The GCSB cryptanalysis section is neither large nor powerful. Established in 1988, it has had major problems with staff retention; most section members have left the GCSB straight after their two-year, all expenses paid training in Australia was over. In early 1996 there were only five staff in the section; twice that number had left.[14]

It is not known what codes are attacked by the GCSB cryptanalysts. All one staff member would admit was some successes, saying that 'we can achieve major things, that the Australians can't, with our much smaller resources'. Another described the work as computer-assisted statistical analysis.

It appears that, as with other sections of the GCSB, the development of the KH section was part of a UKUSA-wide initiative. The section was built up at precisely the same time as cryptanalysis was built up in the Canadian CSE and Australian DSD.[15] For example, the CSE began recruitment of new cryptanalysis staff in late 1983 and early 1984, at the same time as the GCSB; and the first CSE trainees went to the NSA for training in March 1984, within months of the first GCSB trainees going to the DSD.[16] Then, in March 1985, the CSE and DSD simultaneously received their first codebreaking computers from the United States — the powerful Cray computers developed for the NSA.

It is likely that cryptanalysis projects are shared out between the five agencies in the same way as for intelligence collection and analysis. This probably involves the KH staff working on some lower level codes encountered in the GCSB's areas of responsibility, and possibly working on some aspect of a more important and difficult code in collaboration with the cryptanalysts in the other agencies.

The first head of the section (later the manager, H, when it was a separate unit) was an arts graduate, Thomas Weiss, who had applied for a job in Foreign Affairs and then received an unexpected call from the GCSB proposing that he apply for a job there. After his training in Melbourne, he worked in the C cell until the next two trainees arrived back from the DSD. In June 1988 he had a training course at the GCHQ in Cheltenham, experiencing the scale of the cryptanalysis activities there, to help in establishing

GCSB Russian and Japanese linguists have been regularly posted to this building, the headquarters of the Canadian UKUSA agency in Ottawa, as part of increasing links since 1988.

the GCSB section. Mark Kininmonth, a former Hong Kong police officer who joined the GCSB in 1983 as a Japanese analyst in K3, was appointed head of the section after Weiss left in 1990. The current head is a former mathematics teacher, Susan Kelly.

The staff's DSD training focused mostly on computer-based cryptanalysis, but the trainees were also rotated through various other DSD sections to give them an overview of the job. Their training included visits to Australian intelligence stations, among them the DSD's Shoal Bay radio and satellite interception station near Darwin. While they were in Australia the GCSB paid for their accommodation and provided generous allowances.

An applicant for a job in the section in 1990 was told that the GCSB was looking for two or three extra cryptanalysts at that time and wanted people with a 10-year commitment to the job, to build up the necessary skills and experience in the section. Part of the incentive for this would be the opportunities offered to travel to the other agencies.

The interview was to take a full day, with a morning of 'aptitude tests' and then the interview in the afternoon. Then there would be a long period of 'intensive vetting by another government department' (i.e. the SIS). Once he started, the successful applicant would have six months to a year in Wellington and then two years 'overseas' (i.e. at the DSD).

The advertisement for the job had sought a 'Research Mathematician with a minimum of a First Class Honours Degree' and preferably a Masters Degree or PhD. But the GCSB failed to attract qualified mathematicians and, with most trainees quitting soon after their expensive training, in 1992 and 1993 the GCSB lowered its sights and looked instead for staff from within the organisation. Dave Bimler and Mike Keehan, originally hired as programmers in the GCSB's Computer Services Unit, moved to KH without the two years' training at the DSD. Similarly, a linguist from the KE section moved to the section in October 1995 and was sent back to university for part-time study in mathematics.

The GCSB cryptanalysts have frequent contact with their colleagues in the overseas agencies, travelling to conferences and visiting the agencies. In July 1995, for example, KH staff member Stephen Watson mixed with cryptanalysts from the DSD and elsewhere at an Australian Cryptology Policy and Algorithms Conference held at the Queensland University of Technology in Brisbane. Watson, who has worked for the GCSB since 1985, identified himself at the conference as working for the Australian Department of Defence. This was presumably to keep secret the GCSB's codebreaking role.

Developments in encryption technology have meant that, in the 1990s, systems are no longer the exclusive preserve of governments of technologically advanced countries. Good encryption systems, such as PGP, developed privately by American Phil Zimmerman, are publicly available, although they are still used only by relatively few people in the know.

The UKUSA agencies have been attempting to curb the spread of this technology, which is a major threat to their influence, so far without enough success to stop it. In the United States, for example, the NSA tried unsuccessfully to have the 'Clipper' chip (which it could break) made mandatory for all 'secure' American communications systems. In Europe, the GCHQ succeeded in forcing the manufacturers of the new Europe-wide GMS mobile phone system to downgrade its encryption (which, initially, it could not break).[17] In Australia DSD officers at first scoffed at a West Australian, Monty Sala, who claimed to have developed unbreakable encryption software but soon after they turned up at his Perth company and stopped him getting several export sales.[18] And in New Zealand, the GCSB, with input from the NSA, was also recently successful in blocking export licences for encryption software. It remains to be seen how much the public can find a technological answer to maintaining privacy in a world with systems like ECHELON.

Generally, the UKUSA agencies apply a lot of their time to targets that use little or no encryption anyway. Most of the telephone, fax and e-mail communications relayed through international telecommunications networks have no protection and provide easy pickings. Even when the ciphers can not be broken — for example the high-level Russian, French and Japanese communications targeted by the UKUSA alliance — information can still be gleaned by studying an encrypted message. This is part of the job of the GCSB's C Unit.

Signals intelligence interception is a highly technical activity, requiring a lot of work before the actual interception begins. For radio interception, radio officers must know where to search among thousands of different transmissions, all at different times and on and between different frequencies. With satellites, they should know not only what is on which frequency band and when, but they must keep up with developments in the telecommunications industry which change the ways that messages and data are transmitted. Just when they are organised, some of it will change again.

A special unit within the GCSB headquarters does the preparatory work for the interception at Waihopai and Tangimoana. Called the SIGINT Collection Unit (with a manager, Bruce Miller,[19] called C), it has about a dozen staff divided into satellite (CS) and radio (CT) sections.

There are three distinct parts to the unit's work. The first is traffic analysis, providing guidance to the radio officers in the two stations about what, how and when to intercept to catch intelligence of interest. They study what communications are available to be exploited and plan when and how to intercept them. These jobs have gone mainly to experienced intercept officers who learned their skills at Tangimoana and NR1.

The second area of work is maintaining data bases of all the individual targets and their characteristics which have been identified by the traffic analysts. This work is done by operations analysts, who type in and amend details of all the targets in the data bases.

With so many targets to keep track of, a well-organised system is required. The data bases of targets updated in the C Unit and used continuously by the intercept staff at the stations are not just New Zealand data bases. They are fully integrated with the massive computer data bases of worldwide targets maintained by the NSA. James Bamford has described the NSA system, which classifies all the targets in a publication called *Technical Extracts of Traffic Analysis* (TEXTA).[20] TEXTA is the system used in the C Unit. All the information on targets compiled by the C staff, for example, on how best to intercept South Pacific countries, is sent into the central NSA data bases. It is the NSA-supplied TEXTA target digests that are used at the GCSB stations.

The third area of work in the C Unit is done by the Dictionary Manager, who provides the directions to the Dictionary computers inside the two stations and liaises with the equivalent Dictionary staff in the overseas agencies.

When the C cell (as it was then) was established in 1984, Wally Brendon and his small staff of experienced radio officers used hand-written logs compiled at the Tangimoana station for their traffic analysis work. Within a few years the Tangimoana staff provided logs of everything the station had intercepted as computer printouts. These logs include details of when a transmission began, how long it went on for and the transmission frequencies. The unit also uses lots of data and copies of traffic from the other agencies (notably CSE and DSD stations) to help with its work.

During those first years C Unit's role was to support the work of the Tangimoana station. The staff's job was to study the 'externals' of a communication: what type of message it was, who it was to and from, the type and priority of code used, when it was sent, when similar messages had occurred before and so on. This is still what happens — providing information about transmissions that can be used to guide future interception operations. As one of the staff in the unit explained, the job involves searching for patterns.

'If you get them', he said, 'you know when to intercept'.

The UKUSA term used in the C Unit for part of this work is 'technical search', which means 'the search for, identification and acquisition of new or previously unnoticed communications channels'. In other words, the aim of the work is finding communications that can then be intercepted by the stations. This work could include picking up and classifying communications appearing in unusual bands or transmitted by unusual means (e.g. spread across different frequencies).

When Waihopai opened and the GCSB joined the ECHELON system in 1989, the C Unit increased in size and expanded into satellite traffic analysis. The staff in the CS section co-operate with the radio officers based at the Waihopai station, subjecting the satellite channels to traffic analysis. The CS1 staff work out schedules of when certain types of communications are usually transmitted and on which frequencies and channels they will be found. These schedules tell the staff at Waihopai precise times to tune into specified frequency bands on the satellite. They will, for example, identify leased lines and what they carry.

From about 1987 the C Unit included a keyword manager who, together with the K staff, worked out and updated the keywords used in a computer to select out telexes of interest from the large numbers of radio telexes intercepted at Tangimoana. The first keyword manager in 1987-88 was Thomas Weiss, who was given this job after he returned from cryptanalysis training in Melbourne and before the H section was established.

Then, in the second half of 1988, preparations began for introduction of the full Dictionary system. Weiss was joined by Ann Wiseman who, after training at the NSA, became the Dictionary Manager. After the introduction of the Dictionary system, it was her job to receive requests from within the GCSB and from the other UKUSA agencies and enter these keywords (which include telex numbers and so on) into the computer. In 1991, when new Prime Minister Jim Bolger visited the GCSB, he talked to Wiseman's successor, Joy Larkin.

There are equivalent Dictionary Managers in the other four agencies. The GCSB Manager checks and amends the keyword entries that have been made on behalf of the GCSB in the Dictionary computers of the other agencies. It is his or her job to liaise with the K staff on what they want from the system and to help to choose the right keywords for the purpose. Contact is then made with the overseas Dictionary Managers. The work of the C Unit demonstrates vividly how much the GCSB's operations are integrated with the other UKUSA agencies.

The GCSB's Customer Support Unit has the job of distributing the intelligence reports produced by the GCSB and UKUSA allies around the relevant government organisations in Wellington, which are referred to, absurdly, as 'customers'. The L Unit has about 10 staff — including the head of the unit, former Air Force squadron leader Leon Crosse, some customer relations officers and records staff. This unit is the GCSB's main link with the small set of officials and foreign embassy people in Wellington, and an even smaller set of Cabinet ministers, who are cleared to see signals intelligence reports.

Up until 1993, the L Unit received three copies of each report from the GCSB communications staff and these went to the Directorate of Defence Intelligence (DDI), SIS, External Assessments Bureau (EAB) and/or Foreign Affairs, depending on the subject. (The New Zealand-produced reports were sent to the overseas agencies before the local ones. The return copies, received in triplicate back from the sister agencies to confirm the message had been transmitted accurately, were the ones distributed around Wellington.)

The intelligence was carried by a GCSB courier, in the standard black leather bags used by New Zealand intelligence organisations. Most days of the week the silver-haired courier could be seen travelling on foot or by van around the four main intelligence recipients, all located within a few minutes' walk of each other in central Wellington. In 1988, for example, he usually visited the EAB (then called the External Intelligence Bureau) first, then crossed the road to Defence Headquarters. Here he took the lift up to the DDI on the sixth floor and then went up to the SIS on the seventh floor (confirming the GCSB's role as a conduit for signals intelligence to the SIS). Finally he took a shortcut up through an insurance building to Stafford House, the foreign affairs building.

Since 1993 the couriers have mostly been replaced by a paperless on-line system. Customer relations officers from the unit work each day at computer terminals in secure locked rooms inside the EAB and DDI. They select any intelligence reports available in the GCSB computers on subjects requested by the customers (indoctrinated public servants) and sit with them while they read the reports. The main users of this on-line service are staff from the EAB, Ministry of Foreign Affairs and Trade (MFAT), New Zealand Defence Force and probably the SIS (using the DDI terminal located one floor below the SIS headquarters). In 1996 the GCSB officer at the DDI terminal was Shelley Edwards and Desiree Jury was at the EAB.

There is also a headquarters terminal within the L Unit (on the 14th floor), from which intelligence is still printed out and delivered by hand to other users, including some Cabinet ministers, the Ministry of Agriculture and Fisheries, the Ministry of Commerce, Police,[21] and indoctrinated officers in the British, Australian and Canadian high commissions.[22] In 1994, the director said that the GCSB had broadened its 'customer community' during the year.[23]

Here, in a locked room in the Directorate of Defence Intelligence, a GCSB officer provides on-line access to data bases in the Freyberg Building of foreign and GCSB intelligence.

Although it is the L staff's job to help these people get what they want from the system, only the unit staff are allowed direct access to the data base of intelligence reports accessed through their terminals. The users at the EAB and DDI terminals get to read the reports only on the screen. The new paperless distribution system is regarded as being very secure — there are no copies, no one apart from the GCSB officer touches the system and users see only the contents of the reports.

This distribution is the last stage of the Operations Division's work. The process begins with preparation for interception in the C Unit, then there is interception at the stations and the production of intelligence reports in the K Unit. Finally the 'product' is delivered by the L staff to the tiny handful of New Zealanders who ever see it.

Intelligence reports from the other UKUSA agencies arrive electronically, via the GCSB communications staff, and are stored in the GCSB's computer data base of finished intelligence reports. (This data base is separate from the Dictionary data base of raw intercepted reports.) The finished intelligence reports from the K sections also go into this data base. The customer relations officers in L have on-line access to the data base, from which they search for reports wanted by the intelligence users by subject category and keywords.

Recently the L Unit began producing a weekly publication bringing together all the most interesting pieces of signals intelligence information received during the week. This publication, called SIGSUM (SIGINT Summary), has a small circulation among indoctrinated officials in Wellington. One who has seen it says that the intelligence reports printed in it are divided up under such headings as 'South East Asia'.

L Unit also covers liaison with the New Zealand Defence Force (NZDF). Leon Crosse originally held this military liaison position, which was called W.[24] The incumbent shares offices with a number of serving military officers who are based at the GCSB. Crosse's successor as military liaison officer was, until recently, Grant Fletcher, who joined the GCSB in March 1987, a few months after completing his Russian honours degree and as a member of the Naval Reserve. After some years in K2, he had a year of leave doing language training in Japan before returning to the KE section. In 1993 he was transferred to the military liaison job and he was sent for several weeks of training in the United States in October-November 1994. Later, after returning to KE, he was sent to Australia to take up the GCSB analyst posting inside the DSD headquarters.

The current GCSB military liaison officer is Don McMurray, who is called LS. He works with an Army officer on posting from the NZDF called the Staff Officer (Special Operations), who, in late 1995, was Captain Jonty Berry, and his Navy assistant. They work on the 14th floor of the GCSB building.

There have been liaison staff to distribute overseas signals intelligence reports to government departments since long before the GCSB was formed. A two-person section originally did this job but in 1988, following a review of intelligence which recommended that a wider circle of departments should have access to signals intelligence, the section was expanded and named the Customer Liaison Office.

Liaison with foreign affairs staff has certainly increased. Despite the presence of the GCSB terminal at the EAB in the same building, on one morning alone in 1994 the Ministry of Foreign Affairs and Trade visitors' book had four entries showing GCSB staff visiting people there.

The GCSB Operations are supported by high-tech computer and communications systems, engineers and technicians and several specialised security sections which try to keep it all secret. These support functions are covered in the next chapter.

CHAPTER SEVEN

THE ORGANISATION
SECRET STRUCTURES OF THE GCSB

Throughout the researching and writing of this book the GCSB has turned down many dozens of requests for information made under the Official Information Act. Many of the refusals have subsequently been investigated by the Ombudsman. The biggest fight of all was over the GCSB's internal staff newsletters. These are unclassified but promised to provide interesting information about what goes on inside the organisation.

The first time I asked for them, the director, Ray Parker, took the easy option and replied: 'No GCSB staff newsletter exists, nor is there any separate such publication for either of the stations'.[1] It was two years before I confirmed that they really did exist and wrote again. Initially the GCSB released six months of what the director called 'staff circulars', containing some information used in these chapters. Then, realising it had been helpful, the GCSB clammed up completely. All the other copies requested from then on had virtually every meaningful word and letter deleted with heavy black pen.

The Chief Ombudsman agreed to review the decision, a process that should take two or three months. After a year, the GCSB was still urging delay after delay so that it could produce yet another long report, new methodology or expert to prove to the Ombudsman why the information should be withheld. Months later the Ombudsman prised some small concessions from the GCSB, but as the book went to press, three and a half years after the first request, the GCSB was still wrangling with the Ombudsman in an attempt to avoid having to release any more.

Why was it worth so much effort to the GCSB to withhold some unclassified staff circulars? The reasons given by Parker and his security staff were always non-specific concerns about 'operational security'. It was not that the particular information was very sensitive, they argued, but that any information could always be combined with other information to damage national security (what they called the 'mosaic theory').

This policy, and the attitudes that underlie it, have not served the GCSB well. Without their secretiveness, this book would probably never have been written. Had the basic information about the organisation been publicly available, it is doubtful that I or anyone else would have bothered to do all the research and digging that have led eventually to a much more detailed exposé.

The information the GCSB wanted to withhold about organisational structures is available, without a great fuss about national security, in books about the United States, the Australian and even the secretive British UKUSA agencies. The Canadian agency openly lists the names of about 50 top headquarters staff, and the titles of their sections and their secure telephone numbers. This chapter presents organisational information about the GCSB, but now with more detail than any of the agencies would probably be comfortable with.

A crucial step in coming to understand an organisation like the GCSB is investigating the structures. This is easier said than done. In the absence of sources such as the staff circulars, hundreds of different scraps of information have had to be pieced together like a jigsaw to form a picture of the organisation.

The GCSB has four divisions: Operations, covering all intelligence operations and the two stations; Technology, covering all the computer, communications and technical support for intelligence and security operations; Information Systems Security (INFOSEC), covering the non-intelligence work of the bureau that concerns security of government information: technical security, information security, computer security and emission security; and Corporate Services, covering the administration, personnel, finances and security of the organisation and also some policy and planning work. In addition, in May 1995 a small Office of the Director was created, headed by a new Executive Director.

Each division is headed by a director and made up of a number of units (headed by managers), which are in turn divided into sections (headed by section heads). This structure was introduced in 1989 when corporate structures were imposed across the New Zealand public service. From that date each division has had a mission statement, 'assistant directors' have become 'managers' and directors and managers have taken over responsibility for their own budgets.

Corporate-speak is in. There is intelligence 'production' to supply the 'customers' and in his 1994 Christmas message the director congratulated the GCSB staff on the 'improved and expanded range of services and products' provided during the year.

As in overseas intelligence organisations, each staff position at the GCSB is known by an acronym and position number. For example, the manager of the Customer Support Unit is called L, he oversees two sections headed by officers called LC and LS and the positions within these sections are called

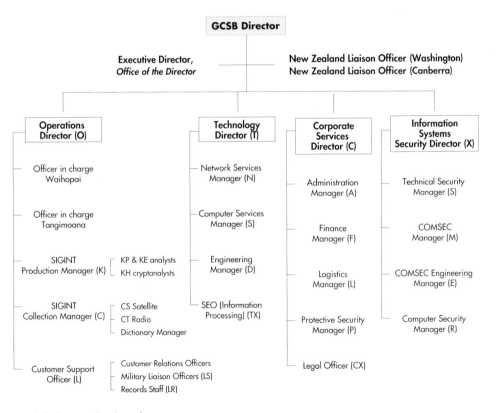

GCSB organisation plan.

LS1, LS2 and so on. This is how the staff are referred to on internal letters, rosters and other documents. (A full organisation plan for the GCSB headquarters, using these acronyms, is included in Appendix A.)

In 1996 the GCSB has about 200 full-time New Zealand staff. About 70 of these are at the two stations, the rest in the headquarters. The senior staff include the Director, the four divisional directors, the Executive Director, the GCSB liaison officers in Washington and Canberra, the officers in charge at the Waihopai and Tangimoana stations, about 15 managers and four Senior Executive Officers. Their names are listed in Appendix A.

In addition there are staff from other UKUSA agencies attached to the GCSB on postings.[2] In exchange GCSB headquarters operations staff are regularly posted or sent for training inside the headquarters of the other four UKUSA agencies. There are also overseas postings of staff from other parts of the GCSB. In October 1994, for example, electronics technician Andrew Vincent arrived back from a one- or two-year posting to the DSD. Two GCSB staff left on overseas postings in the same month. The first was Harvey Jacobs,[3] a senior radio intercept officer at the Tangimoana station, who was posted to the DSD in Canberra to work as a traffic analyst. The other officer posted in October 1994 was a computer programmer, Philip Dorrell, who left for a three-year posting at the GCHQ in Cheltenham, England.

After Operations, Technology (T) Division is the most important division in the GCSB. It covers all the high-tech computer systems that have become central to the GCSB's operations and also the computer-based communication system that links the GCSB to its two stations and the rest of the UKUSA network. Created in December 1994 by combining the previous Information Processing and Engineering Divisions, it now contains all of the GCSB's computing, communications and technical staff, making up about a quarter of the headquarters staff. The Director, called T, is ex-Air Force Group Captain Michael Spring.[4]

The Technology Division is made up of three distinct parts: the Information Centre (known as the 'Infocen') which contains the GCSB's communications N staff; the computer services staff in S Unit; and the D Unit technicians and engineers who were part of the old Engineering Division.

The Information Centre is located in the south-west corner of the 14th floor of the Freyberg Building. This is where the GCSB communications staff maintain communications with the overseas agencies and with the two GCSB stations, exchanging messages, intelligence reports, instructions and

Name		Born	Dates	Position		Location
~~LEIGH KB~~	M	~~16NOV65~~	~~17JAN83~~	~~TECHN~~		ADY
~~LEWIS GJ~~	M	~~30DEC68~~	~~19JAN87~~	~~TECHL CDT~~		ADY
~~MCGUCKIAN JL~~	M	~~23NOV67~~	~~19JAN87~~	~~TECHL CDT~~		ADY
~~TOMKINS MARK~~	M	~~7JAN71~~	~~18JAN88~~	~~CDT~~		ADY
~~WALFORD JC~~	M	~~12SEP68~~	~~19JAN87~~	~~TECHL CDT~~		ADY
~~WHITE DE~~	M	~~14OCT61~~	~~28APR86~~	~~TECHN~~		ADY

007.1   EXECUTIVE/CLERICAL OCCUPATIONAL CLASS

	Name		Born	Dates	Position		Location
09	~~LEWIS KJ~~	M	~~23JUL33~~	~~30JUN87~~	~~DIR MNGMT SPRT~~		HO
	LYNCH LJ	M	19FEB35	16AUG82	DEP DIR OPS ✓		HO
	~~SINCLAIR PA~~	M	~~5JAN48~~	~~12NOV69~~	~~DIR STGC ININL AFF~~		HO
	SMITH CK	M	6FEB34	30JAN79	DEP DIR ENGRG ✓		HO
	~~SMITH KG~~	M	~~20MAY41~~	~~12JAN59~~	~~GEN MGR AFCC~~		HO
	TUCKER WH	M	18AUG50	1MAR82	LISN OFF *(Washington)*		HO
	WILLSON JOHN	M	29AUG35	1MAY85	DEP DIR	COMSEC	HO
08	BRANDON JA	M	19OCT47	19MAR79	ASST DIR	*Policy + Plans*	HO
	CATLEY NG	M	21MAY42	5FEB85	ASST DIR	*COMSEC policy*	HO
	~~GRIFFITHS CLIVE~~	M	~~23SEP41~~	~~13SEP76~~	~~DEP ASST SEC PERS~~		HO
	KEANE BP	M	5FEB47	13JAN86	ASST DIR	*SIGINT*	HO
	~~LAWRENCE PL~~	M	~~22AUG39~~	~~22JAN57~~	~~CH EX OFF~~		HO
	~~MCMAHON KW~~	M	~~27SEP61~~	~~20JAN69~~	~~DEP ASST SEC~~		HO
	ORCHARD JAD	M	22JUN32	2JUL58	OFF IC	*Tangimoana*	HO
	PUNNETT BM	M	7MAR33	8JAN68	ASST DIR	*Admin*	HO
	WAITE CWJ	M	14MAR34	21NOV83	LISN OFF	*(Melbourne)*	HO
07	~~BOWERS PF~~	M	~~17JAN39~~	~~27JUL81~~	~~DEP DIR~~		HO
	~~CAREY DAVID~~	M	~~9FEB47~~	~~28JAN03~~	~~FINL ADVR~~		SGP
	~~CURSON JR~~	M	~~20JUL48~~	~~12AUG74~~	~~ADMIN SERV MGR~~		ADY
	~~DRURY ED~~	M	~~21JUN30~~	~~29MAR55~~	~~CMD SEC~~		PM
	~~GOLDS AT~~	M	~~19MAR38~~	~~14OCT85~~	~~DIST MNGMT SERV OFF~~		ANC SGDO
	~~HOWIE HM~~	M	~~19JAN45~~	~~11FEB63~~	~~DIR FINL CORP SERV~~		HO

Crossing out the names of real Defence personnel revealed the GCSB staff hidden within Ministry of Defence staff lists.

so on. The GCSB communications and encryption systems are thoroughly integrated into the United States network.[5]

Here, for example, long-time GCSB communications officer Neil Worthington (known as NC) sits at a computer screen sending off each intelligence report produced by the K analysts to the overseas agencies. He checks where reports of that subject are to be sent, types in the special electronic addresses for those destinations and dispatches them. The Infocen also acts as the terminal through which raw intercept passes as it is distributed around the ECHELON system.

The eight Network Services Officers work 12-hour shifts, providing a 24-hour, seven day a week link to the rest of the UKUSA network.[6] At night it is the Infocen's lights that can be seen behind heavy curtains on the top floor. This is a high security area with a combination lock on the door and sound-proofing. Apart from the communications staff, no one except the director and a few senior staff are allowed to enter. Across the hall is a vault containing the codes, sent from the NSA in Washington, which are used for secure communications between the UKUSA agencies.

Anyone who believed that the supply of United States intelligence to New Zealand was cut off in 1985 would be shocked by the volume of traffic being received by the Infocen, especially from the NSA. In 1993 it was estimated that a pile of paper a few metres high was spat out of the printer in an average week (most of it, according to one Infocen officer, 'rubbish you could read in the newspaper anyway'). The Infocen staff were receiving a pile of overseas reports (printed out in triplicate) about a metre high each day. This is said to be a larger quantity than before the so-called 'intelligence cut' in February 1985.

A small part of the GCSB Infocen's work is for other New Zealand agencies. For example, both the Directorate of Defence Intelligence (DDI) and External Assessments Bureau (EAB) exchange some intelligence with their British, Canadian, Australian and (probably) United States sister organisations through the GCSB Infocen. The SIS is said to have its own secure intelligence channels.

The Computer Services (TS) Unit, described by GCSB staff as being responsible 'for everything that goes "beep" in the GCSB', develops and maintains all the GCSB's computer systems, from the large multi-user systems to small specialised systems. It is located on the 12th floor of the headquarters building and backed up by technicians who maintain the computer equipment.

The GCSB got its first computing staff and large computer in the early 1980s, but the unit dates from 1988 when there was a rapid growth in this area in preparation for the opening of Waihopai and the Dictionary system.

Computers are now involved in every area of the GCSB's operations. The computer operations supported by the TS staff include: the computers, data bases and terminals associated with the Dictionary system, and Dictionary management activities in the C Section; production codebreaking (feeding runs of encrypted messages through decryption programmes devised by the UKUSA allies); computer support for the K, C and M Sections; administration and management information systems; communications (internal e-mail and externally through the Infocen); and the data bases of finished intelligence disseminated through the L Section.

Each of these operations needs to be planned, special programming projects need to be done to adapt and upgrade programmes acquired commercially and from the UKUSA allies, the day-to-day running of the systems must be checked and staff from other sections must be supported when they use them.

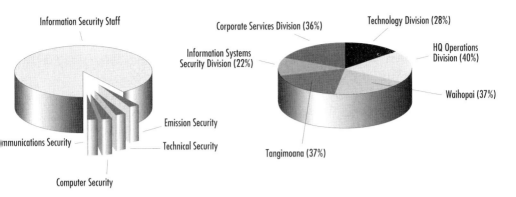

Official documents state that the GCSB has four functions: 'Communications Security, Computer Security, Technical Security and Signals Intelligence'. In reality the first three functions combined account for only a fraction of the GCSB's staff and resources.

The TS Unit has about 10 staff, divided between the TSP Section, which contains the computer programmers, and the TSE Section, which designs and oversees the computer systems. TSH staffs a help desk to assist people using computers elsewhere in the organisation.[7]

The main computer systems currently used at the GCSB were supplied by the NCR and ICL companies. The headquarters computer system (the first hardware for which an NCR Tower was installed in March-April 1988) involves a large UNIX-based computer connected to micro-computers and terminals throughout the headquarters in a network that includes the Infocen. The major components of the computer system are connected by fibre-optic cables because, according to GCSB technical staff, it is impossible for these to be eavesdropped upon.

Intercepted satellite communications from Waihopai are sent across Cook Strait to Wellington, computer to computer, on Telecom lines and enter the headquarters through the Infocen. Radio intercept from Tangimoana arrives in the same way. From here they go by fibre-optic cable into the main computers. More fibre-optic cables link the computers with the Operations Division staff on the 14th floor.

In 1993 the computing staff completed a system for interconnecting all the bureau's computers; as one of them described it, 'getting all the different computer systems to talk to each other'. The movement of intelligence reports between the analyst, liaison and Infocen staff is completely paperless. With all the GCSB's and overseas agencies' top secret information being handled within and between computers, computer security has become of increasing concern within the GCSB. Indeed it is likely that the UKUSA allies made it known that a specialist computer security unit should be built up at the GCSB to protect the New Zealand segment of their global network (the British GCHQ provided the first head of the section).

The third component of the Technology Division are the engineers and technicians in the TD Unit. These electronics and computer specialists are divided into two sections responsible for installing and maintaining all the different types of electronic equipment at the GCSB. They work closely with the technical staff at the two stations.[8]

The Information Systems Security (X) Division is the 'non-intelligence' part of the GCSB, concerned with trying to stop other countries spying on New Zealand government activities. Until 1984, these were the only publicly acknowledged functions of the GCSB, even though they account for only about 10 percent of the bureau's resources.

The Information Systems Security Division has a special and very secret exhibition for the few outside visitors — such as Prime Minister Jim Bolger in 1991 — who are allowed to visit its 13th-floor offices. Here there is a collection of all the electronic bugs that its specially trained technical security staff have detected and removed from New Zealand embassies around the world. Its suitably grim name is the Black Museum. These bugs can be technically very sophisticated and extremely hard to detect. Bolger, who like most people probably imagined bugs meant things like small microphones placed in the walls, was introduced to a whole new dimension of electronic espionage. For example, one of the exhibits in the Black Museum is a system that used the ordinary electrical wiring running through a New Zealand embassy building to detect the tiny emissions produced during electronic typing, allowing it to work out what was being typed as a typist worked.

The division, which makes up about a sixth of the headquarters staff, includes the S Unit for protecting government buildings and communication systems from being 'bugged' (called Technical Security or TECSEC); the R Unit for protecting information in computers (called the Computer Security or COMPSEC); the E Unit for protecting computers and other electronic equipment from interception (called Emission Security or EMSEC); and the M Unit for protecting government communications with encrypting equipment and codes (called Communications Security or COMSEC).

Although these are useful services for any government, it is likely that a lot of the impetus for their development came from the other UKUSA agencies. The rationale would have been that, with the establishment of the GCSB as a part of the UKUSA network, the allies needed to be sure that security systems and procedures in New Zealand were as secure as elsewhere so that this country was not a vulnerable weak link. (The same argument had been used to push for the formation of the Security Intelligence Service 20 years earlier.) These various security functions are attached to the signals intelligence agencies in all five UKUSA countries.

The Director of Information Systems Security since 30 August 1993 has been John Brandon,[9] known within the GCSB as X. Previously Michael Spring (1989-93), John Willson (1985-89) and Dave Hilling (1978-85) have held the position.[10]

The S Unit has two teams of TECSEC inspectors who are sent around the world, travelling on green diplomatic passports, searching for the bugs that become exhibits in the Black Museum. They use high-tech sweeping equipment to check for electronic eavesdropping devices planted in New Zealand government offices, embassy and high commission buildings overseas and GCSB facilities and their communications systems.[11] In government circles this is referred to as the 'Inspection Service'. Since 1992 the TECSEC manager, called S, has been Brian Nokes.[12]

Unlike many other sections, the GCSB's six technical security staff do clearly help New Zealand's interests. They were twice sent to search for bugs in this Paris embassy building after the Rainbow Warrior *bombing.*

TECSEC inspectors made two trips, one lengthy, to Paris between November 1987 and April 1988. Why? This is the period following the *Rainbow Warrior* bombing and subsequent capture of two of the French DGSE agents involved. By the time of these inspections France had broken a 1986 agreement that had allowed the agents to leave prison in New Zealand on the condition that they be held on Hao Atoll in French Polynesia for three years. Both agents were back in France by May 1988, less than two years after arriving on Hao. The TECSEC staff did not find any bugs in New Zealand's Paris embassy, but the special attention was obviously a deliberate safety precaution. The resumption of French nuclear testing in 1995 quite likely prompted similar visits.

Because inspection teams travel with reinforced suitcases full of debugging equipment that includes highly classified technology provided by other UKUSA agencies, they must use special security handling techniques while travelling, including personally loading their suitcases into cargo compartments. One piece of this equipment is a side-scan radar that can detect objects underground and inside the structure of some buildings.[13] Before the GCSB began TECSEC work in 1977-78, this service was provided by British inspection teams regularly visiting New Zealand diplomatic posts.[14]

The M Unit is the centre of all New Zealand government activities relating to communications security. Communications security (COMSEC) is about keeping government telephone calls, fax, and telex secure from eavesdropping by the use of encryption machines and special codes, and also encompasses systems of 'safe hand' transport of classified bags. The M Unit is divided into two parts: M2 and M4.

M2 provides policy and advice for all government organisations requiring communications security (notably the government itself and the foreign affairs, defence and intelligence organisations).[15] The M4 Section distributes the New Zealand and international codes used by all government organisations and arranges safe hand transport for the GCSB in and out of New Zealand.

The COMSEC Manager (called M), Chris Farrow, oversees a set of COMSEC standards and procedures governing all government organisations. These specify which types of 'secure communications' (encryption) equipment to use on more and less secret communications and how the staff in each organisation should handle the codes.[16] There are special procedures for receiving and storing the codes in safes and vaults. The regulations also require regular checks that all the copies of codes are accounted for ('musters') and specify how they should be destroyed.[17]

The M4 Section is like a high-security mail sorting room for the GCSB. Its primary role is receiving, keeping computer records of ('accounting') and distributing COMSEC materials to the various users throughout the New Zealand government structure. Established in 1979, it was known in government circles in the 1980s as the New Zealand National Distributing Authority (NZNDA).[18]

For New Zealand's communications with the other UKUSA countries, and particularly for the constant distribution of raw and finished signals intelligence around the UKUSA communications network, each agency receives the codes ('one-time keys') for each day from the NSA for their compatible communications equipment. The use of common codes allows the five agencies to read each other's encrypted messages.

These codes ('COMSEC material') are received by the NZNDA in special bags from the NSA and distributed to communications staff. In the 1990s the codes are stored on computer disks. There are new codes for each day, which are keyed into the secure communications equipment. For the codes always to be compatible, each day must begin at the same time for all five agencies. The UKUSA agencies use Greenwich Mean Time, called ZULU time, which means that the codes are changed over in the GCSB at noon each day.

Because it has procedures set up for transporting and handling the highly classified COMSEC materials, the M4 Section also handles the movement in and out of New Zealand of all the 'safe hand' bags exchanging other sensitive materials between the GCSB and the UKUSA agencies.[19]

GCSB staff, probably from M4, have the job of regularly supplying up-to-date codes for the secure telephone units in government offices. When Prime Minister David Lange was given one of these secure telephones in the mid-1980s its main function ended up as a humorous dinner story. GCSB staff, always two together, regularly visited his office to update the codes but whenever he tried to use the phone for confidential overseas calls it would not work. The GCSB staff came repeatedly but could not find anything wrong. Then one day, to his great surprise, the secure phone suddenly rang for the first time. When he answered the caller asked, 'Is that Taylors Drycleaning?' Later Lange told the GCSB that if they could not fix the phone he wanted it removed. They asked for one more try and got Telecom technicians to check it. The technicians found that the phone had accidentally been given a toll bar to stop it making long-distance calls.

In the mid-1980s the GCSB's security functions were extended to include computer security (COMPSEC). A computer security specialist was brought from Britain and worked alone on the 14th floor. In 1996 this work is done by the Computer Security Unit headed by the Computer Security Manager, Malcolm Shore, R.[20] Just as the M Unit aims to protect information carried over government communications systems, the R Unit advises government organisations on how to protect the information in their computers.

The COMSEC Engineering E Unit has technical staff who are responsible for ensuring that computers and other electronic equipment holding classified information cannot be spied on electronically. This work is known as

Emission Security (EMSEC), taking its name from faint computer emissions which, when intercepted with the right equipment, allow the image or text on the screen to be picked up at a distance.

The Canadian CSE's EMSEC work has been described as follows:

The CSE is involved in attempting to protect the interception of high-frequency radio signals leaking from computer equipment. These signals sound like interference when picked up on standard radios but can be intercepted by sensitive receivers, recorded, and later unscrambled by sophisticated electronic devices, including other computers. In some circumstances, sophisticated equipment can pick up signals from computer equipment within a two block area.[21]

EMSEC staff test government equipment for emissions, install shielding for equipment holding classified material and advise other government organisations on how to avoid this form of interception. The section is known to other government organisations as the Testing and Advisory Service.[22]

Special computer security policies followed at the GCSB itself include placing electronic shielding around computers, testing all computers for emissions, allowing outside service technicians to see only stripped down components of the computer equipment and smashing computer monitors that are no longer used.

The reason for destroying old monitors is an effect known as 'burn in'. The phosphor coating on a monitor, which forms the inside coating of the glass screen, apparently retains image information in the phosphor charges. This can be retrieved from a discarded monitor, especially when the pattern on the screen has had a constant format (this policy is enforced at Waihopai, for example, where some monitors display a standard format within which instructions are given to the interception equipment).

The Corporate Services (C) Division was formed on 1 May 1995 by an amalgamation of the Support Services and Policy and Plans Divisions.[23] Mostly it does the types of administrative work that occur in any large organisation: typing, personnel, finance, equipment and so on.[24] It also has security sections that work to maintain the GCSB's secrets.

The Protective Security Unit, under manager Mike Loughran (who came from the Air Force police) contains the security guards who work around the clock, seven days a week, in the headquarters building (on 12-hour shifts, 7 am to 7 pm). There is also the senior security officer, Don Allan.[25] The unit is responsible for careful screening and monitoring of staff, for the regulations that require every sheet of secret information to be put away in the

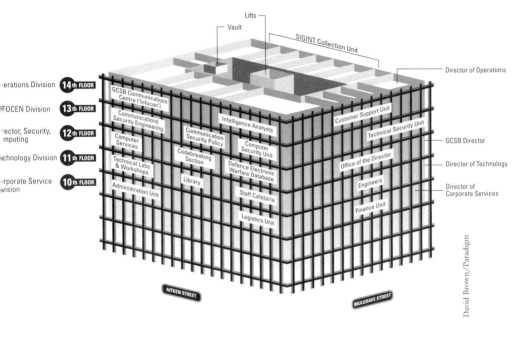

GCSB Freyberg Building Headquarters

Lifts

Vault

SIGINT Collection Unit

Director of Operations

...erations Division **14**th FLOOR

GCSB Communications Centre ('Infocen')

...FOCEN Division **13**th FLOOR

Communications Security Engineering

Intelligence Analysts

Customer Support Unit

...ector, Security, ...mputing **12**th FLOOR

Computer Services

Communication Security Policy

Computer Security Unit

Technical Security Unit

GCSB Director

...chnology Division **11**th FLOOR

Codebreaking Section

Technical Labs & Workshops

Defence Electronic Warfare Database

Office of the Director

Director of Technology

...rporate Service ...vision **10**th FLOOR

Administration Unit

Library

Staff Cafeteria

Engineers

Director of Corporate Services

Logistics Unit

Finance Unit

AITKEN STREET

MULGRAVE STREET

David Brown/Paradigm

The layout of GCSB headquarters in Wellington: inside the most secret building in New Zealand.

correct safe or to be correctly shredded or destroyed, for the electronic access doors that restrict where staff can go within the headquarters and for all the other strict rules, procedures and systems used to maintain what they call 'Operational Security' — or, following the United States military obsession with abbreviations, OPSEC.

The GCSB originally took over the top two floors (13th and 14th) of the Freyberg Building in late 1982 and since then it has expanded down to the 10th. In 1992 there was a major rearrangement of the headquarters layout all the floors were completely refurbished.[26] Physical security throughout the building was also increased. Access to the headquarters is on the 12th floor through a double set of blast- and bullet-proof glass doors, which are operated by a guard inside the reception area; the first door closes behind you before the second opens. (This arrangement is known in the security industry as a 'man trap'.) Strengthened doors were also added on the other floors, video cameras were fitted on the outside of the building and a new security access card system was installed.

The GCSB staff must now carry their internal access cards with them to go from one part of the building to another. They hold the card up to the right place on a door and, when a red light goes out, the door can be opened. But the cards are programmed to allow access only to specified parts of the building and at specified times of day (usually only between 7 am and 6 pm, Monday to Friday) and must be handed in before leaving the building. Since the building's lifts are open to the public, an internal stairway controlled by these access cards provides secure access between floors. To add to the atmosphere, whenever uncleared visitors such as window cleaners or outside technicians visit the headquarters, blue lights flash in the corridors to warn staff of their presence.

These new physical security measures, part of a general tightening of security measures throughout all areas of the organisation, were introduced by Security Manager Steve Smith after he moved into this new position at the end of 1990.

Until then, for example, the staff could move freely between floors and the customer relations staff from L Unit used to walk across to the Parliament buildings and elsewhere alone, carrying the signals intelligence reports in a locked briefcase. But the UKUSA allies insisted that the GCSB introduce higher security for reports taken outside secure areas. Now the L staff have an escort who drives them to each building and waits for them in the lobby.

In 1990 the GCSB introduced monthly staff briefings called, in self-conscious corporate-speak, shareholders' meetings.[27] Held on the 11th floor, they bring together all the headquarters staff and are intended to assist morale by keeping staff informed of what is happening in their organisation. These meetings are brief (less than an hour) and begin with the members of one of the units explaining their work to the other staff. There are then short briefings on issues affecting the staff such as security regulations and wage rounds.

I was shown an uncensored copy of the GCSB staff bulletin describing the first shareholders' meeting on 14 November 1990. It had three 15-minute presentations: 'a brief of a topic of current intelligence' by a member of the Operations Division, a brief on expansion of the headquarters by the Administration Division and a security briefing by the Security Manager. It is typical of the all-pervasive security that each of the presentations was given a separate security classification: 'CONFIDENTIAL' for the second two and 'TOP SECRET codeword' for the intelligence briefing. The latter means it contained information protected by one of the special signals intelligence codewords (see Chapter 12) which are all more secret than TOP SECRET. Since all headquarters staff are invited to the shareholders' meetings, this

```
Director of Law/Defence                          Director O H Bergen ............ 991-7182(S)
  LCol D Couture .................. 995-4585      Director P M Osborne ........... 991-7108(S)

Deputy Judge Advocate General/Materiel           POLICY AND PLANS
  Capt(N) C F Blair................. 992-8044     Director General D E Waterfall ... 991-7247(S)
  Secretary B Grant ............... 992-4114      Director Strategic Planning
                                                    G O'Bright ................... 991-7417(S)
Chief Military Trial Judge                        Director Corporate Policy D Lindley . 991-7242(S)
  Col G L Brais ................... 992-5201
Secretary G Hicks ................. 992-0125      ADMINISTRATION
ACMTJ LCol J S T Pitzul........... 992-0117       Director General M Finner ........ 991-7246(S)
Chief Court Reporter CWO P Crowder . 996-2604     Director Human Resources
                                                    P H Lefebvre ................. 991-7445(S)
CHIEF REVIEW SERVICES                             Director Administration and Finance
  MGen M Terreau ................. 995-8561         D Drew ....................... 991-7420
Admin Asst ........................ 992-0363
                                                  TECHNOLOGY
DIRECTOR GENERAL PROGRAM EVALUATION               Director General M MacArthur ... 991-7178(S)
  P C Skippon .................... 992-4717       Special Asst D G A Ruddick ......... 991-7197
Secretary ......................... 992-4717      Director Telecommunications and Computer
Program Evaluation Directors                        Services W Bailey ............ 991-8603(S)
  N J Black ..................... 996-4534        Director Engineering S Gauthier .... 991-7149(S)
  J E Browell ................... 996-4515
  Capt(N) P J Child ............. 996-0544        INFOSEC
  Dr A A Clark ................. 996-4886         Director General A Pickering ...... 991-7176(S)
  Col W B Fox ................. 996-8185          Director INFOSEC Evaluation and Engineering
  Col A P Humphreys............ 995-0338            Group D McKerrow ............ 991-7215(S)
  Col A W Strynadka ........... 996-4514          R&D Coordinator P Devlin ....... 991-7174(S)
Program Evaluators                                Head, INFOSEC Systems and Equipment
  M Glustien ................... 996-1492           T McKenzie ................... 991-7503(S)
  H Hubley ..................... 996-5664         Head, INFOSEC Standards and Evaluation
  LCol R A Jones ............... 995-1902           B Madill ..................... 991-7220(S)
  LCol J B Knapp ............... 996-4509         Director INFOSEC Support Group
Special Project Officer                             L Bélanger ................... 991-8798(S)
  E E Milbum ................... 995-7958         Manager, INFOSEC Control
                                                    C Caldwell ................... 991-8808(S)
DIRECTOR GENERAL AUDIT                            National Central Office of Records (NCOR)
GENERAL INQUIRIES ............ 995-7641             G Nolan ...................... 991-8804(S)
  J G Van Adel ................. 995-7792/7841    Manager INFOSEC Program Support
Director Audit Program Development                  B Lamarre .................... 991-8791(S)
  P A Cardarelli .............. 995-8640/7841     Manager, Electronic Key Management Systems
Director Audit Policy and Evaluation                S Greaves .................... 991-8714(S)
  L D Stephens............... 995-5395/7841       Manager, Canadian Key Management System
Director Regional Audit Operations                  M Ouellette .................. 991-8701(S)
  R Jolicoeur ................. 995-7841          CKMS User Services .......... 991-8600(F)(S)
Director Special Examinations and Inquiries       National INFOSEC Custodian and Distribution
  S J Davis ................. 995-5483/5-7841       Authority G Dionne ................ 991-8823
Director Review Official Languages                CSE INFOSEC Custodian
  A/Director T C Letellier ....... 992-0270/5-7841   M Brundige ................... 991-8800(S)
                                                  Manager, INFOSEC Services
                                                    R A English .................. 991-7471(S)
                                                  INFOSEC Services Advisor
      COMMUNICATIONS SECURITY                       M Rosplesch .................. 991-7554(S)
          ESTABLISHMENT                           R Special Projects Manager
                                                    W Redden .................... 991-7497(S)
         Confederation Heights                    Manager, INFOSEC Client Services
           719 Heron Road                           R L Stevens.................. 991-7532(S)
          Ottawa K1G 3Z4                          Head, INFOSEC System Consultation
                                                    J Ellis ...................... 991-7470(S)
GENERAL ENQUIRIES ............ 991-7245           Head, INFOSEC System Consultation
                                                    R Hysert ..................... 991-7407
CSE                                               Head, INFOSEC Operational Services
Chief, CSE A S Woolner ......... 991-7241(S)        K Ball ....................... 991-7501(S)
Director Legal Services D Akman ... 991-7243(S)   Head, INFOSEC Client Support Services
                                                    D Davies ..................... 991-7543(S)
SIGINT PRODUCTION                                 Government Secure Telephone Network
Director General C W Hewson ..... 991-7233(S)       (GSTN) ....................... 991-8600(S)
Executive Staff Officer D J Abbott . 991-8508(S)  Manager, INFOSEC Industrial Programs and
Director Customer Services                        Initiatives
  M F White ................. 991-8760(S)           V Muolo ...................... 991-7556(S)
Head Customer Relations Section                   Manager, INFOSEC Industrial Programs
  K Woolner ................. 991-8771(S)           D Connors .................... 991-7520(S)
Head, Customer Relations Unit - NDHQ              Manager, Canadian Industrial TEMPEST Program
  T Larson ................... 945-5069             J O'Callahan ................. 991-7493(S)
Head, SIGINT Current Operations and Support       Manager, Cryptographic Endorsement and
Section                                           Assessment Program
  E Watson ................... 991-8761(S)          J Pavelich ................... 991-7530(S)
Head, Military/IAC Support                        Manager, Trusted Products Evaluation Program
  J Parton ................... 991-8755             W MacLeod ................... 991-7418(S)
Director M B Peart.............. 991-8746(S)      Manager, INFOSEC Standards and Initiatives
Director N R E Brulé ............ 991-7140(S)       D Kimpton .................... 991-7409(S)
                                                  INFOSEC SECURE FACSIMILE . 991-7411(F)(S)
                                                  Library ......................... 991-7188
```

This section of the Government of Canada Telephone Directory, covering the Canadian equivalent of the GCSB, shows it is willing to be much less secretive.

confirms that every member of the staff — from director to accounts clerk — is required to have the special UKUSA signals intelligence clearance.

A wide range of UKUSA-wide security regulations is expected of the agencies in the alliance. Many of these are contained in a document called the *GCSB Manual of Security Instructions Volume I* (Volume II contains the GCSB's Information Processing Security Instructions). Like an earlier publication, a large red GCSB manual called *Standing Orders* which was written in the mid-1980s, it is based on the equivalent NSA manuals. It covers physical security matters such as keeping offices clear and doors closed, security passes, who is allowed access to which areas and documents, what kinds of safes and vaults different classified materials must be stored in and so on. For example, staff members take turns doing 'security duty' before leaving for the day: checking that the vaults are locked, that all classified materials are in safes (signing a card on each safe) and that nothing has been left on a desk or in an unlocked drawer. In the KH cryptanalysis section, for example, there are eight duties on the 'Daily Security Checklist'.[28]

The security instructions also cover personnel security matters such as rules relating to non-GCSB people, again derived from the international regulations. If, for example, GCSB workers are asked about their work, they are advised to say that they work for Defence. If anyone enquires further, they are supposed to report the conversation to the GCSB Security Officer, Don Allan. International regulations also require that if a member of the GCSB believes a fellow worker to be homosexual, they must report this to their superiors (even though homosexuality was decriminalised in New Zealand in July 1986). Very few people report infringements of any kind, however, as special papers have to be filled out and the reporting goes on the individual's own personal file.

When, in the early 1980s, a new regulation was introduced requiring all GCSB staff to be New Zealand citizens, a lot of people rushed to get citizenship papers. Particularly affected were a lot of radio intercept officers who had been recruited from the British GCHQ.

During the 1980s new GCSB recruits were sent to the Security Intelligence Service headquarters to watch what they described as a 'scary' film about security threats. They were warned (with real examples given) of the familiar techniques by which people are induced to become double agents. The main types of 'entrapment' were said to be romantic 'honey traps', ideological influence, blackmail and money lure. The recruits were reminded to report any strange occurrences to security man Don Allan.

Personnel security is centred around the curiously named but long-established practice of 'indoctrinating' and 'deindoctrinating' staff. All new GCSB staff are given a lecture on the security regulations by Don Allan, including which countries they must not visit (such as some East European countries, China, Cuba and Tibet) and the requirement never to talk about their work (under threat of heavy penalty). They must then sign a two-page declaration agreeing to the conditions. (A distinctively New Zealand part of Don Allan's indoctrination briefing, at least for some new staff, has been a warning about the dangers posed by the peace movement in New Zealand and a special warning not to speak to the writer.)

They are then indoctrinated — that is, cleared to see signals intelligence materials and bound by the regulations — until they leave the job. They join a very small group of people around the world allowed to know what goes on inside the signals intelligence alliance — but still only on a 'need to know' basis. Most staff know little about what happens beyond their section.

The list of countries posing a risk to visitors, as defined in a New Zealand Defence Council Order (in the 1980s), was 'Communist Countries': Albania, Bulgaria, China, Czechoslovakia, Cuba, East Germany, Hungary, Mongolia, North Korea, Vietnam, Poland, Romania, Tibet, the USSR, Yugoslavia; and 'Other Countries': Afghanistan, Algeria, Cambodia, Egypt, Iraq, Taiwan, Jordan, Laos, Zimbabwe, Syria and Yemen. GCSB staff say that the list of prohibited countries has changed since the 1989 changes in Eastern Europe.

LITTLE LEAKS...BIG BANGS...KEEP OUR SECRETS SECRET! — a British security poster displayed inside the GCSB headquarters.

Before they leave the job staff must hear another lecture and sign the deindoctrination declaration before they are 'deindoctrinated'. They must not travel to the prohibited countries for 12 months after deindoctrination (24

Bob Leonard

Security officer Don Allan (on right)
indoctrinates all GCSB staff.

months or more for staff in sensitive areas). These rules are strictly enforced; GCSB workers have lost their jobs for infringements, such as travelling to prohibited countries while on leave. In the late 1980s an ex-Navy intercept officer at Tangimoana was discovered by the senior GCSB staff to have been talking to friends about his work. His indoctrination was cancelled and he immediately lost his job.

The indoctrination procedure and many other GCSB security regulations are required and defined by a series of very secret publications called the *International Regulations on SIGINT*. These contain the regulations that New Zealand and the other allies must obey in order to be part of the UKUSA network. They are supplied by the NSA and stored in a vault on the 14th floor of the GCSB headquarters building.

New Zealand intelligence staff say that the New Zealand indoctrination papers follow closely the wording of the British form,[29] but since 1982 have threatened penalties under the Crimes Act rather than an Official Secrets Act. New Zealand indoctrination and deindoctrination briefings also resemble their American counterparts.

One section of the United States briefing is 'a review of the techniques employed by foreign intelligence organisations in attempting to obtain national security information'. During the GCSB indoctrination briefing new staff are shown how easy it is to collect voice vibrations off the glass of windows and the way that emissions produced in the normal operation of computers can be intercepted some considerable distance away with special interception equipment. Also outlined is the 'periodic awareness enhancement' of indoctrinated staff to ensure that they remain conscious of the security regulations. This also occurs in the GCSB.[30]

There are different levels of indoctrination, giving access to signals intelligence reports and documents of different classifications. If one of the agencies (usually the NSA) produces a special type of signals intelligence with its own codeword, then that agency must grant the relevant clearances to individuals in other UKUSA agencies before they can have access to materials bearing those codewords.

Don Allan maintains and updates the list of indoctrinated people in New

Zealand, a list that includes many GCSB, EAB and DDI staff (and some other military staff in intelligence roles),[31] perhaps 20 foreign affairs staff (including usually one diplomat at major overseas posts)[32] and a smattering of director level or security officer staff from other agencies such as the Prime Minister's Department, Commerce and Fisheries. In the government usually only three Cabinet ministers have been indoctrinated (the Prime Minister, Deputy Prime Minister and Minister of Defence) plus, since the mid-1980s, some economic ministers.[33]

Adding all these up, it is still a very small group. Outside the GCSB there are, at any one time, well under 100 people indoctrinated in New Zealand. Outside the GCSB, EAB and Defence intelligence staffs — in other words, not counting professional intelligence staff who are supposedly there to support the rest of the government system — only about 30 people in New Zealand are indoctrinated.

This has major political implications. It affects how government decisions are made and who is included in them. Since indoctrinated people may speak about signals intelligence matters only with other indoctrinated people, and then only on a need to know basis, most politicians and officials (and the public) are excluded. (Even indoctrinated politicians and officials are often judged as not needing to know what goes on within the GCSB.)

But the people working in intelligence organisations can always discuss things with their counterparts in other agencies. I have been shown a copy of an internal document where Tangimoana staff say of an indoctrinated British officer, 'he's one of us', meaning that they could discuss the particular matter with him. Planning and decision-making relating to this most secret intelligence occurs far more between officials in the alliance than within the democratic institutions of the individual countries.

One very senior New Zealand official interviewed for this book expressed surprise when told that the indoctrination regulations are required as part of membership of the UKUSA alliance. He has been indoctrinated but had not realised that they were not just New Zealand regulations. He had never heard of the *International Regulations on SIGINT*.

Even Prime Ministers must take the indoctrination oaths and are bound by them. This creates a curious situation. Even the highest decision-maker in the country cannot speak about things which the alliance has decreed are secret. He or she can discuss signals intelligence matters only with people who have taken the same oath.

CHAPTER EIGHT

SECRET SQUIRRELS
WHO RUNS THE GCSB?

On Monday, 6 March 1995, there was a very important meeting at the GCSB headquarters. On the 12th floor the American flag was on display to greet a special guest — John M. McConnell — the man who controls signals intelligence in the United States. The NSA Director and his wife entered and left New Zealand without publicity for this brief visit to the New Zealand agency. They had two days in Wellington (6-8 March), arranged by the local American embassy, as part of a longer trip to the region. Besides that Monday meeting, McConnell was shown around the organisation and briefed on the New Zealand operations.

John Brandon, who by 1995 had been a GCSB employee for 16 years, was typical of the GCSB director-level staff assembled to meet McConnell at 9 am that morning. Each step of his career, like those of his senior colleagues, had revolved around the NSA. He was appointed in March 1979 to oversee the establishment of the GCSB's first intelligence analysis cells, but he was trained for this role at the NSA, before even taking up his appointment at the GCSB. In early 1985 he was made Assistant Director for Policy and Plans, where he worked as assistant to Glen Singleton, while Singleton was an NSA officer on posting to the GCSB. Brandon's job included rewriting NSA manuals for use in the bureau and transferring and adapting NSA structures, regulations and procedures for the GCSB. Then, in August 1989, he was posted to Washington again, working for three years inside the NSA Headquarters at Fort Meade as the New Zealand Liaison Officer. Since his return in 1992 he has been one of the GCSB's four divisional directors.

The GCSB is but a small component of a system run by the NSA and the other larger agencies. Although few, if any, of the top GCSB staff have ever appeared before a parliamentary committee or in public, their work involves constant interaction with and reference to the overseas agencies. During McConnell's visit to the GCSB he was meeting people who work every day according to rules and systems that originate from his organisation in Washington. The situation was not too far from that of a giant United States parent company visiting its New Zealand office.

The director of the GCSB for its first 10 years, from September 1977 until January 1988, was Colin Hanson, who had become involved in defence intelligence in the early 1960s, halfway through an Air Force career that began in the Second World War. He was introduced to signals intelligence during the 1960s when he was posted to fill one of the positions allocated to New Zealand in the Australian signals intelligence organisation, the Defence Signals Bureau.

By 1974 he had received an OBE, was promoted to group captain and held the position of Director of Defence Intelligence. It was in this role that he pushed for New Zealand's signals intelligence operations to be dramatically expanded, persuading the then Secretary of Defence, John Robertson, to seek government approval to establish the GCSB.

The fledgling organisation initially shared offices with Hanson's previous staff in the Directorate of Defence Intelligence, but soon it outgrew these offices as Hanson, in co-ordination with the UKUSA partners, added one after another new headquarters section and division each year and arranged new collection operations in New Zealand and overseas.

After his retirement, Hanson was interviewed by the *Evening Post*.[1] He told Roger Foley that he had 'entered defence intelligence in 1962 because it gave him the chance to travel overseas. After initial moments of doubt, he became fascinated by it and has been ever since.' He was quoted as saying that that his time at the GCSB had been 'both a job and a hobby'.

The GCSB Director is responsible for some of the high-level liaison with the other UKUSA agencies. According to his colleagues, Hanson was fascinated by the big foreign intelligence agencies and loved visiting them. On the walls of his office he displayed the plaques he had been presented with to mark his visits to the four sister agencies. In addition to frequent visits to the DSD in Melbourne, he went overseas regularly to meet the other agency directors. This included the annual UKUSA directors meeting.[2] As one person interviewed for this book explained, 'People in the intelligence community are like links in a chain, a secret society where people can turn to each other for support. People in the different agencies, especially middle rank people, knew each other well.'

Colin Hanson was unusual because he was not preoccupied with secrecy. Although he believed that large areas of intelligence activity must remain secret for operational reasons, he was not, like some involved in signals intelligence, obsessively secretive. He spoke more openly about intelligence matters than many of his colleagues felt appropriate and he found some of the secrecy imposed on the organisation childish.

He enjoyed his Official Information Act correspondence, engaging in personal and friendly exchanges with some of those who wrote to him. He released some information about the GCSB to the public, but often would not do so because he believed the enquiry had not been framed precisely enough. He enjoyed the intellectual challenge and would often say to his colleagues, 'Why don't they just ask the questions properly and we'd have to tell them!'

Hanson's successor, Ray Parker, is quite different. He appears to regard requests for information from the public as an affront and is reluctant to release information under the Official Information Act.

Ray Parker took over the job on 1 March 1988 and moved into Hanson's office on the 14th floor of the Freyberg Building. He, too, came from the Air Force, most recently as the Ministry of Defence's Director of Defence Communications. In this role, in which he oversaw Defence electronic warfare and communications security, he would already have had considerable contact with the GCSB. In addition, he had also served as Project Manager for the Second Generation Defence Communications Network (SGDCN), which was introduced in the GCSB in the late 1980s. He is in his early 50s, is paid far more than most Members of Parliament and can be expected to stay in the job for some years to come.[3]

It is a common complaint inside the GCSB that the two directors have given most of the top jobs to military old boys, with seniority in the organisation appearing to be linked to their previous seniority inside the military. A stream of such people have ended their military careers with the usual big lump sum payments and walked straight into top GCSB positions. An apparent preference for Air Force staff (both directors were ex-Air Force) has also caused considerable bad feeling over the years among some staff members.

The most important deputy director since 1989 has been Warren Tucker, the Director of Operations. He oversaw all the staff in the headquarters Operations Division, and also both the stations — amounting to over half of the GCSB's staff. On 1 July 1996 he became Intelligence Co-ordinator in the Prime Minister's office. He served, in effect, as the deputy director of the organisation, checking that all the operations are ticking over properly and filling in as acting director when Ray Parker is overseas. This position involves lots of liaison with the other UKUSA agencies. Every year Tucker

The first GCSB director, Colin Hanson, oversaw a dramatic expansion of New Zealand electronic spying between 1977 and 1988.

has traveled to most or all of the agencies in the United States, Britain and Canada for meetings[4] and to Australia several times a year. For example, he spent a week based at the DSD's Canberra headquarters from 6 to 10 November 1995 and brought some DSD staff back with him for a visit to the GCSB headquarters on his return. He has often entertained important signals intelligence visitors from the other agencies, including taking them to visit the Waihopai station.

Tucker joined the GCSB at only 31 years of age, straight from being an

Army major in Defence Headquarters in Wellington. The GCSB selected him because of his electronics expertise (he has a doctorate in electrical engineering) and on 1 March 1982 he became the GCSB's Assistant Director (Engineering), responsible for communications security (COMSEC) engineering. He was also involved in the computer side of codebreaking operations.

The COMSEC engineering work meant trips to Washington, Hawaii and Melbourne over the next two to three years and also involved Tucker in the development of the Tangimoana station. Presumably part of his work was helping with the introduction of UKUSA encryption equipment in the new GCSB communications centres in the new Freyberg Building headquarters and at Tangimoana station when they both began operating later in 1982.

He was later promoted to Director for Policy and Plans, before being posted to Washington in late 1984 as the New Zealand Liaison Officer in the NSA at Fort Meade. He returned from Washington in September 1989 to become the Director of Operations.

The position New Zealand Liaison Officer (Washington) (NZLO(W)) at NSA headquarters, which Tucker filled in 1984-89, is one of the key positions in the GCSB and has been an important part of the careers of a number of influential senior staff. This position is the equivalent of the British, Canadian and Australian senior liaison officers in the NSA.

Held only by very senior GCSB officers, the job personifies the GCSB's close ties with the NSA. The existence of the NZLO(W) demonstrates that the NSA has taken over from the GCHQ as New Zealand's main signals intelligence ally and that the NSA is at the centre of the system. The liaison arrangements also highlight New Zealand's status within the alliance. Britain, Canada, Australia and New Zealand all have liaison officers based at the NSA and, for three of them, vice versa. Only New Zealand does not have a reciprocal NSA liaison officer posted to it.

The NZLO(W)'s work includes regular (although not daily) meetings with NSA liaison staff from the V Group (which deals with liaison). These meetings include discussions about what New Zealand wants from the NSA and what New Zealand is providing to the alliance; new procedures and plans being adopted within the alliance; operational requirements the NSA has which New Zealand could contribute to; and structures and practices in the NSA that might be adopted by the GCSB. They will also include discussions of equipment and software to be supplied by the NSA to New Zealand for specific projects and the GCSB payments and/or NSA subsidies involved.

The NZLO(W) has regular contact with the DSD representative and there are meetings of all the UKUSA liaison staff located within the NSA.[5] There is no evidence that non-UKUSA countries are allowed to have representatives located physically within the NSA headquarters (except perhaps some very close allies like Germany), so the liaison community is very small.

The NZLO(W)s live in Washington DC with diplomatic status and very generous entertainment allowances and other privileges. They work inside the huge NSA Headquarters, at Fort George C. Meade, in the State of Maryland, half an hour by freeway outside Washington. They return to the GCSB at least at the beginning of each year for meetings and also represent the bureau at some UKUSA intelligence conferences in different parts of the world.

There have been six NZLO(W)s to date. The first was Jim Blackford, appointed in 1978 as the GCSB's first Deputy Director of Operations (DDO), responsible for all intelligence collection and analysis for the bureau. Blackford was British, brought in directly from the British signals intelligence establishment (ex-Royal Air Force) to this key position to oversee the development of the GCSB's analysis capabilities. From this vital position, he was made NZLO(W) in 1982 for a two-year term. He left the GCSB in 1987-88.

The second NZLO(W) was Blackford's successor as DDO, Larry Lynch. (Once again the GCSB gave priority to having its top deputy director at the NSA rather than running the intelligence operations of the bureau.) Lynch left the Army (as a lieutenant colonel) to join the GCSB in August 1982. He was NZLO(W) for only a short period in 1984 before being replaced by Warren Tucker. He was then posted straight from Washington to Cheltenham, the GCHQ headquarters, to get more experience of working within the UKUSA network before he returned to be DDO again.

The third NZLO(W) was Warren Tucker, who arrived in Washington in late December 1984, just weeks before the New Zealand-United States showdown over access for nuclear warships. It was known that the conflict was looming, and so for six weeks his family did not unpack their bags because they thought they might be sent home again.

As it turned out, it was Tucker to whom the United States authorities passed on the detailed news of 'intelligence cuts' in late February 1985. Then, when his three-year posting was completed in 1987, he was not brought home. There were still some fears in the bureau that tensions caused by the nuclear row might mean he would not be allowed to be replaced. Rather than risk losing the position, the bureau repeatedly extended Tucker's term until he finally returned in 1989. The fears were unwarranted, however, and he was replaced by John Brandon in August 1989.

John Brandon, son of an SIS agent, was the fourth NZLO(W). In 1983, after completing three years of Russian language courses, he was promoted to the position of Assistant Director SIGINT (ADK). In 1984, while he was ADK, Brandon had a trip to an intelligence conference in Singapore. He became Assistant Director for Policy and Plans (ADP) in March 1985. It was as ADP that Brandon worked under Glen Singleton, adapting NSA manuals for the GCSB. After some years in this job, Brandon was posted to Washington in 1989, at the age of 42. He returned in May 1992 and in August 1993 became the Director of Information Systems Security.

The NSA manuals, such as the ones being adapted by Brandon, are used continuously at the GCSB, both directly and rewritten as GCSB manuals. They are a less visible, but equally important, conduit for alliance influence. The most influential ones in the GCSB are: the *International Regulations on SIGINT*, containing the regulations by which New Zealand and the other allies must abide to be part of the UKUSA alliance;[6] the *United States Signals Intelligence Directives*, which govern all policy and operations of United States signals intelligence and are issued by the NSA Director;[7] and a *National Security Council Intelligence Directive*, which sets out the basic directions for United States intelligence operations. They are mostly very secret documents and are stored in the GCSB vaults. The senior GCSB staff have access to and use them regularly. They are supplied in loose-leaf binders so that they can be updated frequently with new or altered directives from the NSA.[8]

The fifth NZLO(W) was Barry (Bas) Keane, who took over the position in May 1992. Keane took over Brandon's job as Assistant Director (SIGINT) in 1985 while he was still an Air Force squadron leader and did not formally leave the Air Force to join the GCSB until January 1986. In March 1989 Keane was moved to be head of the C Unit, a position he held until June 1991. Then, from June to November that year, he attended a senior staff training course at the New Zealand Air Force college in Auckland, the first of a series of senior GCSB staff to do so.[9] A few months after returning to the bureau he was offered the Washington job. In September 1995, after returning from the NSA, he moved into the new position of Executive Director in the Office of the Director and then, 10 months later, shifted to be the officer in charge at Tangimoana.

The sixth and current NZLO(W) is John Willson, who joined the GCSB in early 1985 directly from the military, where he had been a colonel in charge of Army Operations in Defence Headquarters. He was appointed to the position of Deputy Director of Communications and Technical Security. In 1990 he was made Director of Policy and Plans, P, a position he held until being posted to Washington in June 1995. He will be there until 1998.

The GCSB liaison officer in its Australian sister organisation, the DSD, is another vital position in the workings of the GCSB. The New Zealand Liaison Officer (Canberra) (NZLO(C)) has an office and a small staff within the main Defence Signals Directorate building in the Russell complex in Canberra. This collection of buildings has brought together the headquarters of most of the Australian military and intelligence organisations.[10]

It appears that the original position of Government Communications Liaison Officer (Melbourne) (before the DSD moved to Canberra in 1992-93) grew out of the custom of having a senior New Zealand intercept officer based at the DSD in Melbourne overseeing the New Zealand contingent. Through most of the 1980s this officer was John Orchard, who had had a long career as a radio intercept officer, based at Waiouru since the late 1950s and including a three-year posting to the secret GCHQ/DSD station at Singapore. He was probably in Melbourne by 1982 overseeing the GCSB staff who joined the JTUM Chinese intercept operation that year and was definitely there by 1984 when the first GCSB cryptanalyst trainees were sent for two years of training at the DSD headquarters. Orchard left Melbourne in 1988 to take up the position of Officer in Charge at the Tangimoana station. He stayed in that job until he retired from the GCSB in late 1994 at the age of 62.

Orchard's successor, Larry Lynch, moved to Australia after he was replaced by Tucker as Director of Operations in 1989. As mentioned, Lynch had previously been NZLO(W) in Washington. His term finished in early 1992 and he has since retired.

The first Canberra-based liaison officer, NZLO(C), was Neil Catley, who was posted to the DSD in Melbourne in January 1992 and then moved to Canberra in 1993. Catley is in his early 50s, having joined the GCSB in February 1985 at the end of a career in the Navy. His last job in the Navy, as a lieutenant commander, was as an Assistant Director of Defence Communications in Defence Headquarters, working under Ray Parker who was then Director of Defence Communications.

He was appointed as the GCSB's Assistant Director (Communications Security Policy), a position he appears to have held until his posting to the DSD. Catley returned to New Zealand to take over Orchard's job, as Officer in Charge at the Tangimoana station, in December 1994.

The current NZLO(C) is Keith Smith, who was posted to Canberra in December 1994. He had been the GCSB's Director of Engineering continuously for the preceding 15 years, since that position was first created in January 1979. He was appointed to the GCSB straight from the Air Force, where he had been a squadron leader. As Director of Engineering, Smith oversaw the design and construction of both the Tangimoana and Waihopai stations for the GCSB and many smaller projects as well. Smith's posting is for three years, after which he will be retiring from the GCSB.

Links between the GCSB and DSD occur at every level of operations: the planning and development of the two organisations is closely co-ordinated, as is major equipment purchasing, and information is continuously shared. The GCSB Director and the Director of Operations travel frequently to Australia for meetings with their counterparts. Between these meetings, the NZLO(C) continues the work.

The NZLO(C)'s duties include intelligence sharing and many of the tasks of liaison described for the NZLO(W). He is also responsible for the considerable numbers of GCSB staff who pass through the DSD on training courses and postings.

The intelligence sharing role involves distributing some New Zealand-sourced intelligence to the various Australian intelligence organisations and to the liaison officers from other countries who are based at the DSD. All outgoing safe hand bags and envelopes, on their way to the NSA and other agencies, are initially addressed to the NZLO(C) personally in Canberra. The special secure bags are delivered to him by courier and he arranges for them to go either to the relevant part of the Australian intelligence community or to the other agencies.

The DSD does not have a reciprocal liaison officer posted to the GCSB. As with the position in Washington, the relationship is inherently unequal. In general, joint planning means New Zealanders joining in DSD planning sessions, joint purchasing means New Zealand choosing the same equipment as Australia and co-ordination means New Zealand fitting in with Australian operations.

Chapter Nine

Station NZC-332
Electronic Eavesdropping
From Tangimoana

The Tangimoana station resembles a collection of large, strangely shaped steel sculptures, placed incongruously across a landscape of dry sandhills and small pine forests. The only visible living things are the ever-present sheep, grazing among the antennae.

Beyond razor-topped fences, electronic sensors, security cameras and barred windows, the neon lights in the operations building shine day and night. Here, intercept officers sit with headphones, searching for and recording radio messages picked up through the different antennae, spying on communications from across a large section of the globe.

At any time they may be recording Vanuatu government telex messages, monitoring military communications in New Caledonia or tuning into a Russian ship's radio frequency at its usual reporting time — providing some of the communications that are then sorted, decrypted, translated and written into reports by the headquarters staff in Wellington. Often the Tangimoana officers are intercepting communications from more distant areas for the overseas agencies: East Timor (although it cannot be picked up very well) or the Bougainville Revolutionary Army for the DSD, Asia and

Friendly South Pacific governments, Russian shipping and French nuclear testing have been major targets of the Tangimoana station.

elsewhere for the NSA, GCHQ and CSE.[1] The intercept staff, mostly from military backgrounds, do not question the targets they are asked to monitor. They just follow whatever instructions come from Wellington or overseas: 'that's what we're paid for'.

The station is located 150 kilometres north of Wellington in sandhill country near the small beach township of Tangimoana, not far from the Ohakea Air Force base at Bulls. The sophisticated antennae are designed to pick up high frequency (or short wave) radio signals from ships and land-based transmitters around the Pacific and beyond.

About 70 of the GCSB's 200 staff work at the two collection stations: Tangimoana and Waihopai. Between them these stations target two of the main types of long-distance communications: high frequency radio, where the messages are transmitted as radio waves between transmitters and receivers; and satellite, where the message is transmitted up to a satellite and back down to a receiving satellite dish.

Within the UKUSA alliance the Tangimoana station is known by a very secret 'station designator': NZC-332. Even in the GCSB, many staff would not know this name. Inside the five-country signals intelligence system, all participating stations have such network names to identify them. These station designators are typed at the top of each report transmitted within the network, showing the station where a particular intercept was made and the stations and other locations to which it is being sent.

Most station designators have three letters and three numbers and are made up as follows: two letters indicating the country, one letter indicating what sort of staff run the station and some numbers (usually three) signifying the particular station.[2] Thus New Zealand's civilian-run station at Tangimoana is NZ - C - 332. Likewise the old NR1 station was NZC-331 and Waihopai is NZC-333.

The Tangimoana station can be visited by turning off State Highway One between Foxton and Bulls towards Tangimoana Beach, then turning left into the gate of a Landcorp farm block a kilometre before Tangimoana township. A sealed road then leads you to the buildings and antennae. Until the discovery and exposé of the station by Owen Wilkes in 1984, New Zealanders had no idea that their country was involved in spying on other nations' communications. While Wilkes was visiting a nearby farm, a friend suggested that he go for a walk along the beach to see a new facility run by 'secret squirrels'.

NZC-331	GCSB NR1 station
NZC-332	GCSB Tangimoana station
NZC-333	GCSB Waihopai station
NZC-334	GCSB mobile station
NZC-335	GCSB mobile station
UKC-102	UK civilian-run Singapore station
UKC-201	UK civilian-run Hong Kong station
UKM-257	UK Army-run station at Ayios Nikolaos, Cyprus
UKC-1000	UK civilian-run telex interception site in Palmer Street, London
USA-38	US Air Force-run Misawa station in Japan
USD-110	US Yakima station in Washington State (probably)
USD-1000	US Menwith Hill station in north England
USD-1025	NSA special liaison officer at GCHQ Cheltenham HQ
USF-778	US Bad Aibling station in Germany

These top secret designators are used within the UKUSA network to identify the various intercept stations.

The antennae at Tangimoana receive radio waves in the high frequency range, named before the much higher very high frequency (VHF) radio and ultra high frequency (UHF) satellite frequencies were used. Unlike these higher frequencies, which can only be used to transmit in a straight line (i.e. short-range or to and from a satellite), high frequency (HF) radio can transmit right around the world with the signals bouncing back and forth between the earth and the upper atmosphere.

For most of this century HF radio has been used extensively for long-distance communications between countries and by ships and aircraft. HF radio has been used principally to transmit messages in Morse code and by telex, the two main targets of Tangimoana interception.

But even as Tangimoana was opening in 1982, technological changes were reducing the significance of HF radio. In 1982 the first Inmarsat satellite services were introduced for ships at sea — Tangimoana's main target — and satellite communications were being used by more and more countries. By the time the Waihopai station opened, only seven years later, the use of HF radio by ships and South Pacific countries was declining rapidly.

According to GCSB staff, in the early years of the station about 80 percent of their work was interception of Morse code communications. But there was a 'big drop off' in the use of Morse around 1989 and in the early 1990s Morse has virtually died out in New Zealand. Only its continued use by Russian shipping keeps Morse interception going at Tangimoana.

The result has been a series of cuts to the Tangimoana staff since 1992, with some sections being restructured out of existence. In 1996 the once busy operations building has empty rooms. The communications staff were all made redundant or transferred in July 1995, the training unit was closed in 1993, the technical unit has been halved and, over the last five years, the intercept staff have been cut to a fraction of their previous numbers. From a staff of about 80 in the early 1990s, the station is left with only about 35 staff in 1996.[3]

Nonetheless HF radio will continue to be used for the foreseeable future by shipping and aircraft, at least as a back-up by isolated communities and extensively by the militaries of the world as one strand of their communications networks. The role of Tangimoana in GCSB interception has reduced but will continue.

The station's assigned 'surveillance area' covers the entire Pacific Ocean, Antarctica, the Southern Atlantic, including the Falkland Islands, and the southern Indian Ocean to South Africa. 'You can see how powerful the station is, it almost covers three quarters of the globe.' The main volume of

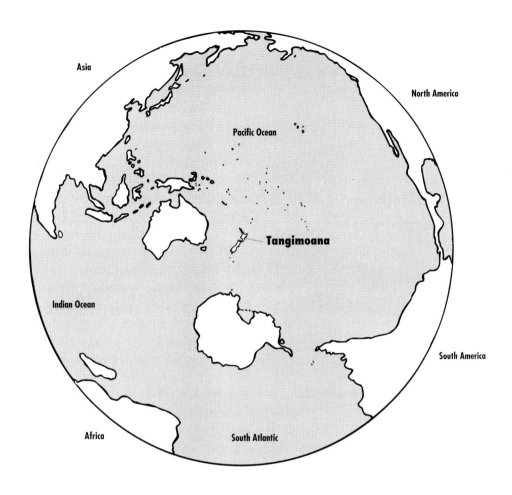

Tangimoana's surveillance area covers over half the earth's surface, not just the primary South Pacific region. In addition, about 10 percent of interception is of special targets outside this area for the overseas agencies.

Tangimoana's work, though, comes from the South Pacific region.

The majority of the station's work, and that of its predecessor at NR1, has been interception of shipping: 'If it moved, we listened to it'.[4] Of all the shipping in the Pacific, however, the Tangimoana interception has mostly targeted Russian vessels. The view presented by the GCSB hierarchy has been that even Russian fishing trawlers 'should be regarded as part of the Russian Navy'.

When Prime Minister David Lange returned from his one trip to

Tangimoana in mid-1985 he reassured his colleagues about the harmlessness of the station, explaining that, as unlikely and absurd as it sounded, the station was targeted '135 percent on Russian fishing boats'. The proportion was a joke but it remains true that a major component of the station's work, throughout its existence, has been monitoring the regular radio messages sent back to Russia from Russian fishing boats around New Zealand.

The station also intercepts radio messages sent home from Russian bases in Antarctica and communications between the bases. All 10 Russian bases — Russkya, Mirnjy, Molodzenaya and so on — are targeted at their regular reporting times, which results in large quantities of intercept, including administrative reports, weather reports and reports from scientific ships in the region to the bases. The most interesting information collected has been reports about Russian exploration for oil and minerals in Antarctica.

Over half of the station's staff have been cut in the 1990s following target countries moving from radio to satellite.

In the mid-1990s HF radio is still used for nearly all communications by Russian fishing vessels; only a small number of new vessels use the costly Inmarsat satellite systems. Also, Russian fishing vessels still use Morse extensively. A Russian fishing trawler engineer spoken to in April 1994 confirmed that Morse is still used on most ships for telegram-style official and private messages back to Russia. Radio telex is used for longer messages such as catch reports for fishing companies.

Another priority target has been the occasional visits by Russian research ships to the South Pacific. When a Russian research vessel is in the region (and often after it has openly notified the New Zealand government that it would like to visit) the New Zealand military issues a secret 'PIC warning' to all New Zealand Navy vessels, major defence bases (including the Defence Scientific Establishment), a range of Australian organisations and the United States Commander-in-Chief for Pacific Forces, 'any allied warships on New Zealand station' and the GCSB.[5]

The New Zealand Defence Force refuses to reveal the meaning of 'PIC', claiming it to be an important national secret.[6] It stands for potential intelligence collector — primarily the Russian research ships that visit Wellington and other New Zealand ports. According to a Defence source, such vessels have sometimes entered forbidden areas, but the cases that have been publicised do not appear very threatening.[7] Similarly, when a Russian icebreaker was sent from Vladivostok to help Russian ships caught in ice in Antarctica, Tangimoana monitored the vessel each day, taking an interest in every detail of its trip.

In addition to Russian shipping, the station has increasingly monitored Japanese and other shipping, including fishing trawlers. Occasional special operations also occur, such as monitoring the controversial Japanese plutonium transport ship that passed through the South Pacific and close to New Zealand in 1993.

For a period in the late 1980s, under the Labour government, one of the station's priorities was monitoring foreign fishing vessels using drift nets in the South Pacific. The intelligence collected was used as part of New Zealand's diplomatic efforts to stop this environmentally destructive practice.

Most of Tangimoana's interception of shipping has been of vessels in the South Pacific. But there are also requests from the other UKUSA agencies, which give the frequency, time and location of a ship in which they are interested. All these requests are acted on. Very occasionally there are also requests from New Zealand Customs to look for a particular vessel.

East Timor and Bougainville are targeted for the Australian DSD.

The other area of communications intercepted for analysis at the GCSB headquarters are from South Pacific countries and French South Pacific territories. The French communications targeted by Tangimoana are military communications: radio messages between French Polynesia and Paris, between French territories including Moruroa Atoll and military communications in New Caledonia. The main French language targets during most of the station's existence have been communications concerning French nuclear testing.

Tangimoana tried in mid-July 1985 to monitor the French terrorists who sank the *Rainbow Warrior* as they sailed away from New Zealand on the yacht *Ouvea* (after the police had identified the yacht). The staff listened to all the marine frequencies and attempted to monitor other French vessels with which the *Ouvea* might be in contact, but picked up nothing at all: 'zero'. They presumed the yacht used satellite communications; but if the NSA intercepted any maritime satellite communications at its Yakima station, they were not passed on to New Zealand. (Tangimoana also failed to give any warning of the Fiji coup.)

Interception of communications between and within South Pacific nations and their communications with the rest of the world has mainly involved government and military telex communications. There is very wide targeting: from political telexes in Melanesia, to Fiji Army communications, to Tongan patrol boats communicating with their headquarters. There has even been some monitoring of private ham radio operators in the South Pacific (and New Zealand ones) if they are communicating to or from areas of interest (e.g. internal conflict within a Pacific Island nation). By the mid-1990s, however, nearly all non-military radio communications from South Pacific nations have been replaced by satellite. Tangimoana does not monitor the Japanese or other foreign embassies in Wellington. None of the embassies use high frequency radio for long-distance communications.

A radio officer at work in the station's Operations Centre.

In addition to its primary role of South Pacific interception, it is routine for Tangimoana to assist other UKUSA stations with their interception tasks. As one of the workers explained, 'We can pick up transmissions from Tangimoana which other agencies cannot because of our siting.' The nature of HF radio propagation means that the station at Tangimoana can sometimes receive signals from quite different parts of the world more clearly than other spy stations nearer to the source. Radio reception is always clearer at night, without interference from solar activity, and so, for example, Tangimoana at night may be the best place to pick up communications from a distant location where it is daytime. Also there may be storms or other disturbances in the atmosphere affecting reception elsewhere. In these cases Tangimoana can be requested to intercept targets in another agency's area. About 10 percent of the station's interception is of targets right outside the Pacific region. It is routine, Tangimoana staff say, that 'If the Yanks can't hear somewhere from

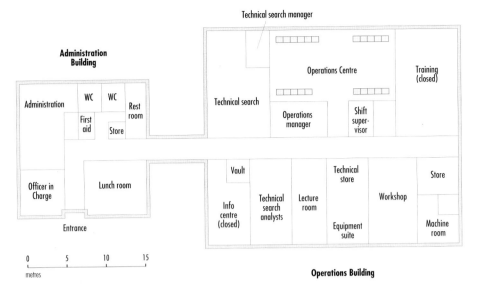

Inside the secret Tangimoana station: it operates as a wholly integrated component of the allied network. A detailed guide to the layout and workings of the Waihopai and Tangimoana stations is contained in Appendix B.

their stations, they ask Australia or New Zealand.'

Raw intelligence gathered at Tangimoana is sent, heavily encrypted, to the GCSB Head Office in Wellington along normal Telecom lines (the whole station was once cut off when a cow chewed through the cable). The raw intelligence includes large quantities of telexes intercepted automatically by special equipment at the station which are sorted by the Tangimoana Dictionary located in the Wellington headquarters. As part of the ECHELON system, the Tangimoana collection schedule (i.e. schedule of who to spy on when) optimises collection for the whole network and the Dictionary computer automatically sends raw intercept to the overseas agencies according to their keyword specifications.

The intercept officers — known as radio officers or ROs — make up most of the staff and are at the centre of the station's operations. There are about 20 of them working shifts; only five years ago there were about 50. They work in the Operations Centre, a room about 15 by 10 metres in size, with the interception equipment around three of the walls. The job is said to be '95 percent boredom', sitting with headphones on for hours swinging manually through the frequencies, listening for assigned targets.

For Morse interception, the radio officers sit at the old radio consoles and first manually locate the target transmitter (usually a Russian vessel).

This involves searching for the right frequency because the ships change frequency often, both to improve transmission quality and to try to hide the transmission. The officers then listen to the Morse message, slowly typing the transcribed message onto their computers, which, at least until recently, were as old as the station.

Once the complete message is on the screen, the officers type at the top who the message should go to (usually the NSA, GCHQ and so on) and send it through the station's internal computer network to the duty officer. After he has checked it, it is sent off to the Wellington communications staff for distribution around the UKUSA network.

For telex communications, there is specialised receiving equipment designed to be compatible with target communications equipment. For example, French military communications, including those concerning French nuclear testing, have been intercepted by special telex machines which the radio officers set to the right frequency and then leave to intercept automatically all the telexes on a particular communications link day after day. The Dictionary computer does the selecting.

Some equipment is designed to filter out radio messages that the sender is trying to disguise. At Tangimoana this equipment has regularly been used for Russian and French communications. For example, the transmitting equipment may break the message up and send different parts over different frequencies among other messages, or may remove certain parts of the frequency range of a message and send those separately. Special interception equipment is used to capture and reconstruct the target messages. Even more

Tangimoana organisation plan

156

sophisticated equipment is needed to detect and filter out messages where there is a continuous transmission of meaningless noise against which real messages are occasionally superimposed. This situation is encountered when the station intercepts certain land targets inside Russia for the NSA.

Often the intercepted messages are encrypted. In these cases the radio officers are recording gibberish — long, meaningless streams of letters or five-letter groups. The encrypted messages are simply sent on to the Wellington headquarters.

The shift supervisors allocate a series of tasks to each radio officer. For the first part of the morning it may be Russian trawlers during their standard reporting time, then a period intercepting Japanese ships at their known reporting times, later Chinese ships north of Fiji and so on through the shift. There are carefully worked out collection schedules determining the day's tasks. If the task is new, the supervisor gives the radio officer the TEXTA details for that target on a card, showing the technical details of frequencies and transmission characteristics for the target transmitter. (TEXTA, the 'Bible of the SIGINT community', is the computer-generated digest of intelligence targets from all over the world. It is provided and regularly updated by the NSA and supplied to the station on microfiche.) Addressee lists are also received from the overseas UKUSA agencies, specifying which types of intercept should be sent to each.

Another area of the operations building, occupying offices beside and across the corridor from the Operations Centre, contains technical search officers and analysts. Their job is not interception but studying the immense clutter of radio traffic picked up by the station to identify possible targets for future interception.

The station's orientation has also been reinforced through recruitment of foreign signals intelligence staff. Between 1979 and 1981, as Tangimoana was being designed and built, large numbers of new radio officers were appointed and trained. About a fifth of the new staff were signals intelligence personnel recruited from the British GCHQ; a smaller number came from the Australian DSD. Most of the Tangimoana supervisor positions have been filled by these experienced overseas staff. Among the Australians are officers who worked as Army intelligence collectors in Vietnam (based at Da Nang and elsewhere) and there are British staff who worked in GCHQ stations in Hong Kong and Cyprus.

In general, the technology used by intelligence agencies is advanced compared with commercially available equipment, but at Tangimoana much of the equipment used until the mid-1990s would be regarded as obsolete.

This has been a common complaint among the staff, that no money has been spent on equipment since soon after the station opened. For example, for several years radio scanners have been available that can search through the radio spectrum and microprocessors that automatically transcribe Morse code. But, these tasks have been done manually at Tangimoana.

A major new computer system is, however, being introduced to the station in 1996 which will allow a lot of the interception and processing of communications to be done automatically. One of the radio officers, Ian Prisk, moved to headquarters to help plan the new system and other staff have been sent there for training. The new computerised systems are designed to maintain the station's level of operations with the reduced staff. The radio officers have been told that the new equipment will allow each of them to intercept about eight different targets at once.

It is strange, isolating work. The workers at the station cannot talk about their jobs in their communities or even to their families. Permanent shift work further disrupts social contact. Once you take the job, staff say, 'they own you'.

There are five main types of antenna scattered across the fields around the Tangimoana station, each designed for operating under certain conditions and against different targets. Mostly they are connected by underground wires back to the operations building. The types of antenna are no secret — others just like them are used for military and intelligence purposes all over the world.

The specific models can be looked up in military communications manuals in a public library (notably the annual publication, *Janes Military Communications*). Indeed, the first time I nervously visited the station in 1984, not at all sure which aerials did what, my investigation was assisted by finding metal labels at the base of most of the towers stating the antenna type, the manufacturer's name, technical details about its capabilities and even the GCSB's customer order number. One of the antennae, a large circular antenna array, is part of the station's high frequency direction-finding (HFDF) system. The radio officers work at 'bearing and display consoles' connected to this antenna, calculating the direction from which a target signal is being transmitted. Information gathered in these HFDF activities is shared directly with the other agencies and overseas stations as part of direction-finding collaboration.

High frequency direction-finding (HFDF) is a distinctly different activity from the rest of the work of a signals intelligence station. It is not about communications intelligence — the content of what is being communicated — but purely about trying to locate and identify the radio transmitters. The main users of HFDF intelligence are military authorities and the main target of the UKUSA HFDF network has always been Russia. HFDF capabilities contributed directly to the Cold War.

The previous GCSB station at Waiouru had no direction-finding capability. Tangimoana joined the Pacific and Indian Ocean network of HFDF facilities built up in the late 1970s and early 1980s, and specifically targeted

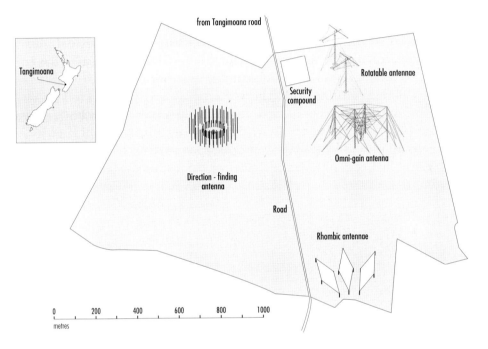

The various antennae, supplied by United States and British companies, are designed for different types of eavesdropping.

on the Soviet Navy, late in 1982. Although HFDF is a signals intelligence activity, Tangimoana's HFDF findings have been fed into a different system from the rest of the station's product and are analysed and used within separate, military organisations.

A direction-finding antenna is of little use on its own. It can estimate the *direction* from which a radio signal is coming, but it is only when this information is put together with direction bearings taken from other stations that, by triangulation, the *position* of a Russian ship or submarine can be estimated. Since New Zealand has only one such antenna, the one at Tangimoana, it goes without saying that it operates routinely and continuously within a network of other intelligence stations with direction-finding capabilities. To date New Zealand governments have denied or evaded comment on these links.

The Pacific HFDF network is made up of a ring of stations operated by the United States and its allies. HFDF circular arrays have been observed in Hawaii, California, Canada, Alaska, Japan, Okinawa, the Philippines and Guam; plus three Australian stations and Tangimoana in New Zealand. The HFDF intelligence from this network is sent to regional centres, which correlate ocean surveillance information from their assigned geographical areas.

New Zealand HFDF intelligence goes to the US Joint Intelligence Center, Pacific, in Hawaii, which has computer data bases including information on US and allied navies, 'free world merchant shipping, communist navy, communist merchant shipping and communist fishing vessels'.[8] This last category helps to explain Tangimoana's long-term interest in Russian fishing boats.

This information goes directly into the United States system; there is no section at the GCSB headquarters concerned with this intelligence. It is collected primarily for the allies and also goes to a separate ship movements data base established in 1981 by the New Zealand Defence Force. As part of the HFDF network, Tangimoana has regularly received instructions as to which frequencies to monitor and sent its HFDF results back to the overseas centres. The Tangimoana HFDF information was also sent to the Naval Maritime Intelligence Centre in Washington DC (now incorporated into the Office of Naval Intelligence), which was responsible for the preparation and dissemination of reports within the United States military on the positions of all naval vessels, but particularly Russian ships and submarines.[9]

Greenpeace/Midgley

Tangimoana was a small part of a US-co-ordinated system for tracking Soviet subs (above) and ships, including nuclear ones, in the Cold War.

The Tangimoana HFDF system was installed as part of Cold War intelligence gathering for the United States. Established primarily for tracking Russian ships and missile-carrying submarines, the HFDF network was part of the infrastructure for nuclear war. Tangimoana was only one small component in a relatively remote region, but part of the network nonetheless.

But although the system in theory remains available to help the allies in some future conflict (and could be upgraded), gradual corrosion of the antenna in the sea air has made it increasingly inaccurate and unreliable. Staff who operate it describe it as 'bloody useless', saying that it frequently malfunctions (requiring outside technicians to be called in), gives inconsistent results and, even when it does work, can only be expected to give an accuracy of about 10 percent. The radio officers do use it continuously as part of their work, but they will take a few 'shots' and compare them to estimate the direction. Staff say that whereas there were large numbers of requests from other agencies for HFDF work in the early 1980s, these are now rare.

Tangimoana's HFDF capabilities are occasionally used in emergencies to locate ships and yachts that are overdue or in distress in the South Pacific. The GCSB has installed a special direct telephone line into the station for this purpose. In an emergency the duty officer from the Maritime Safety Authority dials this Tangimoana access number, then a security PIN number he or she has been allocated, and the call goes through to the Tangimoana operations staff at any time of the day or night.

The Tangimoana staff are given the frequency on which the vessel is believed to be transmitting (e.g. the international distress frequency) and an approximate position if available. The radio officers then use the station's HFDF equipment, together with other HFDF facilities in Australia and elsewhere, to estimate the position of the vessel. They say that they get such requests from New Zealand government organisations about five times a year.

One Maritime Safety Authority staff member said the accuracy of the system allowed a position to be given to within about half a nautical mile; GCSB staff say the system is much less accurate than this.

The Tangimoana HFDF system's foreign connections received publicity in August 1990 when, during a protest weekend, peace movement activists broke through the gate into the station. Some of them managed to get to a room containing the equipment for the direction-finding system and came away with the main manual for setting up and operating the HFDF circular antenna array. It was a 150-page internal operating manual from the British signals intelligence agency, the GCHQ, provided for use at the New Zealand station.[10] The individually numbered copy of the manual — Copy No. 137 — was stamped as arriving at Tangimoana on 17 November 1982, but it had been around and regularly updated, with amendments signed and dated on the inside cover, since March 1974 — the year that new UKUSA HFDF installations began to be established for the Pacific-Indian Ocean network.

The activists decided to return the manual (which was, after all, the property of the British government) and other GCSB papers to the gate of the station after the protest. But unfortunately the documents never got back in one piece. That afternoon the neighbouring farm manager found the two parcels by the gate and dropped them off at the station. The officer in charge misunderstood the gesture. Placing the 'suspicious parcels' gingerly on the grass outside the main building, he closed down interception operations at the station and moved the staff to the farthest corner of the building. An Army bomb disposal team was rushed from Wellington and blew the packages up.

> *The Prime Minister today visited the RNZAF Base Ohakea and opened the new communications station at Tangimoana.... The advent of this station will significantly improve defence communications in New Zealand. Because of the classified nature of defence communications this station, like other defence establishments, will not be open to the general public.*[11]

This brief press release was issued by Prime Minister Rob Muldoon's press secretary in 1982 after he had opened the new Tangimoana station. It was an announcement designed to mislead and to go unnoticed.

In the 1960s radio officers at the NR1 station at Waiouru heard talk of plans to relocate the station to the coastal area of the Manawatu region. This area was discussed as being a more attractive location in which to live and work and a natural area for radio reception owing to the 'conducting stratum' for radio waves in the low-lying country. But the funding was never available.

Then, shortly after the GCSB formed in 1977, planning for the new station began. According to Australian researcher Des Ball, the decision to set up the new station 'was made in discussions between New Zealand, United States and Australian intelligence officers at Irirangi in 1977 and 1978'.[12] The exact location, on the coast in the Manawatu, was finalised in 1979.

The site chosen was on land that had been owned by the state since 1869 when the Maori native title was 'extinguished'. By 1979 it was a Lands and Survey Department farm development block, a small area of which the Ministry of Defence was allowed to use for the station. After the station was discovered in 1984, the Defence Council hastily designated the land a 'Defence Area', protected by strict regulations that allowed trespassers to be searched and detained. In May 1992 the GCSB took ownership of the 171-hectare area now occupied by the station. Although the land is now protected only by ordinary law, the GCSB managed to restrict public use of the road that runs through the middle of its land.[13]

Design work for Tangimoana was done in early 1980 and by late 1981 the operations building was completed. Although Muldoon opened the station on 18 August 1982, erection of the antennae was not completed until September and it seems that the station was not fully operational until early the following year (the NR1 station continued to operate until at least the end of 1982).

The construction was overseen by the GCSB's Deputy Director for Engineering, Keith Smith, together with two Army officers, Colonel Rob Dickie and the Ministry of Defence's Assistant Director for Works, Major Jasonsmith. According to locals, a number of American and Australian personnel were involved during the construction. GCSB director Colin Hanson named the new development Project Acorn, 'acorn' being a familiar codename for signals intelligence activities around the world. Construction workers building the station in 1981-82 wore T-shirts featuring this name, with the result that they were jokingly referred to as 'secret squirrels'.

These small dishes were the first sign of planning for the move to satellite interception.

The official name for the station, the Defence Communications Unit (Tangimoana), was clearly an attempt to mislead the public by associating the station, which is only a few kilometres from the Ohakea Air Force base, with the Air Force communications group of the same name. In fact, there are no transmitting aerials, only receiving ones; Tangimoana is not for communications, only eavesdropping.

Some of the new staff for Tangimoana were trained at the old NR1 station, others at a temporary GCSB station established in early 1980 in a disused Air Force communications station in Whitemans Road adjacent to the Ohakea Air Force base. The Whitemans Road station was partly a training establishment for about 30 of the new radio officers recruited for Tangimoana and JTUM in Melbourne, and partly an operational station taking over some of NR1's interception duties in 1982 before Tangimoana was fully operational.

In mid-December 1985 two 3-metre dish antennae were installed temporarily at the station behind the operations building. The peace movement suggested incorrectly that they could be a new communications link for the station via a United States military satellite. Prime Minister David Lange denied this and issued a press release saying, with deliberate obscurity, that 'trials were being conducted at the base to measure the electrical noise throughout the radio spectrum in the Manawatu region'.[14] The dishes were aimed towards geostationary satellites above the Equator in the central and eastern Pacific. What the Prime Minister had not explained (and in fact was never told himself) was *why* the GCSB was suddenly interested in doing electrical noise trials in the Tangimoana region.

The answer to this question came three years later when news of planning for a second GCSB station leaked to the public. The electronic noise trials were part of early studies relating to a whole new area of interception: satellite communications. Tangimoana had originally been considered as a site but was rejected. As more and more of the station's targets began using satellites, planning was underway for what would become the Waihopai station.

CHAPTER TEN

UNDER THE RADOME
WHAT HAPPENS AT WAIHOPAI

In the early 1600s a French gunsmith devised a new firing mechanism that would become the standard for the next 200 years. Unlike the cumbersome matchlock, where a wick had to be lit, the new design had a flint attached to the cock of the gun which, when it struck the hammer, produced sparks to ignite the gunpowder. Hence its name, flintlock.

Simple yet effective, flintlock muskets could be constructed cheaply and therefore in large numbers. In the 1600s and 1700s the new guns were taken to every corner of the world by the British, French, Spanish, Dutch and Portuguese as they established a new world order, carving up the world into their respective empires.

In the 1990s military technology is much deadlier than the once dominant flintlocks, but the causes of war and military repression have not changed substantially: gaining access to cheap resources, maintaining spheres of influence, competing over philosophy and religion. In the 1990s, however, intelligence capabilities are often as much a source of power and influence as military forces.

Each station in the UKUSA intelligence network has a special secret codename that identifies the intelligence collected there. The GCHQ Hong Kong station's intelligence was codenamed GERANIUM. The NSA Yakima

The Waihopai station consists of the operations building, a services building and a single dish under the large radome. Inside the operations building powerful computers do most of the work, producing intelligence with the top secret codename, FLINTLOCK.

station, set in the midst of canyons and desert next to an Indian reservation, produces intelligence called COWBOY. Intelligence from the Waihopai station was given an inexplicable yet strangely apt codename: FLINTLOCK. Intelligence collected at the station for the UKUSA alliance is identified by this word and by Waihopai's station designator, NZC-333.

The Waihopai station, located in the Waihopai Valley near Blenheim, in the north-east corner of the South Island, is by far the most important intelligence facility in New Zealand. Opened just a few weeks before the Berlin Wall fell in 1989, the station was part of the GCSB's entry into the ECHELON system: the 21st-century electronic spy network.

In the ECHELON system the codenames are used to identify the Dictionary at each station. The Waihopai computer contains the FLINTLOCK Dictionary and the GCSB also has keywords placed in other Dictionaries such as the COWBOY Dictionary at Yakima.

Unlike much of the work of the UKUSA radio interception stations, Waihopai (and its sister stations) are targeted not on some enemy's military communications, but on all the ordinary telephone calls, faxes, telexes and Internet and other e-mail messages sent by individuals, groups, businesses and governments around the world.

Waihopai has a large dish antenna that is locked onto the target satellite. Its receiving equipment is then tuned into some of the frequencies on which the satellite is transmitting and large banks of processing equipment break the signals down into individual telephone calls, faxes, computer data communications and telexes. Everything is then fed into the FLINTLOCK Dictionary computer to search for messages of interest.

When news of the planned station leaked out in late 1987, the then GCSB Director, Colin Hanson, had a press release ready for the Prime Minister explaining the rationale for the new station. The station was said to be the outcome of an intelligence review that followed the defence and intelligence split between New Zealand and the United States in 1985: it would provide 'greater independence in intelligence matters for New Zealand'.[1] This and other public explanations were deceptive. Waihopai provided greater capability, but not independence. The global intelligence collection system was being expanded by the UKUSA allies and New Zealand's new station was to be but one small, integral part.

The Waihopai station represented a new level of integration into UKUSA. Around the world UKUSA stations like Waihopai now work as an integrated collection system: GCSB staff automatically receive some intelligence from other stations in the network; and NSA intelligence staff sitting at Fort Meade outside Washington DC have an automatic, 24-hour flow of raw FLINTLOCK intelligence fed into their computers according to their pre-programmed requirements.

The Waihopai station is targeted on Intelsat civilian satellite communications in the Pacific. Its target is the Intelsat satellite located at 174 degrees east — Intelsat's primary Pacific Ocean area satellite, which carries most satellite telephone, telex and Internet transmissions for the countries of the Pacific and between nations on the Pacific rim. As described in Chapter 2, this Intelsat 701 satellite replaced the earlier 510, at 174 degrees east, which was Waihopai's target for its first five years of operation.[2]

Since the 1960s international satellite communication of telephone calls and telex for most countries has been synonymous with the Intelsat system. Intelsat is an international co-operative with shares owned by the telecommunications organisations of most of the world's nations. It has ringed the world with satellites for international telecommunications.

These communications satellites are positioned in a ring around the Equator, far out in space about 36,000 kilometres above the earth (the diameter of the earth is 12,750 kilometres). Known as geostationary satellites, they

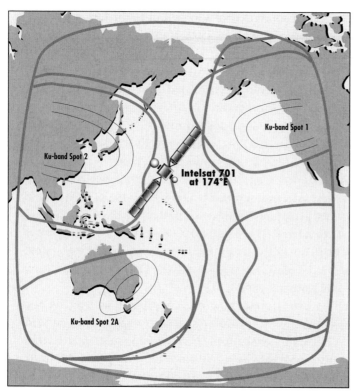

Waihopai's big secret is what satellite it is intercepting. It is this international communications satellite at 174 degrees east. (The lines show the areas of the Pacific covered by the satellite's various beams — one beam covering the whole Pacific, other beams covering a half or quarter of the region and spot beams for areas of heavy comm- unications traffic.)

have been launched into an orbit where they revolve around the earth at exactly the same rate as the earth is spinning; this means that they sit station- ary above a particular spot on the Equator.[3]

The other communications satellite of known interest to the UKUSA agencies in the South Pacific is the Inmarsat-2 mobile communications sat- ellite at 178 degrees east, which is probably intercepted at the Yakima station. Inmarsat (an international co-operative, like Intelsat) has provided satellite communications for ships and other mobile users since 1982. There are four main geostationary Inmarsat satellites positioned around the world (East and West Atlantic, Pacific and Indian Ocean Areas), each with a 'global' beam down on to the hemisphere in its view.[4]

In 1993 orders were made for a new series of Intelsat 8 satellites to service the Asia-Pacific, Intelsat's fastest growing region. It is planned that sometime in 1996 Intelsat 801 will replace 701, and 802 will replace 703 (with 701 and 703 being moved to new locations).[5] Waihopai and Geraldton will be retargeted accordingly.

After plans for Waihopai became public, there was a lot of speculation in the news media about what the station's targets would be. But, until now, the target has remained secret. For example, after peace researcher Owen Wilkes suggested Intelsat, a Telecom executive, who worked with Intelsat receiving equipment, described as 'laughable' suggestions that Intelsat might be a target. Getting useful intelligence would in practice be too hard, he argued, like 'getting a needle from a haystack'.

What specific communications are targeted by Waihopai? Under the UKUSA agreement, signals intelligence tasking authority (specifying which agency spies on what) was traditionally divided up between the five member nations partly by geographical area and partly by subject. These divisions have never been strict: radio waves do not obey such boundaries, historical connections lead to responsibilities such as the British in Hong Kong and, more recently, United States spy satellites have provided global monitoring.

In the age of the ECHELON system, collection duties mostly involve monitoring some large component or components of the international telecommunications system — in Waihopai's case one satellite carrying tens of thousands of messages. As such, Waihopai is potentially collecting intelligence from a very wide geographical area and on every conceivable subject. What is specifically collected is determined by all five agencies according to the keywords they have had placed in the FLINTLOCK Dictionary.

New Zealand's area of responsibility is mapped out in one of the GCSB's

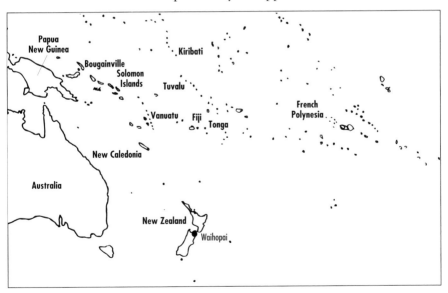

All South Pacific nations and territories pictured (except UKUSA ones) are continuously intercepted at Waihopai.

internal manuals. It shows that the area of the world covered by the GCSB for analysis includes most of the South Pacific from French Polynesia across to and including New Caledonia, Vanuatu and the Solomon Islands. West of there is the Australian DSD's responsibility, including Papua New Guinea, East Timor and Indonesia. So during the government crises in Vanuatu in the second half of the 1980s the GCSB was responsible for producing intelligence reports based on communications in Port Vila; and in the 1990s most reports on the Bougainville conflict came from the DSD.

The South Pacific is very vulnerable to satellite interception because, although some radio links are still used, most telecommunications in the area rely on satellite. While up to 90 percent of New Zealand's international telecommunications are carried by undersea cable rather than satellite (because of their huge capacity the cables are much cheaper), satellite communications are ideal for isolated islands. Only Fiji has access to the ANZCAN undersea cable, which it uses for about half of its international communications, the other half being satellite. (The UKUSA agencies spy on cable communications by other methods — see Chapter 2.)

All South Pacific island groups, no matter how small, have earth stations linked to the Pacific Intelsat satellites. This includes every nation and territory from Papua New Guinea across to Tahiti in French Polynesia. They are served by the Intelsat satellites' global and west hemisphere beams which are designed for wide areas of low traffic. Antarctic communications can also be picked up.[6]

Every user of the Pacific Intelsats is vulnerable to interception by the UKUSA stations. According to GCSB staff, no codebreaking is usually required, since most South Pacific communications are sent 'en clair'. Often not even translation is required. Except in French areas, English frequently serves as the lingua franca between island groups.

The main constraint on interception in the South Pacific is a UKUSA regulation that prohibits collecting signals intelligence where the source is a national of any of the five UKUSA countries. The GCSB analysts are told to abide by this regulation strictly — but a series of revelations elsewhere make it clear that the other allies do not.[7] In the GCSB's section of the South Pacific the regulation stops interception of American Samoa (United States), Norfolk Island (Australia) and the Cook Islands, Niue and Tokelau (New Zealand). Western Samoa would also be regarded as problematic since many Western Samoans are New Zealand citizens.

Taking these factors into account, the GCSB is responsible for producing intelligence reports for the UKUSA alliance about: Fiji, which is the largest of the South Pacific island nations and base for various regional and international organisations, embassies and so on; New Caledonia and French Polynesia (France is the only colonial power in the region which is not a UKUSA member); Vanuatu and the Solomon Islands; all the smaller nations including Kiribati, Nauru, Tuvalu and Tonga; Antarctica; and some foreign ships in this region.

The specific intelligence collected for the GCSB is what reaches the KE and KP staff in the Operations section at the GCSB headquarters. They see communications from all the South Pacific governments, from individuals and political groups, from diplomatic posts in the region, from many companies and international organisations active in New Zealand's section of the South Pacific, and from French territories, with an emphasis on military intelligence (including ship and aircraft movements, troop rotations and, most important, nuclear tests at Moruroa and Fangataufa). They also receive intelligence on the South Pacific nations' military forces and anything on Antarctica. GCSB's long-term interception and analysis of Japanese diplomatic traffic from this region also remain important.

The reason for a division of analysis responsibilities between the UKUSA agencies has been proposed by Owen Wilkes:

> One can imagine that local GCSB analysts sitting in Wellington will be far better at remembering and picking out significant personal names, at correctly hearing place names, at understanding Pacific accents and languages, at understanding the significance of an island conversation. Imagine how difficult it would be for a bored analyst in, say, Fort Meade in Maryland, to remember who [New Zealand unionist] Ken Douglas is, or who [Kanak activist] Susanna Ounei is and so on. In Maryland it would be hard to remember whether Apia is the capital of Tonga or Samoa, whether Vanuatu is on our side or theirs, etc. It would be far better to let the Kiwis sort out all that, and just send over the daily summaries.[8]

The GCSB operations staff have very detailed lists of what is carried on all the individual satellite channels on the Pacific Intelsats. Waihopai's target satellite, Intelsat 701 at 174 degrees, carries virtually all the international communications of the nations and territories in the GCSB's area of the South Pacific: the Solomon Islands, Vanuatu, Kiribati, Nauru, New Caledonia, Tuvalu, Fiji (except for its undersea cable communications), Tonga, Samoa, Niue, the Cook Islands and French Polynesia. Similarly, it carries all the international communications for various countries and territories in the DSD's area to the west, including Papua New Guinea. It is the South Pacific region's satellite.

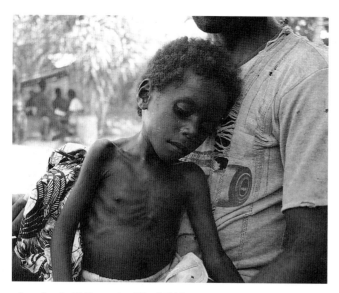

A seriously ill Bougainville child has no access to medicine owing to the military blockade by Papua New Guinea. All Papua New Guinea and Solomon Island communications concerning the Bougainville conflict have been intercepted and passed to Canberra, where they have assisted Australia (which is backing PNG) in its questionable role there.

Some South Pacific countries also use Intelsat for domestic communications but mostly these are not accessible from Waihopai. The domestic satellite link between Fiji and Rotuma uses the Intelsat 701, and is targeted, but all other domestic services use other satellites. Domestic links in French Polynesia are said to use the Intelsat at 180 degrees (which mainly carries television) and the Solomon Islands and Papua New Guinea use Intelsat 703 at 177 degrees, a target satellite of the DSD's Geraldton station.

The Solomon Islands use this satellite for inter-island communications, as does Papua New Guinea (PNG) for communications to several remote islands and regions. These communications have been carefully targeted by the DSD's Geraldton station throughout the Bougainville conflict.

Intelsat 703 has 10-20 channels allocated to Bougainville, including a small number of circuits for use by the Bougainville Revolutionary Army/ transitional government at Arawa and others for use by the PNG defence forces located at Loloho. Other domestic PNG communications are also available to the DSD from this satellite.

Any Solomon Island domestic communications relevant to the Bougainville conflict have also been targeted by Geraldton, but are sent automatically through the ECHELON system to the GCSB analysts, who are responsible for UKUSA reporting on the Solomon Islands. The finished intelligence reports, prepared by the GCSB's KP staff, are then sent back to the DSD.

South Pacific countries are very small Intelsat users by international standards. Most of the enormous capacity of Intelsat 701 is used for communications between the larger Pacific Rim countries. As the Intelsat

Corporation's information on Intelsat 701 says, the satellite is used by 'most long distance carriers in the North America and the Asia-Pacific region' and it serves 'the west coast of the United States, every country from the Russian Far East south to New Zealand, and almost every island in the Pacific'. It also carries 'a significant amount of Intelsat Business Traffic (for private line applications)' and, in total, it links to 'seventy three earth stations in 31 countries'.[9]

It is clear what this means. Waihopai's target satellite mostly carries communications of countries outside the GCSB's reporting area — including a wide range of political, military, business and private communications of many different countries, large and small, of interest to the overseas agencies. Whenever the allies have asked, Waihopai would have intercepted these communications for them.

Intelsat 701 carries some of the main trade communications in the world,

Waihopai Operations Building

The first time you see the main operations room at Waihopai it can be a strange and unsettling experience. It is a huge room with a handful of workers during office hours but most of the time no people at all. Banks of very sophisticated equipment and spaceship-like control areas run themselves. The only movement comes from constellations of small blinking red, green, orange and white lights. The equipment is supplied by the UKUSA allies and wholly integrated into their system — you could just as well be in the United States.

almost entirely involving countries with which New Zealand has good relations. New Zealand, through the Waihopai station, is doing the physical spying on some of these countries for the allied agencies, without having any control over what is then done with the intelligence. Because of the way the ECHELON system is organised, New Zealand does not have access to the intelligence that the NSA or other agencies get from Waihopai. Generally, the GCSB has no way of even knowing what they are getting. It is up to those agencies whether they subsequently share the information with New Zealand.

We can only guess at which foreign and military policies of the United States and other allies are being assisted by the spying occurring at Waihopai. Only a tiny number of GCSB staff know what keywords have been entered for the allies and even they probably have little idea of their political significance. There is, in practice, no New Zealand control over much of the station's output.

The types of communications intercepted by the Waihopai station in-

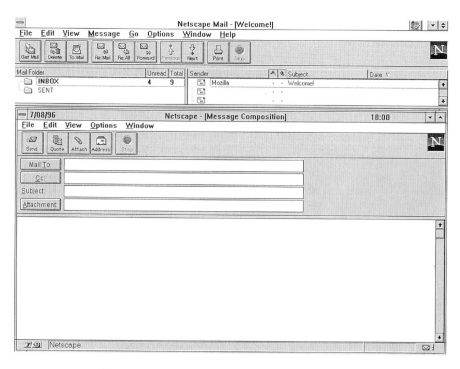

Internet users are continuously intercepted. They do not have to be specifically targeting you; the Dictionary picks out any messages containing one of the agencies' keywords.

clude telexes, faxes, electronic mail and computer data communications. Internet, of course, is an area of interest. Because the GCSB lacks the resources to analyse large amounts of audio intercept, Waihopai does not intercept international telephone traffic on behalf of the GCSB — although it may do so for other UKUSA agencies. By targeting only written words, the Waihopai computers can do the work of searching for interesting information among the millions of messages pulled down from the satellite.

It is not known at present whether Waihopai intercepts telephone calls for the other agencies and sends them on to the agencies for analysis. Tapes are no longer required for audio interception as voice can be stored digitally in a computer. Telephone intercept could be sent overseas through UKUSA communications channels in digital form. If this is the case — and I believe it is likely — NSA equipment inside the Waihopai station will be listening automatically to all the telephone conversations intercepted there and extracting all those in which specified keywords are spoken. The Waihopai station is certainly intercepting large numbers of telephone channels since these are where fax and data communications are carried.

Finally, it needs to be mentioned that Intelsat 701, intercepted at Waihopai, is also used for New Zealand's international communications.

Does the Waihopai station spy on New Zealanders? The GCSB is primarily set up to collect *foreign* intelligence, but it is currently unclear whether it is also used against New Zealand citizens. The KE and KP Section staff, who process all foreign intelligence reports produced by the GCSB, say that they are instructed not to report on any New Zealander's communications selected by the Dictionary: 'If any information is sourced from a member of a UKUSA country, you don't use it'.

But operations against New Zealanders would not be handled through the normal reporting channels anyway — which is why it has been hard to find out if any are occurring. In practice such operations would be assigned a special codename, only two or three directors and one or two operations staff (probably from C Unit) would be indoctrinated to have access to information about them and no one else would ever need to know. It is routine procedure to protect secret operations within an intelligence agency in this way.

There is ample evidence that the other UKUSA agencies turn their collection capabilities against their own citizens. During the Watergate affair, for example, it was revealed that the NSA, assisted by the GCHQ, routinely intercepted the international communications of such prominent anti-Vietnam War activists as Jane Fonda and Dr Benjamin Spock.[10] Similarly, official papers leaked in 1983 to an Australian journalist, Brian Toohey, revealed that the DSD had been used to intercept telephone calls made by an Australian political activist involved in the East Timor independence campaign.

The clearest indication that Waihopai could be used to eavesdrop on New Zealanders is found in one of the denials. While discussing plans of the new station before a parliamentary select committee in 1988, the Co-ordinator of Domestic and External Security, Gerald Hensley, was asked about this possibility. His careful reply was that he could give a 'complete assurance' that the Waihopai station 'would not be used *without lawful authority* to eavesdrop on New Zealanders' (emphasis added).[11]

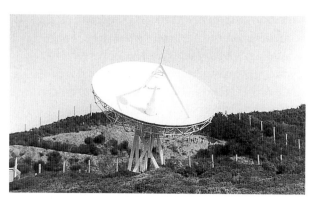

A Telecom New Zealand earth station. The 1977 SIS Act makes it legal to use Waihopai to spy on New Zealanders.

The 'lawful authority' exists in the New Zealand Security Intelligence Service Act, which allows the SIS to obtain a warrant to intercept New Zealanders' communications; Section 4(3) states that any such warrant may include: '(b) A request to any person or persons or class of persons to give such assistance as may be specified in the warrant in making the interception...' This is the clause that requires Telecom staff to install telephone taps for the SIS. It can equally be a legal directive for GCSB staff to list someone's name and telephone number on the Waihopai computers (and the Dictionary watch lists of every other UKUSA station around the world, for that matter).

This is the arrangement in Australia where the DSD co-operates with the Australian Security Intelligence Organisation (ASIO) on some intercepts. Other papers leaked to journalist Brian Toohey, and published by him in 1987 under his tongue-in-cheek 'Archival Early Release Scheme', included a document, stamped UMBRA and Australian Eyes Only, describing 'General principles for warrants' for when the DSD intercepts Australians' communications.[12]

The main DSD operations against Australians involve intercepting telephone calls in and out of Australia (ASIO intercepts the internal calls), but the NSA is even freer, operating according to a 'one terminal rule': if a United

States citizen calls someone overseas, it is regarded as fair game. No warrant or special authorisation is required. The NSA recently won a court case upholding this rule.[13]

Of course no warrant is required for New Zealanders to be intercepted by the other UKUSA agencies (and they are not as scrupulous about the non-UKUSA citizen rule). This loophole, which has been regularly exploited by the overseas agencies to help each other carry out 'deniable' internal spying, may also have been applied to New Zealand targets. The interception could even occur at Waihopai, after a keyword on one of the other agencies' Dictionary lists had picked up a New Zealander's communications.

In the mid-1980s New Zealand received an American intelligence report based on interception of leading New Zealand trade unionist Ken Douglas while he was on a trip for medical treatment to the Soviet Union.[14] It is not known whether the SIS, which would have received this report via the GCSB, had requested the surveillance and, if so, whether this was under a warrant signed by the Prime Minister. The SIS is also said to have obtained information via the GCSB on funds being given to the Socialist Unity Party by the Soviet embassy in 1979.

The Waihopai station provides an unprecedented potential for spying on New Zealanders' international communications. Its interconnection with a worldwide network of similar stations multiplies this potential. There are no legal impediments and such interception would be almost impossible to prove.

Ever since the Waihopai station was first announced there has been discussion about its legality under New Zealand and international law. Its legality under the 1982 Nairobi International Telecommunications Convention (Article 22) is ambiguous.[15] In relation to New Zealand law there is an interesting story to be told.

In April 1988 an opponent of the planned station wrote to the New Zealand Auditor-General asking that he investigate whether the government had lawful authority to build the station.[16] The letter pointed out that, under the new Telecommunications Act and Radio Regulations introduced the year before, the GCSB needed a licence to install and operate the station. It noted that section 24 of the regulations stated:

no person who receives any radiocommunication not intended for that person shall —

a) make use of the radiocommunication or any information derived therefrom;

b) reproduce or permit to be reproduced the radiocommunication or information derived therefrom;

c) disclose the fact or existence of the radiocommunication.

The Auditor-General replied that the expenditure on the station to date had been only for buildings and works — not the actual radio receiving equipment — so the regulations did not yet apply. Before the radio communications equipment was installed the GCSB would need to have obtained an appropriate licence. The matter appeared to end there.

Information released later by the Ministry of Commerce under the Official Information Act shows what happened next. The challenge had alerted the GCSB to the need for a licence. With installation of the Waihopai receiving equipment due to start about April-May 1989, the GCSB wrote to the radio licensing authority (the Ministry of Commerce) in January 1989 with an extraordinary request. It asked for licences for both Waihopai and Tangimoana and requested that each include a specific written authorisation to do the three things quoted above, which the regulations otherwise forbade (no such licence had previously existed for Tangimoana).

The ministry accepted the applications. Two weeks before Christmas 1988 (between the initial challenge and the licence application) the Telecommunications Act had been amended, limiting the discretionary powers of the licensing authority. In a memo on the GCSB application discussing the 'privacy issue', the manager of the section concerned noted that: 'the radio management statute has now been constrained to be related to the effective and efficient management of the radio spectrum, and thereby giving us virtually no powers to judge or enquire into the purposes or intent of the applicants'.[17]

So, since 1 April 1989, Waihopai has had a 'satellite, reception only' licence covering 'such frequency bands as allocated to the Fixed Satellite (Space-Earth) Service'. Under the 'terms, conditions and restrictions' on the licence it states:

This licence authorises the Licensee to receive radiocommunications not intended for the Licensee and to:

a) make use of the radiocommunication or any information derived therefrom;

b) reproduce or permit to be reproduced the radiocommunication or information derived therefrom;

c) disclose the fact or existence of the radiocommunication.[18]

There are two striking things about the planning for the Waihopai station. One is that it was part of a UKUSA-wide expansion of interception of civilian satellite communications. The other is that it occurred throughout a period of New Zealand-United States political conflict over nuclear ship visits when the public was being led to believe intelligence ties had been severed. Internally it was being seen, in part, as a way of demonstrating commitment to the intelligence alliance; to the public it was being presented as the pursuit of greater independence to compensate for exclusion from the alliance.

Plans to expand the system for civilian satellite interception were underway by 1984, with Prime Minister David Lange first told of the proposal for a new New Zealand station about late 1985. But he was never told by his officials about the degree of the new station's integration into the UKUSA system. He was being sold the station with the same line about enhanced independence that he later used in public (together with arguments about co-operation with Australia).

Officer in charge, Colin Waite, had a two-year posting at the DSD in Melbourne in preparation for running the station. The station's chief engineer, Paul Bruckel, came from the British GCHQ.

The first public sign of the planning may have been in December 1985, when the GCSB began testing satellite reception using the two small microwave receivers at the Tangimoana station.

The bureaucratic push for a satellite interception station came through an official review of external intelligence. The government initially called for the review in early 1985 in response to the so-called intelligence cut and by January 1986 the review was nearly completed. Then, suddenly, it was extended for a whole year to allow a review of all New Zealand external intelligence collection and analysis.

A major reason for this extension was that the Australian government was also in the middle of a major review of its military and intelligence policies. New Zealand's reviews of both intelligence and defence would be delayed to see what the Australians (who had no alliance problems) were doing. In practice, the two reviews became the means of recommending to the respective governments all the developments that the intelligence and defence establishments on each side of the Tasman already wanted.

The attitude of New Zealand officials to the Australia-New Zealand relationship at this time is apparent in a confidential 1986 government paper, which said that the relationship depended on New Zealand's ability to 'share good analytical intelligence gathered from its area of specialisation, the South Pacific, with the Australians. It is important that the New Zealand Intelligence Review results in an outcome which ensures a continuing capacity in this regard.'[19] They knew that a system useful for Australia was a system useful to the whole UKUSA alliance.

The intelligence review was undertaken by the New Zealand Intelligence Council (made up of senior military and public service staff), and the top secret report that resulted was written by its chairman, Gerald Hensley. Officially titled 'A Review of New Zealand's External Intelligence Structure and Requirements', it was known internally simply as the 'Hensley Review (Intelligence)'.

The first part of the Australian review was a one-person report by Paul Dibb, ex-director of the Joint Intelligence Organisation. His report has the intelligence sections edited out and states merely that 'continuing investment in new technology will be required to maintain the effectiveness of the DSD'.[20] This phrase was specifically meant as a reference to a new satellite interception station.[21]

A comparison of the Australian and New Zealand reviews clearly shows New Zealand following Australia. Australia decided to develop a Defence Electronic Warfare Data Base (DEWDAB) and so did New Zealand (with the same name and acronym). Both decided on increased use of SAS personnel for intelligence missions, towed arrays for anti-submarine surveillance and to improve signals intelligence interception and analysis.[22]

The Labour government's strategy of replacing its lost United States military ties with closer links to Australia was being eagerly picked up by Australian and New Zealand officials. It provided the pretext they needed for maintaining the alliance orientation of New Zealand's foreign and defence policies despite the ANZUS break.

In July 1986 Dibb was invited to New Zealand for discussions with government officials who were preparing the New Zealand defence review. His longest meeting, however, was not with Defence officials, but with Gerald Hensley (10.30 am-12.30 pm on Friday, 25 July). What was said during this discussion is not known, but there is little doubt that improved signals intelligence interception, meaning satellite communications interception, was on the agenda. Later that year GCSB staff were present at meetings in the DSD where planning for the Australian station occurred.[23]

The Hensley review was presented to David Lange in March 1987 but its contents have never been made public. It recommended changes to the system of intelligence oversight and various other items such as establishing DEWDAB and increased use of the SAS, mirroring the Australian review. Its most significant rec-

Gerald Hensley wrote a top secret report recommending that Waihopai be established.

ommendation was indeed that a satellite interception station be built. Although Lange still had to be convinced of the need for the station,[24] the GCSB was by then well advanced in its planning.

Although in 1986 the GCSB had obtained only limited approval to investigate possible sites for a station, in early 1987 Colin Waite was posted to Melbourne for two years as a special liaison officer with the DSD to prepare for his role as officer in charge of the new station. During this period, too, detailed design and planning took place under the control of the GCSB's Director for Engineering, Keith Smith.

The GCSB initially considered building the satellite interception station at Tangimoana with the existing station,[25] but the sandy soil could not support a heavy dish. After that they searched the country for possible sites within a 30-kilometre radius of military bases (the bases providing support services), eliminating site after site because of problems such as electrical interference from urban areas. In September 1987, farmer Don McDonald advertised 36 hectares of his land in the Waihopai Valley and the GCSB leapt at the offer.

Perhaps awaiting the possible election of conservative government, the GCSB did not ask for government approval for the station until straight after the general elections, which took place in August that year. Lange approved the construction of the new station on 4 November 1987, two months after his party had been returned to government. The land was bought later that month for $210,000.[26]

By then planning for the station had been going on in secret for some years. The GCSB Director, Colin Hanson, aware that construction of the station could scarcely go unnoticed, prepared the Prime Minister's state-ment announcing the station.[27] This was delayed while funding was finalised, but the news leaked out anyway.

Farmers in the valley, who had heard about the purchase, contacted their local MP, Doug Kidd, who happened to have close ties with Defence. He rang the Secretary of Defence, Denis McLean, who gave an unauthorised briefing about the station over the telephone. Within days, the MP asked a question in Parliament and the story was out.

The sister station in Geraldton, West Australia, was planned, built and now operates in tandem with Waihopai.

Construction of the station be-gan a few months later in April 1988. A year later the main build-ings were completed and Colin Waite returned from Australia to take command of the station. Be-tween May and August 1989 the dish was assembled and fittings and computers were installed in the buildings.[28] There were public pro-tests at the site throughout the construction, making it the first intelligence base in the world to be protested against during its construc-tion.[29]

According to the GCSB, the station was opened on 8 September 1989 by Prime Minister Geoffrey Palmer in a brief ceremony in the operations building. The opening of the by then controversial station occurred without publicity. A spokesperson later said that Palmer 'had addressed a few remarks to the people working there but this had not been any sort of opening cer-emony'.[30] Palmer, who had replaced Lange as Prime Minister just weeks before, was the only politician present and the GCSB Director, Ray Parker, gave the main speech.[31] The Director of Domestic and External Security, the Chief of Defence Staff and the Director of the Prime Minister's Office were the only other visitors.[32]

During its planning the station was called Project Delta, referring to a large military camp with that name located nearby during the Second World War. It is now known officially as the Defence Satellite Communications Unit (Blenheim).

In January 1988 recruitment began for all the new staff required to op-erate the station. This included the technicians and other workers for Waihopai

182

and also a considerable number of new computing and technical staff in Wellington for the GCSB's entry into the ECHELON system. The head-quarters staff included programmers, systems analysts, several managerial staff and extra engineers and technicians.

In March 1987, the same month that the Hensley review recommended a New Zealand satellite station, the Australian government announced plans to 'enhance our independent intelligence capabilities by establishing a large satellite communications station in Western Australia' which would 'contribute to Australia's security in our area of strategic interest'. The station would be Australian-owned and staffed and operated by the DSD.[33]

Planning for the two stations had been proceeding in tandem. The DSD had preliminary discussions with its government about the plans in early 1986, at the same time as Lange first heard about Waihopai. The first construction contracts for Waihopai were advertised in March 1988, and the following month for the Australian station, which was to be built in Geraldton, halfway up the west coast of Australia. Construction of both stations began later that year.[34]

The Geraldton station (officially called the Australian Defence Satellite Communications Station, ADSCS) opened in 1993 with four antennae and 125 staff, including 10 from the GCHQ.[35] It targets the second Pacific Intelsat, 703, and the two main Indian Ocean Intelsats, at 60 and 63 degrees east. Its fourth target is likely to be the new Intelsat positioned, in 1992, at 91.5 degrees east, between South East Asia and India.[36]

When the Geraldton station was opened on 10 September 1993, four years and a day after Waihopai, both the GCSB Director, Ray Parker, and the Operations Director, Warren Tucker, were present.[37] They flew to Australia for a week, meeting up with their DSD counterparts in Canberra. Then, with top DSD staff, they went to Geraldton for an afternoon to see the Australian Minister of Defence, Robert Ray, officially open Waihopai's sister station.

Speaking at a post-Cabinet press conference on 2 March 1987, as Geraldton was announced in Australia, Prime Minister David Lange reacted to suggestions by the Minister of Defence that New Zealand was considering satellite surveillance:

There's been no decision made as to that step; in fact that is a critical considera-tion and the question really for New Zealand's purposes is whether we even purport to be capable of gathering intelligence from a vast well, or whether we are selective in gathering our intelligence. I tend to the view that we should be selective.

It is no secret from publicity abroad and in particular from the United Kingdom that it is possible for some technology to be used to absolutely saturate one's computers with details which are then triggered out by certain key words which are locked in. I don't conceive that New Zealand should have a role for that. It's trying to get a cup of water from the Niagara.[38]

Only eight months later, Lange approved the project. A senior public servant, quoted in a 1988 article, explained the decision: 'It's not a question of a foreign power [placing pressure on the Government] but of the international intelligence community wanting to be assured that New Zealand will keep up with the play in collecting signals intelligence'.[39]

This sums up the predicament of a small nation like New Zealand in an alliance of larger nations. It would have been hard for New Zealand to say 'no' when the allies suggested that it should contribute to the new collection system. If New Zealand wants to remain part of the alliance it must assure the 'international intelligence community' (that is, the United States, Britain and Australia) that it will play its part. And, simply because of their relative size and power, this generally means *its* part in *their* plans.

A source within the Australian intelligence community at the time of the ANZUS conflict described it like this: while building Waihopai would have a spin-off for New Zealand's national interest, in building Waihopai the country was 'paying [its] membership to the intelligence club'.[40]

Ten years later, a membership payment was due again. About March 1995 a small dish antenna appeared at the western end of the Waihopai operations building with cables leading into the main operations room.[41] It was facing skywards towards the geostationary satellites above the central Pacific. Just like the two small

Marlborough Express

Once completed, the dish was covered by a radome to hide which satellite it was targeting. Staff say a second dish is being planned.

dishes which appeared behind the operations building at Tangimoana 10 years earlier, it is likely to be a sign of the next major expansion in GCSB interception.

The logical next development at the Waihopai station has always been a second large dish and associated processing equipment to enable the station to monitor both main Pacific Intelsat satellites for the alliance at the same time. The DSD's Geraldton station will then concentrate entirely on Indian Ocean and Asian satellites. It would be a safe bet (and on-site measurements support this) that the small test dish which appeared at Waihopai is pointing at Intelsat 703, the Pacific Intelsat presently targeted by Geraldton. A great deal of preparation and planning will be needed before a second permanent dish can be erected.

When I wrote to the GCSB in 1995 asking about the second dish, I was told that the antenna, which had arrived at the station in July 1990 but was by then wired up outside the operations building, was 'in storage at the station'.[42] I wrote again and this time Ray Parker replied that the dish was being 'used aperiodically for operational tasks information about which I decline to provide on the grounds that to do so would be likely to prejudice the security or defence of New Zealand'.

A few weeks after the station was announced in 1987, the Director of the GCSB, Colin Hanson, told a meeting of Waihopai Valley farmers that it would not be unreasonable to expect another dish to be added at some stage: 'If we're going to stay in the game in the years ahead then in all probability there will be another dish'.[43]

The current GCSB director has refused to say whether the GCSB's 1995-96 budget includes funding for a second large dish, saying only that there were no plans to install one at the station before July 1996. The inside story at the station, according to the workers there, is that a second antenna is planned for not long after that.

CHAPTER ELEVEN

THE FACTS IN THE FILOFAX
MILITARY SIGNALS INTELLIGENCE MISSIONS

On 5 April 1994 a child walking along Ferry Road in Days Bay, Wellington, found and took home to her father a thick black filofax diary that was lying in the long grass beside the road. It had been there for two or three weeks, long enough for the rain to wash away most of the ink writing inside, but pages of neat pencil notes remained that gave a very rare view of the inner workings of the New Zealand military.

The filofax belonged to an Army major, Scott Turner, who had moved into a nearby Ferry Road house the month before. His business card in the diary described him as the New Zealand Defence Force Assistant Director of Electronic Warfare, a position he had held for two months.

The electronic warfare title was intriguing enough for the child's father, who was not a fan of the military, to decide to show the filofax to journalists. At first impression a confusing collection of military acronyms, it turned out to contain more information about secret New Zealand spying operations than had ever reached the public.

What Turner's filofax revealed was a third area of GCSB operations, besides those at Tangimoana and Waihopai, which had previously been completely hidden. This is the interception of other countries' *short-range*

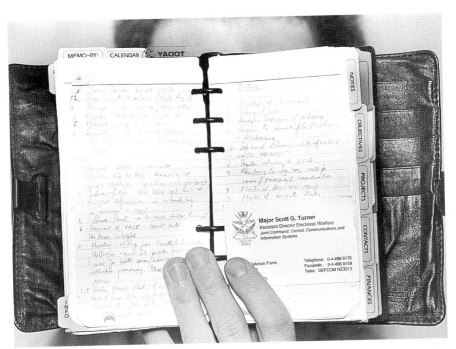

This filofax diary, found in a Wellington street, revealed a new, highly secret area of New Zealand overseas spying operations: covert Navy and Army intercept missions for the GCSB.

radio communications, such as military and political VHF radio communications. Because short-range radio signals in other countries cannot reach the GCSB stations in New Zealand, special intercept units have to be sent close to monitor them. The GCSB has been training and directing New Zealand Defence Force (NZDF) units for these special signals intelligence collection operations.

The filofax contained names and times for a series of meetings between Turner and senior intelligence staff (including from the GCSB and Directorate of Defence Intelligence), notes of a trip he made to Auckland-based intelligence units and, most revealing, careful lists of everything he was doing in his job.

According to the Director of the GCSB, Ray Parker, who is legally required by the Official Information Act to make information available unless there is a stated reason for withholding it, 'the GCSB does not receive support from the New Zealand Defence Force'.[1]

Yet Turner's work plan specifically referred to: a new 'Collection Agreement with the GCSB' (and 'finding out about extant [existing] collection agreements'), a 'CDF Directive for NZDF Support to the GCSB' (CDF is the Chief of Defence Force), a 'CDF Directive for Special Collection Operations', an 'Annual Forecast of Special Collection Operations' and 'Signal[ing] to GCSB the Training programme'.

The 'special collection operations' are interception missions carried out by Defence electronic warfare operators. They are trained for this work inside the GCSB and elsewhere and then use special eavesdropping equipment on missions into other countries. The GCSB decides on the collection targets and the NZDF operators bring back tapes of intercepted communications for analysis.

The filofax contained notes of Turner's meetings with each of the Army and Navy units involved in this work. It named a number of officers who had been indoctrinated for signals intelligence duties, described new intercept equipment being sought and included a note he had written to himself to get 'GCSB feedback on the operators, tape quality etc' of the Navy units' work.

Ian Jones

GCSB director Ray Parker: 'The GCSB does not receive support from the New Zealand Defence Force'.

The government and Defence chiefs refused to comment at all about these NZDF special collection operations and the links with the GCSB revealed in the filofax. The only reaction from any Defence spokesperson was the following statement: 'Electronic warfare is a long-established, legitimate and entirely normal part of military operations. It is not spying.'[2] The first sentence is mostly true. The second is false.

Electronic warfare operators are indeed a part of modern military forces. Their job is military-oriented signals intelligence: locating, intercepting, recording and analysing emissions from the radars, communications equipment and electronic weapon systems of other forces.

The operators detect radio transmissions and radar emissions, they attempt to work out the location and identity of the source and they collect information either from the content of communications or from the physical characteristics of the emissions about the systems being used. All these functions are called electronic support measures (ESM). Their job also includes trying to jam or confuse the other forces' ESM and other electronic systems (these are called electronic counter-measures or ECM). Their work is often linked to targeting and defences against being targeted during military exercises and warfare.

Each Navy frigate has six to 10 electronic warfare (EW) personnel, the Army has a 21-person EW troop and the Air Force also has an EW capability. Their duties include all the different aspects of electronic warfare operations listed above — including collecting information from the content of intercepted communications. In other words, spying. What Turner's work plan revealed is that, of all these activities, the spying ('special collection operations') in support of the GCSB is a major part of the New Zealand Defence Force's electronic warfare work. The revelations contained in Turner's filofax have been confirmed from a number of other sources.

Work Plan

CDF Directive for Special Collection Operations

CDF Directive for NZDF Support to GCSB

Annual Forecast of SCO

Defence and Single Service Intelligence Requirements

Review of EW Policy Paper

Training System

Language Training

Filing System

Signal to GCSB theTrg programme

Minute to ACOPS re COMSEC monitoring

Laptop funding

Paper to reorg Coll Mangement within HQNZDF

Auckland Visit Report

NZSOC SOPs

SPINDRIFT Letter – *partly done.*

Sanitisation JOINT VENTURE
letter to GCSB

This page from Major Turner's filofax directly contradicted Ray Parker's statement (opposite).

The GCSB started training and using New Zealand Defence Force EW operators for intelligence collecting missions in 1986. In that year an Air Force squadron leader, Leon Crosse, was seconded to the GCSB's P Section to arrange the training of Navy EW operators in preparation for signals intelligence operations from Navy frigates. Crosse was later appointed to the GCSB's staff in January 1988 as a one-person section for liaison with the military about these special missions. He was called W. (The filofax recorded Turner meeting with Leon Crosse at 10 am on 2 February 1994, one of his first meetings after taking up the job.)

Initially, in 1986, two Navy EW operators went to the GCSB headquarters for several training periods, each lasting a few days. They were especially indoctrinated for signals intelligence work. Navy EW staff have been involved in these operations ever since.

The GCSB was following the example of the other UKUSA agencies, all of which use Navy ships for signals intelligence missions. A top secret 1983 memo, prepared by the Australian DSD for Foreign Minister Bill Hayden and leaked to a journalist, told of just such a mission. It described how HMAS *Cessnock*, with a team of DSD operators and equipment, sailed into the waters north of Australia in December 1983 to monitor the Indonesian armed forces during their operations in East Timor. The aim was to 'provide a unique opportunity to establish the audibility in the Darwin area of Indonesian VHF/UHF tactical communications from Irian Jaya, the Aru Islands, Ceram and the East Lesser Sundas, including Timor, and thus their potential for exploitation for signals intelligence'. The memo went on to say that the 'cover story' for the operation was that the ship was 'conducting enhanced surveillance operations in response to reports that illegal fishing has been in progress'.[3] This leak gave the first positive proof that Australian Navy ships were involved in DSD signals intelligence operations. There is also a long history of United States naval ships being used in this way.

HMNZS Canterbury: *GCSB-trained and directed Navy operators work in an off-limits room behind the bridge.*

The first mission Leon Crosse co-ordinated was a trial for the EW operators which, like the Australian DSD operation, was aimed mainly at investigating the potential for exploiting different countries' communications for later signals intelligence missions (i.e. seeing what was available to intercept). Ships are used because they can patrol close enough to intercept short-range VHF and UHF radio communications.

A six-week tour of the South Pacific by the frigate HMNZS *Canterbury* was chosen for the trial. Between 20 June and 27 July 1986 the *Canterbury* visited Fiji, Tuvalu, Tonga, the Cook Islands area and Western Samoa, with the EW operators following GCSB instructions as to when and against whom they were to collect intelligence. They worked in a locked room, directly behind the bridge, on the port side of the frigate. This room contained classified equipment connected to aerials above the deck. It was off-limits to other crew, earning the EW operators the nickname 'secret squirrels' from fellow crew members.

Crosse and the GCSB regarded the trial as a success and after their return brought the EW operators in for extra training for future missions. New Zealand frigates had begun going on annual six-week South Pacific tours and the GCSB decided to plan a special intelligence task for each of these trips.

The Navy purchased US$12.5 million of new electronic warfare equipment for the four New Zealand frigates from a United States manufacturer and this was installed between 1986 and 1990. *Canterbury* was fitted with the new equipment in 1986, presumably before the South Pacific trip, followed by the frigates *Wellington*, *Waikato* and *Southland*.[4]

The following year's collection mission was planned for the frigate HMNZS *Wellington*, again presumably after it had had the new EW equipment installed. But as the *Wellington* approached its first port of call, Suva, Fiji's 14 May 1987 military coup occurred. Faced with a serious military crisis, what was to be the second trial became the GCSB's first real ship-based intelligence collecting operation.

The *Wellington* arrived at Suva two days after the coup, on 16 May, and stayed at the Walu Bay berth until ordered to leave a week later. Then, along with Australian warships, it patrolled just outside Suva beyond the territorial limit until it left the area four days later on 27 May. Being in such a position would have enabled continuous interception of short-range communications.

Because the *Wellington* was scheduled for ceremonial duties in Western Samoa and then a military exercise in the Tokelau Islands, and the Navy did not want to disturb its plans, the GCSB had to prepare hastily to continue intelligence collection from a second ship, HMNZS *Monowai*, the Navy's 90-metre oceanographic ship. The government had directed the *Monowai* to sail to Fiji in case there was a need for emergency evacuation of civilians.

The *Monowai* was undergoing major maintenance at the time and had to have its propellers reassembled quickly and hull work completed. It left New Zealand on 23 May and rendezvoused with the *Wellington* in the patrol area on the 27th. It then spent five days in Suva, until ordered to leave, and another six days after that on the patrol line.

The GCSB arranged additional intercept equipment and had crews shuffled around to get experienced EW operators for the *Monowai*. The GCSB also sent an Australian Navy signals intelligence officer on this voyage. The

New Zealand Defence Force

Navy frigates Wellington *(pictured) and* Canterbury *are designated as GCSB mobile stations (NZC-335 and NZC-334). Covert interception occurs while the ships are visiting ports and transiting through areas.*

captain was decidedly unhappy about his presence (especially when he wore an Australian uniform on deck), being already uneasy about the presence of two Special Air Service (SAS) intelligence collectors who had joined the trip without government knowledge. The Australian officer was a analyst from the GCSB's K2 cell, on a two-year posting from the DSD to the GCSB and had previously been posted to the British GCHQ. He had probably had previous experience of ship-based signals intelligence collection in his DSD work.

A confidential section of a 1986 New Zealand Defence review proposed that portable EW modules be developed for intelligence purposes for deployment by ship, land or air, and noted that the Royal Australian Navy 'has such a module which has been used successfully for surveillance of Soviet naval vessels'.[5] (The New Zealand Navy was still seeking such a module in 1994. Major Turner's filofax contained notes of a meeting with the Navy in Auckland at 9 am on 2 March 1994, where he had discussed purchase of a 'SASE — COMINT [communication intelligence] Suite', about which 'Commander Anson [was] unhelpful'.)[6]

The *Monowai* EW operators intercepted Fiji military radio communications both from within the port and from the patrol line just south of Suva and north of Kadavu Island. At least six Australian Navy vessels were also part of the patrol at various times, including HMAS *Sydney*, HMAS *Woollongong*, HMAS *Paramatta* and the same HMAS *Cessnock* that was used for the DSD mission in 1983. There is no doubt that at least some of them were also doing signals intelligence work.

On 7 June the *Monowai* left the patrol and headed to Nukualofa in Tonga, to meet a New Zealand military plane which would take some people back to New Zealand. The *Monowai*'s log records the ship arriving at 4 pm and at

4.15 extra personnel — '30 in number' — departing for the airport.[7] The extra electronic warfare and GCSB staff were among them.

A second coup occurred in Fiji on 25 September 1987. The *Monowai* was ordered to recall its ship's company from leave that evening and sailed from New Zealand the next day. It returned to the same patrol line off Suva and motored up and down there from 30 September until 10 October. The *Monowai* crew called it 'Operation Déjà Vu'. Again the official story was that the ship was there in case the situation deteriorated and New Zealanders needed to be evacuated, but the requirement to patrol so close to Suva was clearly to allow another special collection operation.

There have been six-week naval trips to the South Pacific nearly every year since, usually by the frigates *Canterbury* or *Wellington*[8] and the intercept collected has been sent from the Navy to the GCSB headquarters, where it was seen and reported on by K Unit analysis staff. Throughout this period groups of EW operators from the *Canterbury* and *Wellington* were sent for training in the now closed training unit at the Tangimoana station.

This is not an ad hoc arrangement between the Navy and the GCSB. The areas on the frigates used for these operations are called GCSB mobile stations. The main frigates used for these operations, the *Canterbury* and *Wellington*, have been assigned UKUSA station designators — NZC-334 and NZC-335 — so that the intelligence they collect can be identified wherever it ends up in the UKUSA network. The use of the 'C' — meaning they are civilian stations — in the designators is significant. Despite the Navy staffing, they are definitely *GCSB* mobile stations, with all the training, tasking and analysis controlled by the GCSB.

In 1987 a collection of new aerials was installed on the roof of the operations building at Tangimoana.[9] The purpose of these at first seemed inexplicable, for they are suited only to picking up short-range communications from the area around the station. It is now obvious that they were put there for use in training the Navy intercept staff. The aerials, which resemble some of those you would see on a frigate, are used to listen to all the VHF radios, cellular telephones and other communications within range. This is not serious spying (and some of the local monitoring is just done for fun) but it is precisely what the operators are learning to go and do in foreign ports.

In contrast to a fixed station, on a frigate the targets change as the vessels visit different countries or pass through different areas. As a GCSB officer said, 'Their tasks change as they change positions themselves.' He explained how, for example, as the frigate goes up the coast of Australia the operators will be listening to Papua New Guinea; then, as it passes north of Australia, they may be listening to East Timor. Each country the frigate visits in the South Pacific and elsewhere is also targeted (except UKUSA country territories), even while the ship is moored in the port of one of New Zealand's friends and is being officially welcomed by the local authorities. The annual New Zealand frigate deployments to South East Asia also involve signals intelligence collection. This work is presumably directed by and passed on to the Australian DSD, since this is its area of responsibility.

The Australian Navy clearly has signals intelligence missions to South East Asian waters. One of these missions came to light in 1993 publicity surrounding sexual harassment of crew on the Australian frigate HMAS *Swan*. The case involved women sailors who were harassed while the *Swan* was in South East Asia and around Hong Kong in 1992. During the inquiry it was revealed that two of the women were 'Chinese language specialists' and that they were working in a 'specialised and classified area'.[10] By the time of the inquiry one of these Chinese language specialists had been posted on to HMAS *Harman*, home of the DSD's HF radio interception station outside Canberra.

Army EW operators were the next to be trained to support the GCSB. Most of the New Zealand Army's EW personnel are based with the SAS (the military's other main covert intelligence collection unit) at the RNZAF Hobsonville base in Auckland. Although all operational Army units have an EW capability, the main EW unit is the 21-person 53 Electronic Warfare Troop at Hobsonville. This unit has a troop headquarters and four detachments that can be sent separately on missions.[11]

In the mid-1980s the Army, like the Navy, took steps to increase its EW capabilities. The Army's Tactical Electronic Warfare Project, 'intended to enhance the Army's capability to gather intelligence by electronic means'[12] and completed in 1990-91, included $2.75 million of new EW equipment approved by the government in January 1990.[13] As with the Navy, planning for the new Army EW equipment began in 1985-86;[14] and, also like the Navy EW developments, details of the Army equipment are classified.

By 1991 the GCSB was training these Army EW personnel for intercept work. In that year an issue of fortnightly *Army News* carried a feature about pay rates, and buried in the midst of paramedic qualifications and heavy equipment repair were the various types of EW skills: EW Analyst, EW Reporting, Advanced Intercept and 'GCSB Intercept'.[15] This shows that there are courses designed by the GCSB for Army EW personnel, training them to undertake special collection operations. Like the Navy operators, groups of Army EW staff have indeed had occasional GCSB training courses at Tangimoana. The courses for Army operators began in the 1990s. No Air Force operators have received this training.

Military sources have confirmed that Army EW operations involve GCSB-directed interception projects carried out during military exercises and assistance programmes in the South Pacific and elsewhere; and possibly trips by Army EW personnel into other countries on special projects.

Major Turner had a meeting with the Army EW Troop in Auckland on 1 March 1994. The discussions included indoctrination of troop members, courses, participation of the troop in an exercise in the Cook Islands called 'Tropic Twilight' later that year and an 'intercept range upgrade from 2MHz - 1 GHz'. Turner noted that only three members of the troop — a senior sergeant and two sergeants — were currently indoctrinated. These would have been the three operators available for special collection operations at that time.

The EW unit has close links with the Australian Army's 72 EW Squadron based in Cabarlah, Queensland (which is also the location of one of Tangimoana's Australian sister stations). Since 1990

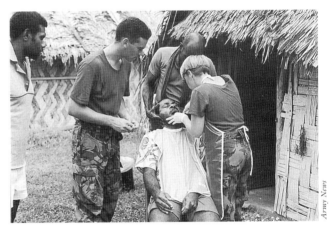

Military aid in Vanuatu: since about 1990 some Army units sent overseas include covert GCSB-trained interception units.

this co-operation has included sharing training and exercises. Operators from the New Zealand EW troop attend the Australian Regular Officers Basic EW Course in Cabarlah. Also during the early 1990s, 10 operators took part in Australian EW exercises.[16] In August 1992 an Army EW operator attended an EW course in Canada.[17] And the filofax notes referred to an exchange of EW personnel between the New Zealand Navy and the Royal Australian Navy. In October 1993 the New Zealand troop held its own exercise, called Exercise Ultra.

The Air Force also has EW capabilities in the form of the EW maritime surveillance capabilities on its Orions and EW systems on the Skyhawks. But there is no evidence of GCSB-Air Force EW links. It is noteworthy that Major Turner had no meetings with Air Force staff during his visits to Auckland intelligence units (despite flying in and out of Auckland through the Orions' Whenuapai base).

New Zealand agreed to buy five Lockheed Orion aircraft in 1964 as its contribution to a worldwide United States anti-submarine system. Orions are long-range patrol aircraft designed with stacks of electronic equipment for detecting (primarily Russian) submarines. In addition to a large American fleet of Orion aircraft, American allies like Canada, Australia and New Zealand were encouraged to buy Orions and operate them over the segments of the world's oceans allocated to them in the American system. There is little point in having them today.

The final element of the Defence EW resources is the Defence Electronic Warfare Data Base (DEWDAB), which was established in the first half of 1990, although the official opening date was 18 February 1991. According to the then Defence Minister Warren Cooper, 'it contains technical information about weapon systems likely to be encountered by New Zealand forces, and is used to programme self-defence systems used by our forces'.[18] But this is only part of the story.

Although operated and funded by the military, the data base is actually located inside the GCSB headquarters in Wellington (in a secure locked-off area). Containing lists of targets for NZDF signals intelligence missions and their technical characteristics, it is closely linked to the intelligence collection activities. It shares offices with the GCSB and NZDF liaison staff who co-ordinate these missions.

Into this computer data base is put any information collected by Defence EW operators about other nations' communications and weapon systems. This includes the radio frequencies and operating procedures used in the South Pacific countries on which the Navy and Army missions eavesdrop, accumulating information to assist future spying operations. It will also store large quantities of EW information provided to New Zealand by other countries. The Australian DEWDAB was developed in tandem with the New Zealand one.

The Officer in Charge of New Zealand's DEWDAB for its first five years was Squadron Leader John Lawton, who had had an Air Force career in defence electronic systems. In 1995 Flight Lieutenant Jeff Price took over the position. The unit has two other staff: Price's assistant (a non-commis-

New Zealand Defence Force

Papua New Guinea-Bougainville peace talks, June 1990. New Zealand boasted about its neutral mediator role in hosting peace talks on these three Navy ships. But, in fact, the GCSB has been spying on both parties before and after the talks, and the frigate accommodating the PNG delegation is equipped as a GCSB intercept unit.

sioned officer) and a 'data insertion clerk'. Its establishment cost $1 million from the Defence budget.

Before moving to the DEWDAB job, Lawton was the Staff Officer (Electronic Warfare) at the Defence Headquarters in Wellington, Major Scott Turner's predecessor in charge of military EW activities. The position of Staff Officer (Electronic Warfare) was established in 1987, at the same time as all the other developments in EW capabilities were occurring, and upgraded to Assistant Director in 1989.

As Assistant Director Electronic Warfare, Major Turner is responsible for developing EW policy for the New Zealand Defence Force and co-ordinating and managing the activities of all the units involved in EW work. He is responsible for two staff, a military officer called Staff Officer (Special Operations) and his assistant. Based at the GCSB headquarters, these two liaise with GCSB staff to co-ordinate special collection operations by the Army and Navy EW staff. They share offices on the 14th floor with the GCSB's defence liaison officer — an officer who himself came from a career in Navy electronic warfare — who is part of L Unit.[19]

Army electronic warfare developments in New Zealand are determined largely by following the four intelligence allies, in this instance in the context of the 1964 four-nation ABCA agreement (America, Britain, Canada, Australia), of which New Zealand has been an associate member since 1965. Although it is rarely heard of or discussed, this agreement is very influential in integrating the New Zealand military into the American alliance. ABCA ensures that the militaries in the different countries standardise their equipment, training, doctrines and so on to allow joint operations. For the smaller allies it invariably means following the larger allies.

ABCA is implemented through a series of working groups, including one on electronic warfare. It is through the meetings every 18 months of this working group, and contacts between meetings, that planning in New Zealand is guided by the allies. Because the United States benefits from having New Zealand electronic warfare policy and capabilities shaped to its needs, New Zealand participation in this joint planning continued despite the public announcement in February 1985 of a full severing of New Zealand-United States military ties.

New Zealand attended the April 1985 working group meeting in Brisbane and the following meeting at Fort Huachuca, Arizona, on 9-16 September 1986. Since then New Zealand has been at meetings in London (April 1988), Montreal (September 1989), Sydney (May 1991), Fort Huachuca (October 1993), Auckland (October 1993) and Fort Huachuca (June 1995).[20] In the rotation of meeting locations around the five nations, New Zealand would normally have been the host in 1988. It was obviously left out on that occasion to maintain the appearance of no New Zealand-United States defence co-operation.

Electronic warfare co-operation between Australia and New Zealand was cemented in a formal Memorandum of Understanding on Defence Communications-Electronics Co-operation, signed in April 1985. This covers military communications systems and electronic warfare and calls for the 'closest possible' liaison and approach to all aspects of these activities — 'to the best advantage and mutual benefit of both countries'. This included 'specific projects of co-operation', training and a 'similarity of approach extending into systems and equipments and to the timing of their acquisition'. Both parties 'recognise the continuing importance of membership of those international military forums which deal with communications-electronics interoperability and other matters' — in other words, that this Australasian co-operation should occur within a wider alliance framework regulated by agreements such as ABCA.[21]

The memorandum prepared the way for the expansion of New Zealand EW capabilities that began in 1985, in effect specifying that all the developments occur in parallel with Australia. It also stated that officials from the two countries should meet to implement the joint planning. One such get-together, the Australia-New Zealand Communications Forum Meeting, took place in Wellington on 12-13 March 1987, hosted by Group Captain Ray Parker, then the Director of Defence Communications. Until shortly before it had been called the ANZUS Communications Forum.

Arranged by the military and intelligence bureaucracies in the countries concerned, agreements and meetings like these are in practice all but invisible to Parliaments and to the public. Yet they are frequently far more important to what actually happens in the military and intelligence organisations than the official policy statements made by governments.

Together the various defence EW elements contribute to the GCSB's signals intelligence collection capability. Although by far the bulk of the collection occurs at the two stations, the defence EW units, as we have seen, have the advantage of mobility. They can move close to a target of interest to intercept short-range radio communications, civilian and military, and visit areas of potential future interest to collect information about communications systems and electronic military equipment, which is stored on the central data base to aid future operations. The cost of these activities in effect adds millions of dollars every year to the GCSB budget.

CHAPTER TWELVE

WHAT ARE THE SECRETS?
THE INTELLIGENCE PRODUCT

All the countries, organisations and individuals that have become targets of the GCSB are contained in a very secret three- to four-page document known simply as the Target List. This describes individually each of the specific types of communications that are to be intercepted by the GCSB stations at Tangimoana and Waihopai and by other special interception missions.

The Target List is one of the few documents revealing GCSB operations ever seen outside the organisation. Even then, only a few people within the upper echelons of government organisations have ever seen it. There are a very small number of copies outside the GCSB, stored in safes in key areas of the intelligence and security bureaucracy.

The list of targets is divided up first by country, then by functional categories within each country, and then, within each category, the specific targets are listed (stating the type of communications the GCSB is trying to intercept). For example, under the country Fiji the functional headings could include 'Fiji Government', 'Fiji Defence Force', 'South Pacific Forum', 'United Nations Development Programme' and so on — all of which are GCSB targets based in Suva. Each of these is then broken down further. For example, the 'Fiji Defence Force' category could include 'Fiji Defence Force communications with the Sinai', 'Fiji police radio communications', 'Fiji patrol boat communications' and so on. In total, the list has dozens and dozens of individual targets of this type.

The Target List (as seen outside the GCSB) is probably produced only once a year, at Budget time, when the GCSB is required to justify its operations to the Officials' Committee for Domestic and External Security Co-ordination, a committee made up of the heads of Defence, Foreign Affairs and the SIS.

This chapter looks at the intelligence produced on the basis of this list: who it is shared with overseas, what it looks like and how they ensure that the right pieces of intelligence reach the right users throughout the alliance. It then looks at the intelligence received by the GCSB from each of the overseas agencies, describing in detail the most secret intelligence that comes from the United States, Britain, Australia and Canada.

As we have seen, the main areas of GCSB intelligence collection include a wide range of political, military and economic intelligence from the South Pacific, obtained by targeting all the independent South Pacific countries and French territories. Outside powers present in the region are also targeted: diplomatic posts (notably Japanese ones), ships (notably Russian ones), non-UKUSA nation bases in Antarctica, French military activities and international organisations active in the South Pacific.

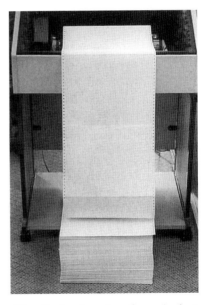

The types of communications being intercepted include information that is crucial to the countries and organisations concerned, revealing their plans, negotiating positions, internal problems, political personality issues and so on. There can be a definite advantage in knowing this information (and a disadvantage to whoever is spied upon). This is why intelligence sharing arrangements are not neutral; by their nature they involve taking sides in political, economic and military conflicts and competition between nations.

There are, therefore, important issues at stake about how the intelligence produced by the GCSB is used in New Zealand and who it is shared with. GCSB staff gave two examples.

New Zealand receives the equivalent of a few metres deep of intelligence reports from overseas each week, most of it from the gigantic NSA in Washington.

201

The first concerns Vanuatu. Whenever someone in the Vanuatu government sends a telex or fax it can be intercepted by the GCSB. This interception has, for example, revealed how Vanuatu intended to approach negotiations on treaties and trade matters. Referring to specific cases in the 1990s, a GCSB intelligence officer explained that although he felt New Zealand was definitely 'monitoring situations' rather than meddling, Australia, with which all the intelligence was being shared, was quite likely to be using the information gained from Vanuatu communications to interfere and 'throw its weight around'.

The second example is from the mid-1980s when the small independent state of Kiribati was negotiating a fishing agreement with the Soviet Union. Fishing agreements represented one of the few ways in which Kiribati could attain some economic independence, but United States fishing boats had been refusing to recognise its 5 million square kilometre exclusive economic zone and were fishing illegally.

Proposals that the agreement include shore facilities for Soviet fishing boats led to alarmist publicity in Australia and New Zealand about the implications of a 'Russian base' in the South Pacific. This was despite the fact that large numbers of Soviet fishing boats used New Zealand ports, where the business they brought was welcomed.

A GCSB officer says the 'right wingers in the bureau [GCSB] worried a lot about this' (Kiribati). Tangimoana was directed to monitor Kiribati intensively and large quantities of communications relating to the agreement were intercepted and shared with the UKUSA allies. Diplomatic efforts (aided by this covert knowledge) were made to stop the plans. By March 1985, the Kiribati government had dropped completely any offers of shore access for the Soviet fishing boats.

So, of everything that is collected, how does the GCSB assess which parts to send into the UKUSA network?

The answer is very simple. The GCSB passes on to its UKUSA allies virtually everything they request. There is no screening process.[1] Intelligence collected and analysed in New Zealand is sent immediately to the American, British, Australian and Canadian agencies and to a range of other military and intelligence addresses in these countries. In the United States, the NSA then distributes New Zealand reports through the rest of the American intelligence and military system, deciding where it should go and who should have access to it.[2]

In addition to the four UKUSA agencies, GCSB staff say that interesting pieces of New Zealand signals intelligence are regularly sent to United States naval commanders in the West Pacific, the Commander-in-Chief of the United States Pacific Command in Hawaii, individual American military services, the Australian and New Zealand liaison officers at the NSA, the GCSB liaison officer in the Australian DSD, the Australia/New Zealand intelligence unit in Singapore (ANZMIS) and, until recently, the GCHQ office in Hong Kong. New Zealand intelligence reports, where relevant, are passed on throughout the rest of the UKUSA countries' intelligence and military organisations and perhaps even to their close allies, notably NATO countries like Germany.

In 1978, a year after the GCSB was formed, the head of the Australian Office of National Assessments, Bob Furlonger, wrote in his annual report that 'our intelligence partners, notably the US, are not very active in the South Pacific and look to Australia and New Zealand in this region'.[3] The logic of the UKUSA intelligence sharing system, when you are the smallest member, is that you give what is asked for. If New Zealand began withholding large amounts of intelligence because it interpreted its interests on some things as being different from other UKUSA nations (as the larger agencies routinely do) its commitment to the alliance would soon be questioned.

David Robie/Lindon Publishing

Large quantities of GCSB intelligence about Walter Lini, former outspoken Prime Minister of Vanuatu, and his nuclear-free government were provided, unscreened, to the intelligence allies.

Inside the closed UKUSA world a curious system of codewords and procedures adds to the mystique of the alliance. On secret intelligence reports, for example, the five agencies have secret codenames corresponding to the five vowels in the alphabet. Using the call sign for each vowel, the GCHQ is known as Alpha Alpha, the DSD is Echo Echo, the GCSB is India India, the NSA is Oscar Oscar and the CSE is Uniform Uniform. The choice of other codewords is also interesting. The main security codewords used in the UKUSA agencies are MORAY, SPOKE and UMBRA. These and other security codewords, following the same UKUSA numerology that has five vowels for the five alliance agencies, always have five letters.

The writing of finished intelligence reports is the work of the K analysts at the GCSB. Their reports follow special UKUSA procedures and are written using a distinctive telegraphic style and jargon. Each report is headed with several lines of abbreviated information and uses language intended to minimise ambiguity.

Three distinct types of signals intelligence reports are produced by the UKUSA agencies: reports, gists and summaries. Reports are direct translations of intercepted messages and have such titles as: 'Message passed between X and Y concerning ...'. Their lengths depend on the extent of the message intercepted. Gists are the intelligence reports produced when a full translation is not deemed necessary. Part précis, part translation, they begin with sentences such as: 'Following is GIST of ...'. Gist is a special signals intelligence term that has had a precise meaning within the United States-British intelligence system at least since the 1940s.[4] Most of the reports and gists produced by the GCSB and other agencies are about half a page in length, but many are only one paragraph, containing a snippet of information.

Summaries are compilations of the information that has already appeared in individual reports and gists, usually over some regular period of time (e.g. weekly or monthly). For example, at one time the GCSB's K4 section (now KP) was producing a weekly summary on French troop movements and transfers in New Caledonia. In the United States the NSA produces large numbers of regular summaries of the intelligence it collects, causing some controversy within the intelligence community over whether the NSA should only do collection and leave analysis to other organisations.

Although no 'sanitising' (an intelligence term referring to the removal of references about where and how information is acquired) occurs in the production of these various intelligence reports, there is a strict rule about not naming New Zealand citizens. Other agencies have the same rule. All such names are replaced by double brackets, for example, '...((the director of a large New Zealand company))...'. According to GCSB staff, this rule is motivated not by concerns about civil rights, but by concerns in the NSA about American citizens demanding access to intelligence reports about themselves. If reports do not contain citizens' names, there is much less chance that the NSA could ever be required to release the reports under the freedom of information laws.

GCSB K unit staff are trained to use standard UKUSA headings for the reports, gists and summaries they produce. Each report is headed up with several lines of abbreviated information including the following: the originating agency, the 'date-time group', the title of the report (like a newspaper headline) and details of which organisations the report is to go to. There are also lines of technical instructions, such as 'ZYN CCCC' and 'BT' for begin or break text, and sometimes two lines stating where the intercepted message was going to and from.

The date-time group (DTG) uses a 24-hour clock set to Greenwich time ('ZULU time') and gives the date, time and month as eight numbers with a Z on the end. A report sent at 3.15 am on 19 November (the 11th month) would have '19031511Z' written at the top.

There is, as well, a set of figures at the top of each report, such as 'FJM25546', indicating a particular military target in Fiji. These are TEXTA designators (described in Chapter 6), which show the nationality, type and individual classification of every interception target — ship, embassy or office — from which the communication came.

The agencies, stations and other addresses the report is to go to are referred to using more special codes (described in the next section) or may be individually listed using their abbreviations or station designators. For example, a particular report may be addressed to all four other agencies, to some major intercept stations in the Asia-Pacific region and to the GCSB's liaison officer at the NSA. These details, on each report, are used by the communications staff to send the reports to the correct recipients.

TOP SECRET
Information or material the unauthorised disclosure of which is likely to damage national interests in an *exceptionally grave* manner.

SECRET
Information or material the unauthorised disclosure of which is likely to damage national interests in a *serious* manner.

CONFIDENTIAL
Information or material the unauthorised disclosure of which is likely to damage national interests in a *significant* manner.

All intelligence reports handled at the GCSB are classified higher than TOP SECRET. The staff believe much of it is overclassified.

In addition to these, all signals intelligence documents are labelled HVCCO (Handle Via COMINT Channels Only) and security codewords are written or stamped at the top and bottom of every page, defining the sensitivity of the document and how it should be handled. The three main UKUSA signals intelligence classifications (there are less often used higher ones too), from least to most secret, are: SECRET MORAY, SECRET SPOKE and TOP SECRET UMBRA.[5] All of these are more secret than TOP SECRET, yet the definition of TOP SECRET used by all the UKUSA nations is: 'information or material the unauthorised disclosure of which is likely to damage national interests in an *exceptionally grave* manner'. There has been a lot of talk between GCSB staff about how many documents, especially United States ones, appear to be overclassified. Reports received by the GCSB from other agencies are mostly headed with all these lines of information, but include routing indicators such as 'YORKNZL', which indicates that the report is being sent to some New Zealand organisations ('NZ'); in this case to L, which stands for the Directorate of Defence Intelligence.

Occasionally reports more secret than UMBRA are seen at the GCSB. Documents stamped GAMMA in bright red are NSA reports containing intercept of high-level Russian communications. They have a very limited distribution, as do DRUID reports, which are produced by 'third parties' to the UKUSA agreement (e.g. Germany, Denmark, Norway, Japan and South Korea). Some senior GCSB staff, including Operations Director Warren Tucker, have been cleared to see DRUID reports.

A combination of some of the most advanced technology in the world and massive expenditure of public money results in the UKUSA network producing staggering quantities of intelligence reports. A highly organised system is required to get each type of intelligence produced to the intelligence and military organisations in each country that wants it.

Each UKUSA agency asks each of the other agencies to provide it with all the intelligence reports it produces on particular subjects of interest and specifies to whom within its government system each type of information should go. (This is exchange of finished reports, produced by analysts within the UKUSA agencies, not of the raw intercept which is distributed within the ECHELON system and described in Chapter 3.) For example, a category of New Zealand-sourced intelligence such as 'Russian research vessels' might be requested by all four agencies, the United States Commander-in-Chief of Pacific Forces, other Australian stations, the Australia-New Zealand defence intelligence unit in Singapore and any number of other individual military, diplomatic or intelligence units.

On the basis of these requests each of the five countries has built up a distribution catalogue that lists all the categories of intelligence it produces. Under each category heading is a list of all the organisations in the five UKUSA countries which should be sent reports produced on that subject. Some subject categories have hundreds of addressees around the world, from organisations such as the NATO Command right down to individual intelligence officers in an American embassy.

United States intelligence couriers from the NSA escort bags off a US Air Force plane at Christchurch airport.

The UKUSA agencies in New Zealand, Australia, Canada and Britain each maintain such a catalogue, built up from the other agencies' requests. But the NSA is in a league of its own. Its worldwide network of eavesdropping stations, spy satellites, underwater listening devices and so on is so big that its distribution lists fill three large blue folders. These are regularly used by the K Unit analysts.[6]

In each country's catalogue, using the international phonetic alphabet, every specific subject category (e.g. 'Russian naval ship movements in the Baltic Sea') is given a two- (occasionally three-) word call sign (e.g. Hotel Bravo). These are ordered alphabetically, starting with 'Alpha Alpha', then 'Alpha Bravo' and so on through the alphabet.

Under each category, so ordered, are listed all approved recipients of reports on that subject in the United States and other countries. These pairs of words serve as 'routing indicators': on the top of an outgoing report from one of the agencies they indicate to the communications staff all the places where that report should be sent.

These addressee catalogues provide a comprehensive list of all the UKUSA stations and facilities around the world, since all of them are on an address list for some categories of intelligence. The British catalogue, for example, lists all the British stations, including the equivalent of New Zealand's Waihopai station at Morwenstow. They are also said to show all kinds of interconnections, from which United States agent in a particular embassy is interested in a certain subject, to the fact that the NSA sends some categories of intelligence to the Canadian Security Intelligence Service.

These mechanics of intelligence sharing could sound sensible and uncontroversial; actually the foreign policy significance of this system is immense. Virtually all information on a requested subject will automatically be sent by New Zealand to any UKUSA agency that has requested it. When the subject is the internal politics of Vanuatu or the economy of the Solomon Islands, and the intelligence New Zealand collects could affect the way those countries are treated by one of the UKUSA countries, no one in the GCSB has the job of judging whether or not it *should* be passing on this or that report. According to GCSB staff, in all but exceptional cases the distribution list is followed.

The intelligence from the other UKUSA agencies is regarded as extremely valuable by the Wellington intelligence organisations. It used to arrive, hundreds of pages a day, off the big printer in the GCSB communications centre. In recent years it has appeared on the screens of the liaison staff.

By far the majority of foreign reports — referred to within the UKUSA agencies as 'product' — arriving at the GCSB come from the massive intelligence machinery of the NSA. Only a bit comes from the Canadians (CSE) and somewhat more from the GCHQ. The DSD provides more than these two but still far less than the NSA. Overall, according to a senior New Zealand diplomat, 'so much is pouring in that it doesn't get read by the people who could use it'.

The reports from the NSA reflect the global military, political and economic interests of the United States government. While the other four agencies have geographical responsibilities within the UKUSA network, the NSA possesses global intelligence collecting capabilities. The NSA deliberately spreads the workload by dividing analysis work for different regions and subjects between the agencies. But GCSB staff say that the NSA collects over the whole world anyway and its analysts will still produce reports on any interesting intercept (whether or not it is covered by another agency).

There are reports arriving at the GCSB from the NSA on a very wide range of countries and issues. According to the people reading them, most of this information, apart from its top secret classifications, is little different, in breadth and composition, from the information publicly available in news-

Many of the United States reports concerned Russian forces, for example in Cam Ranh Bay, Vietnam.

papers and through other open and readily accessible media.

Large quantities of reports are produced about any crises of concern to the United States government: the Iran-Iraq war, Soviets in Afghanistan, Libya, Panama, Poland and Eastern Europe in the late 1980s, Iraq and North Korea in the early 1990s and so on. Also, of course, there was extensive coverage of Soviet activities around the world during all this period.

When an event occurs such as the shooting down of the Korean airliner KAL007 in 1983 or the bombing of the Pan Am jumbo jet over Lockerbie in 1988, the GCSB receives a stream of reports about it as the NSA sifts through all the intercept from that period looking for evidence. With KAL007, the NSA transcripts of Soviet communications provided to the GCSB were said to have shown that the Soviet fighter pilots knew they were shooting down a civilian aircraft (but the intelligence sources were silent about media reports that the aircraft had been deliberately directed into sensitive Soviet airspace).

When international negotiations are taking place the NSA produces large quantities of reports of intercepted communications from the other countries involved, including details of their negotiating plans. The GCSB has, for example, received reports about GATT negotiations and about such meetings as those of the International Whaling Commission.

This intelligence has some relevance to New Zealand, as do the small amounts of NSA material on the South Pacific. The GCSB has requested that the NSA send on anything it picks up about the South Pacific; although ex-Prime Minister David Lange has said that 'New Zealand's contribution matched for usefulness any intelligence about the region the Americans ever gave us'.[7]

At least until the early 1990s, the main preoccupation of the NSA was Soviet intelligence. Most of this was completely irrelevant to New Zealand; although occasionally reports classified GAMMA were received containing transcripts of intercepted conversations of high-ranking Soviet officials relating to New Zealand.

Much more often, the reports were about Soviet military activity in the northern Pacific: weekly reports about and position reports for the Soviet Pacific fleet, reports about military units in Vladivostok and at Cam Ranh Bay in Vietnam and any contacts between Russia and South Pacific nations. The Soviet military reports were the most valued by the Directorate of Defence Intelligence (DDI), as were the large hard copy documents received from the NSA describing all Soviet ships.

The NSA also regularly provided three or four types of documents that arrived at the External Assessments Bureau and DDI stamped ELINT (electronic intelligence) and consisted entirely of long series of numbers. These included intelligence collected by American ocean intelligence satellites (the CLASSIC WIZARD system, which gives the positions of intercepted vessels). The information from these satellites came as long computer readouts containing screeds of figures, each set representing one sweep of the satellite over the Pacific. They are not photographic satellites. Instead, detectors on the satellite intercept and calculate the position of all radar systems operating in the ocean area beneath them. The positions of radars indicate where the ships are and the characteristics of the radar (such as its frequency) are analysed to work out what kinds of vessels they are.[8]

Other ELINT documents contained tracking data for Soviet intelligence satellites — EORSAT (Electronic Ocean Reconnaissance Satellite) and COSMOS satellites — presumably so that New Zealand military authorities would know when the satellites would pass over.

One particularly alarming piece of United States intelligence was delivered to recently elected Prime Minister David Lange by his head intelligence official, Gerald Hensley, in 1984. Hensley rushed into Lange's office saying that there was an unconfirmed report that the Soviet Union had launched a nuclear ballistic missile attack on the United States. Lange, stunned, sat signing letters while the minutes dragged on. Finally Hensley returned and explained that it had been a false alarm.[9] When Lange publicised this event in his book, *Nuclear Free — The New Zealand Way*, Hensley told journalists that he could not recall it. He later explained to the staff in his office that 'one doesn't talk about those things'.

Rainbow Warrior, *1985: 'not one scrap of intelligence' warning of the bombing came from the intelligence allies.*

Of special interest to the SIS are the United States reports on worldwide terrorist activities and a regular worldwide watch list of terrorists. The SIS has about 20 reports a day addressed to it from the UKUSA allies — although, again, these are apparently of little relevance to New Zealand.

On the one instance of international terrorism when signals intelligence might have helped New Zealand — the 1985 French operation to bomb the Greenpeace ship *Rainbow Warrior* — nothing came from the UKUSA intelligence agencies at all: 'not one scrap of intelligence', according to intelligence staff. Similarly, the GCSB operations gave no warning at all.

The lack of intelligence warning of a large foreign operation inside New Zealand is surprising. Either the massive UKUSA intelligence system actually gathered no information or, as was suggested in news stories at the time, the United States and British intelligence authorities may have withheld some information to punish New Zealand for its nuclear-free stand earlier that year. One explanation raises questions about the usefulness of the system to New Zealand, the other about its reliability.

The piles of incoming reports from the NSA consist mostly of daily reports, but also regular (weekly or monthly) summaries of the daily reports. It was some of these summaries (for example the weekly summary on world terrorism) that were cut by the NSA in 1985 during the ANZUS crisis. Withholding the summaries was essentially a token punishment, since New Zealand still received the reports from which these were compiled. Selective withholding of reports, such as those about preparations for the *Rainbow Warrior* bombing, would have been much more serious.

The reports received from the DSD cover the countries in Australia's area of responsibility within the UKUSA network. They include the South West Pacific (for example, the Solomon Islands and Papua New Guinea) and South East Asia.

There is extensive interception of the ASEAN (Association of South East Asian Nations) countries (Thailand, Malaysia, Singapore, Indonesia and the

East Timor: Australia and New Zealand intelligence agencies know much more about Indonesian actions than they tell the public. This photograph shows Indonesian paratroopers over East Timor, 1981.

Philippines) but not American territories in Micronesia. ASEAN meetings receive special attention, with communications of the countries involved being intercepted to reveal the topics discussed, positions being taken and policy being considered.

Indonesia was a major target of the DSD during the 1980s. The GCSB received regular reports on Indonesian government activities in West Papua and East Timor. The governments of Australia and New Zealand know far more about Indonesian actions in these areas than they choose to reveal publicly. Malaysia is also regularly targeted, including information about operations of the Malaysian secret service.

During the late 1980s and 1990s the conflict between the Papua New Guinea government and the secessionist Bougainville Revolutionary Army has been extensively monitored by the DSD, as have the government communications in the neighbouring Solomon Islands. Large quantities of this intelligence were provided to New Zealand. In 1988 the DSD established the new signals intelligence station near Bamaga, at Cape York on the north-east tip of Australia, specifically to monitor this conflict. It has been operated remotely from the DSD station at Cabarlah since 1990.[10]

The DSD has also provided the GCSB with large quantities of reports about Russian naval, scientific and commercial ships in the West Pacific and Indian Ocean.

Finally, like the GCSB, the DSD has responsibility within the UKUSA network for analysing sections of the worldwide interception of Japanese diplomatic communications. The DSD produces reports on interception of Japanese posts — the JAD intelligence — within its geographical area of responsibility and possibly elsewhere.

The most valued British intelligence received are the minutes of the Joint Intelligence Committee, which arrive at the GCSB from Whitehall every Friday.

British High Commission

The relatively small numbers of intelligence reports received from the CSE in Canada have mainly concerned Russian shipping in the North Pacific and the CSE's share of JAD intelligence analysis. Even when this is not of great interest to the New Zealand intelligence users, the Russian and JAD reports are still received as part of routine co-operation between analysis cells in the different UKUSA agencies working on the same subjects (allowing them to see what is being produced on their subject elsewhere).

The CSE, like the DSD, occasionally provides intelligence reports on a 'New Zealand Eyes Only' basis, because they contain information about the United States.

The reports received from the GCHQ cover areas of concern to the British government around the world. Thus, during the 1980s, for example, the SIS was receiving a major weekly report via the GCSB communications centre listing Libyan people in Britain. The GCHQ also occasionally sends on reports based on intercept of South Pacific communications, but this is a low priority area for the GCHQ.

The most comprehensive coverage of events around the world is contained in the minutes of the British Joint Intelligence Committee (JIC) which arrive in New Zealand every Friday. These contain summaries of all the situations around the world that interest the British government. After the ANZUS crisis in the mid-1980s, pieces of these minutes would occasionally be missing, suggesting that there had been discussion and/or intelligence presented of which New Zealand was the subject. Similarly, sections of the minutes are occasionally marked 'New Zealand Eyes Only' because they contain criticism of the United States. The GCHQ provided New Zealand with large quantities of intelligence about the Argentinian military during the Falklands War.

A final interesting document provided by the GCHQ is stored in a vault inside the GCSB headquarters. Called *Public References to SIGINT*, it lists all the security breaches since the Second World War when signals intelligence secrets have been spoken or written about in public. The document is large — about 10 centimetres thick — and quotes all the offending excerpts from books and articles together with the date and place of publication and the author. Similarly, transcripts of information disclosed on radio or television are also given, with details of where and when the breach occurred.

It is said to be a very comprehensive record of everyone who has ever mentioned anything regarded as classified about UKUSA signals intelligence. Someone who has read it recalls that James Bamford (author of *The Puzzle Palace*) is there, as are the Australian researcher Des Ball and, several times, New Zealand researcher Owen Wilkes. (There are also said to be entries concerning this writer.) Its comprehensive worldwide coverage shows that individual agencies like the GCSB make it their business to report to the GCHQ on perceived breaches by the citizens of their own countries.

Read as a whole, it apparently adds up to quite a good history of signals intelligence in the UKUSA countries, partly because over time a lot of correct information has reached the public, and also because it includes editor's notes, which elaborate on the breaches. *Public References to SIGINT* is classified SECRET SPOKE and is seen only by senior people in the GCSB.

There is no doubt about the volume of intelligence New Zealand receives from the other UKUSA agencies. The more pertinent question, left to the final chapter, is: how useful is this intelligence?

CHAPTER THIRTEEN

WHO WATCHES THE WATCHERS?
OVERSEEING THE INTELLIGENCE AGENCIES

For many months in 1984-85 Dr Peter Wills, a physics lecturer and part-time researcher into intelligence activities, had been bombarding the Prime Minister and the newly exposed GCSB with Official Information Act requests about the bureau's activities and overseas links.

One of these requests concerned a small reference to New Zealand in the voluminous records of military construction hearings before the United States Congress's Committee of Appropriations.[1] The record showed that the United States Department of Defence had waived US$29,942 of charges to New Zealand, relating to the design and development component of supplying 'HGX-83 COMSEC' equipment. The waiver was granted because the department judged that supplying the equipment would 'significantly advance US interests in standardisation'.[2]

The small reference concerned a large development. The equipment in question was encrypting machines for use in GCSB communications centres that were then being set up in the new Freyberg Building headquarters in Wellington and at the new Tangimoana station. The date of the purchase was 21 July 1982, just before the opening of the new communications centres. Until then the Ministry of Defence had handled GCSB communications. The new equipment would, for the first time, connect the GCSB directly into the UKUSA network.[3]

Peter Wills suspected that the equipment could be for the GCSB and so wrote asking the government about it. The reply prepared for Prime Minister David Lange by one of his officials began by noting the number of official information requests Dr Wills had been writing and said: 'In view of the consistent responses you have received to all the above correspondence it should be clear to you that the Government means what it said when it used the phrase — the detail of the operations of the GCSB... is, and will remain, secret'. Taking umbrage at questions in Dr Wills' letter about government access to intelligence information held by officials, the letter went on: 'As Prime Minister, and Minister with broad responsibilities for intelligence and security matters, I assure you that I have ready access to all information, wherever it is held in Government. I will also reiterate that I have been briefed fully on the GCSB....' The letter then explained that the HGX-83 waiver 'was merely a refund of over-payment' and that the equipment was to be used in the Ministry of Defence's 'new second generation communications network'.[4]

The contracts for supplying equipment for this network were not even signed until two years after the HGX-83 equipment arrived in 1982 and the system was not operational for another five years after that — years after Lange's letter.

The Prime Minister's intelligence officials were putting untruths in his mouth to hide the United States co-operation in New Zealand signals intelligence communications — and in doing so were demonstrating that the Prime Minister is anything but fully briefed on the GCSB.

Ten years later, on 19 December 1995, members of the parliamentary press gallery were invited to an unprecedented off-the-record briefing on the eighth floor of the Beehive. That evening new legislation was being introduced to Parliament to 'increase the level of oversight and review of intelligence and security agencies' by creating a new parliamentary oversight committee and a position of Inspector-General of Intelligence and Security. The usually elusive directors of the GCSB and SIS, Ray Parker and Don McIver, were present with the head of the Prime Minister's Department, Simon Murdoch, to explain the legislation to the journalists.

The news of the legislation was strictly embargoed until 7.30 that evening, when Jim Bolger introduced it to Parliament. Seven thirty is also very close to deadlines for the morning newspapers, leaving little time for analysis or seeking alternative views. All the papers ran uncritical stories, closely following the briefing they had received three hours earlier. The limitations and drawbacks of the bill only become apparent on closer reading.

Headlines such as 'NZ spies come under new watchdog' and radio stories about spies 'coming in from the cold' created the desired public impression: that the new legislation was a significant advance for control of the intelligence organisations. The fact that the bill was welcomed by the usually secretive bureaucrats at the briefing should have been warning enough that it was not.

David Lange spent half a day at the GCSB headquarters in mid-1985 trying to find out for himself what was going on. Many important operations and developments remained secret.

The Labour government years from 1984 to 1990 were a period of rapid expansion of New Zealand's secret intelligence activities and alliance links. This was not Labour policy and nor was it pushed by anyone in the government. Much of it occurred without the government even being informed.

The intelligence officials did not tell the government about New Zealand's entry into the ECHELON system, the most significant development since the GCSB was established, Singleton's role while he was an NSA officer in the GCSB, various developments in military signals intelligence operations, most details of the GCSB structures and changes to these, various important GCSB targets (e.g. Japanese diplomatic intelligence), Navy and SAS intelligence missions after the Fiji coup, how large a proportion of GCSB staff and resources goes to intelligence operations, and the use of the Waihopai station by overseas agencies and its integration with the global network. If more information were available, this list would certainly be longer.

Where the government knowingly agreed to some developments, it believed it was compensating for diminished alliance links after the ANZUS conflict. Unwittingly, Labour oversaw increased integration into the American-led intelligence alliance, a situation maintained, with a similar lack of knowledge, by the National government that came to power in 1990.

The arrangements for control of secret intelligence activities in New Zealand initially appear reasonable. The highest politician in the land, the Prime Minister, is the minister in charge of all intelligence matters. A high-powered officials committee, and now the new parliamentary committee, review the annual reports and finances of the intelligence organisations. Since intelligence operations are by nature secret, only people with special clearances are allowed to know what goes on and, even then, only on a need to know basis.

Yet the effect of these arrangements is to remove intelligence activities almost entirely from democratic control; the public has almost no information about or influence over what occurs and, in respect of intelligence, it makes little difference which government they elect. As the Labour years showed, these arrangements have also, to a considerable extent, removed intelligence activities from government control. Information is regularly withheld by government officials so that New Zealand's elected 'decision-makers' do not know what is going on.

Control of the New Zealand intelligence organisations, before and after the 1996 oversight legislation, is highly centralised. Usually only the Prime Minister is allowed knowledge of the organisations' operations and his close staff and ministerial colleagues are told almost nothing.

The Prime Minister is perhaps the busiest person in the country, dealing with continuous meetings, public engagements and crises. Every available gap in a packed schedule is filled with phone calls and hurried discussions with staff. There is little time to think, let alone probe deeply into issues where the officials are secretive or inclined only to provide information and advice that suits their preferred policies.

David Lange once spoke publicly, in September 1988, about the attitude of his officials:

> *When we took office in 1984 it was taken for granted by the government's advisers that we would change the anti-nuclear policy. They had no doubt about it. They just assumed that when we were confronted with what they called the realities of global power politics we would back off. When after several months it started to sink in that we were serious, they started to get heavy.... It is not easy to be told all the time by people who are advisers to the government that what you are doing is wrong and dangerous.[5]*

A senior government official from the period described some of these officials, notably from Foreign Affairs, as 'not just determined but downright nasty'. They were, he said, highly political, sure they were right and very clever at getting the government to do what they thought should happen. It is not easy for a single, busy politician to stand up to a determined bureaucratic agenda.

The best interests of the intelligence alliance were represented in this process by a powerful network of past and current Foreign Affairs officials. Two of the most influentially placed ex-Foreign Affairs men during this period were Gerald Hensley, the head of the Prime Minister's Department and later intelligence co-ordinator, and Denis McLean, Secretary of Defence.[6] Both were highly critical of the nuclear-free policy and strong defenders of the American alliance.

The culture of the Foreign Affairs ministry tends to be rigid and conservative. New staff soon learn that noting carefully what the United States and Australia are doing helps their career prospects; independent thinking does not. In

Ministry of Foreign Affairs and Trade: a condescending attitude to politicians and contemptuous attitude to the public.

my experience, many also develop a condescending attitude to politicians ('who come and go') and a contemptuous attitude to the public. Former Foreign Affairs and Trade officials are found throughout the small New Zealand government bureaucracy in various important roles affecting foreign policy.[7] A familiar phrase, when inter-departmental calculations are being made, is 'Don't worry, he's one of our people.'

These attitudes are present in the Officials Committee for Domestic and External Security Co-ordination (DESC),[8] which oversees external intelligence activities. Although this committee is at times the scene of inter-agency competition (for example, over how the intelligence budget is shared between the various agencies), it is inconceivable that it would ever question the intelligence alliance.

Even this committee is told little about what actually occurs at the GCSB. The DESC officials see papers on GCSB operations only once a year — the GCSB's brief Annual Report and Corporate Plan.[9] Copies are handed out by Ray Parker at the beginning of one meeting and collected up again at the end. Also, about March each year the committee gets to discuss the GCSB Budget estimates for the year, amounting to five to 10 pages of information which it discusses during one two- to three-hour meeting.[10] These are the

219

papers that the parliamentary oversight committee will see. According to people on the DESC committee, they provide very little insight into what is occurring inside the GCSB. Other important documents are never seen.[11] There have been various instances during these brief appearances before the DESC committee when Ray Parker has frustrated the officials by refusing to provide even them with information.

Prime Ministers hardly ever visit the GCSB. Lange did visit the head-quarters twice and Tangimoana once, trying to find out for himself what was happening. The longest visit was in mid-1985 when he spent half a day visiting most sections in the headquarters and talking to the staff. (Many GCSB staff were impressed by the visit. Jim Bolger made a less probing prime ministerial visit in 1991.) But Lange never found out about many of the most significant activities and links. If the GCSB and military chiefs hold back information on highly secret things, the Prime Minister has no other way of finding out. In many instances he would not even know what questions to ask.

The intelligence officials are adept at giving Prime Ministers pieces of interesting information designed to persuade them of the value of the organisations concerned. For example, on 20 December 1995, the morning after the new intelligence legislation was introduced, former Prime Minister Sir Geoffrey Palmer spoke at length on National Radio in enthusiastic support of the SIS and GCSB. Asked whether New Zealand needs the GCSB, he replied:

> There is no doubt that in this modern electronic age that agency fulfils a very important role.... It has made contributions in the past in New Zealand's welfare in many different ways. I remember, for example, as a minister getting information about how much tuna was being caught by drift-net fishing from these means. Now that was a very useful and important piece of information in New Zealand's campaign against drift-net fishing.

During his time as Deputy Prime Minister and then Prime Minister Palmer was also Minister for the Environment, with a strong personal interest in subjects such as drift-net fishing. It is clear that the intelligence officials knew environment-oriented intelligence would appeal to Palmer and the Labour government and worked hard to produce some for them. Tangimoana intensively monitored fishing boats using drift nets for a while, to useful effect. But it was not and is not the main work of the GCSB.

In his one year as Prime Minister (1989-90), Palmer opened the Waiho-pai station and was in charge of the GCSB as it was integrated into the

ECHELON system. He was told practically nothing about these developments and was unaware of their significance. He may or may not have been aware that most of the GCSB's work at that time was making small contributions to foreign operations against Russia, China and Japan.

How do the intelligence officials justify withholding information from the Prime Minister of the country? Just as 'operational security' is a catch-all justification for withholding information from the public, so the officials feel justified in providing information to the Prime Minister only on a 'need to know' basis.

The need to know principle — one of the fundamental concepts in the intelligence world — makes some sense within an intelligence organisation for keeping secrets secret. The basis of needing to know in these cases is very clear: people need to know something only if this is necessary to get the work done. But when it is applied to the government, Parliament and public, the principle is perilously unclear. What criteria should be used to judge whether they need to know and who makes the decisions?

Currently these crucial decisions are made by the public servants and the basis appears to be purely pragmatic. This means that, unless he specifically insists on being given certain information, the only time a Prime Minister really needs to know anything is when funding is being sought. If the Prime Minister does not really need to know about something, even as central as, say, the ECHELON system, why take the unnecessary risk of the information leaking by telling him? Why risk any disagreement?

A well-placed GCSB officer says that more information is actively withheld from Labour than from National governments, since Labour is seen as being less in tune with the orientation of the intelligence agencies. But they say National governments ask fewer questions anyway and are usually comfortable about leaving the officials to run things. So the effect is much the same either way. There is little doubt about how the need to know principle would be interpreted by officials if a less compliant future government were thought to be threatening the alliance by attempting to investigate and change the intelligence agencies. The 1996 Intelligence and Security Agencies legislation (described in the next section) was part of preparations for just such a possibility.

Another obstacle to effective government control is the unnecessarily high level of secrecy imposed on all intelligence matters. The need to maintain secrecy deprives the Prime Minister of people with whom to talk over issues and from whom to get alternative advice. Even on a relatively minor question such as the HGX-83 equipment, how could a busy Prime Minister ever check whether the letter drafted on his behalf was correct? The officials' power is increased by the Prime Minister's isolation.

Prime Ministers are bound by the indoctrination regulations that prohibit them from discussing intelligence matters with non-indoctrinated people: which means most other politicians, all but one or two of their staff, members of their party and the public. Lange, for example, was known by his staff to have had no one — friend, staff or colleague — with whom he discussed intelligence matters.

Intelligence staff argue that this is in part a problem of Prime Ministers' own making. Senior intelligence staff who served during several administrations described how Prime Ministers 'love receiving secret intelligence and they often don't want to share it with their Cabinet Ministers'. They tell a recurring story. The Prime Minister, who may have said all kinds of things about intelligence in Opposition, receives his first briefing from one of the intelligence heads. When they have finished, the official offers to brief some of the Cabinet ministers (often the Minister of Defence) so that the Prime Minister has colleagues to discuss things with. The Prime Minister reflects for a while, and then says he thinks he will just look after it himself for now. The officials say this story has repeated itself several times over the last 25 years, with Prime Ministers from both main parties. They assume that the Prime Ministers see information as power and also do not trust their fellow ministers to look after classified intelligence.

Frank O'Flynn, Minister of Defence 1984-87: GCSB staff were specifically instructed that he not be given any signals intelligence.

During six years of intelligence expansion under the Labour government, two ministers on the Cabinet Domestic and External Security Committee said they were shown almost no papers concerning intelligence. A few ministers were indoctrinated to see selected External Assessments Bureau reports containing signals intelligence (never raw intelligence from the GCSB) and the reports were brought to them by an EAB official who waited while they read them and then took the papers away again (Lange had expanded this practice). But they were seeing only a fraction of the product and were told nothing about the intelligence operations.

Some ministers are arbitrarily branded as unreliable. An example of this was the 1984-87 Minister of Defence, Frank O'Flynn, one of the few Ministers of Defence in New Zealand history who actively questioned the advice he was getting from his officials. He was indoctrinated by GCSB Director Colin Hanson and then wondered why he never saw any secret intelligence reports. GCSB staff say they were specifically instructed from above that he should not be given any signals intelligence.

Most Members of Parliament have not even known the name of New Zealand's largest intelligence agency.

Later O'Flynn asked his Chief of Defence Staff, Ewan Jamieson, 'Where's all this secret intelligence I'm supposed to see?' Jamieson replied politely, 'It's in the briefings we give you.'

A senior public servant interviewed for this chapter summed up the situation succinctly. He said centralising control of intelligence activities on the Prime Minister suits officials very well because the Prime Minister cannot control them, but their status is enhanced by being able to say that they are acting with his or her authority.

Almost all news stories about the Intelligence and Security Agencies Bill presented the legislation in the same way:

New Zealand's spies are edging out of the shadows, with legislation setting up a new watchdog and requiring them to report to a committee of MPs.

The bill introduced to Parliament by Prime Minister Jim Bolger last night updates security legislation for the post-Cold War era and responds to years of criticism that New Zealand's intelligence services get too little scrutiny.[12]

In the past parliamentary select committees have theoretically had the job of reviewing the intelligence organisations' activities during parliamentary Budget hearings. The EAB has been reasonably open during this process, but not the GCSB, SIS or military intelligence units. Here is a quote from one such session in 1988 where the co-ordinator of intelligence, Gerald Hensley, was being questioned about the GCSB, in the news because of protests during the building of the Waihopai station:

Jim Sutton (committee chair): "You're not going to tell us how much you're spending, how much you want us to approve; you're not telling us who's spending it, but nevertheless you feel we should approve this expenditure."

Hensley: "That's true."

Doug Kidd: "The source of the money is Parliament, and the presumption is that we don't need to know, we won't be allowed to know, we're not considered worthy of clearance even on a selective basis, and yet some public servant, only remotely answerable to us, is cleared by other public servants to know."

Hensley: "That has been Government policy."[13]

Also in 1988, Parliament's Foreign Affairs and Defence Committee unanimously urged that the GCSB be accountable to Parliament. It recommended that 'the House examine the method by which the GCSB reports its expenditure and annual activities to Parliament and, in order to meet public concern, strongly advocates that clearer lines of accountability be established for the justification of the expenditure of this money through Vote Defence'.[14]

The following year, for reasons related to restructuring of the Ministry of Defence (where GCSB expenditure had been hidden until then), the Prime Minister approved the publication of an annual budget figure for the GCSB. But Parliament's influence did not increase. For example, in February 1995 a select committee tabled the following two-sentence GCSB report in Parliament: 'The Government Administration Committee has conducted the financial review of the performance of the New Zealand Security Intelligence Service in 1993/94 and has no matters to bring to the attention of the House. The committee recommends that the House take note of its report.'[15] This careless duplication of the SIS review tabled the same day summed up the perfunctory nature of the GCSB review.

Although the GCSB is located only 100 metres from Parliament, most MPs could not even tell you the name of New Zealand's largest intelligence organisation. Yet of the 66 separate government departments and organisations for which Parliament approves the budgets each year, the GCSB's is relatively large, coming about midway down the list; it is larger than 27 others reviewed by Parliament such as the State Services Commission, the Ministry of Housing and the Department of the Prime Minister and Cabinet.

The intelligence officials have also applied the need to know principle to

MPs. When John Blincoe, one of the few MPs with an interest in intelligence matters, asked the GCSB for permission to visit the Waihopai station in 1994, Ray Parker replied, without referring the request to the Prime Minister:

> *It has been the policy of successive Governments that information concerning the facility should be disclosed strictly on the basis of a demonstrated "need to know". While I fully understand your interest as a local Member of Parliament, I am unable to accept that fact alone as evidence of such a need.*[16]

The 1996 intelligence oversight legislation at first appeared to be a significant improvement on this situation. The legislation created a committee of MPs, the Intelligence and Security Committee, to examine the 'policy, administration and expenditure' of the GCSB and the SIS and to receive and consider their annual reports. This committee includes both government and Opposition members.

At the same time the position of Inspector-General of Intelligence and Security, to be held by a retired High Court judge, was created. The Inspector-General investigates the activities of the GCSB and SIS to ensure that they do not break any New Zealand laws and investigates complaints about whether they have adversely affected any New Zealanders.

On closer inspection, however, it is clear that the legislation was carefully designed to give only token influence to Parliament and to prevent any important new information reaching the public or the politicians. Each 'opening up' clause is accompanied by clause after clause of conditions and restrictions that serve to entrench secrecy and unaccountability.

To begin with, the five-person Intelligence and Security Committee is chaired by the Prime Minister or someone he or she appoints, two other members are chosen by him or her (giving an automatic majority) and one of the other members can be nominated only with his or her agreement. Prime Ministers, and the officials who advise them, have total control over the committee,[17] removing much of the point of having this parliamentary check and balance to government oversight.

Next, the committee's functions are strictly confined to general policy and reviewing the finances. The legislation specifically states that the committee cannot enquire into any matter that is 'operationally sensitive'.[18] If politicians cannot review who is spied on, what intelligence is collected and who it is shared with, their role in overseeing intelligence organisations is all but irrelevant. Even if they are briefed on some general intelligence targets, they cannot check this information or discover what they are not being told.

The committee members will be indoctrinated, which means they cannot pass on any secret information they do receive to their colleagues or the public. Indoctrination restricts politicians more than it assists them. Even if members of the committee find out about something they do not agree with, they are prohibited from doing anything with that information outside the committee.

The legislation says far more about the information to which the committee is not allowed access than that which it can see. Unless specifically overruled by the Prime Minister, the GCSB and SIS do not have to supply any 'sensitive information' to the committee; and it is left to the directors of the two organisations to decide what is covered by the legislation's broad definition of sensitive information.[19] 'Sensitive information' basically includes all information about the organisations' operations.[20] The Prime Minister is given no right to overrule the officials if the information comes from another agency. The legislation also ensures that the committee has no independent staff to help its investigations; staff are appointed by the head of the Prime Minister's Department.

Restricting access to information in this way is crucial to rendering the committee ineffective. In the aftermath of publication of the Pentagon Papers and of Watergate, the United States Senate's Church Committee undertook an extensive investigation into illegal activities and abuse of power by the United States intelligence organisations in the 1970s. In the preface to its final report it wrote: 'The most important lesson to be derived from our experience is that effective oversight is impossible without regular access to the underlying working documents of the intelligence community. Top level briefings do not adequately describe the realities. For that the documents are a necessary supplement and at times the only source.'[21]

In New Zealand, the Inspector-General of Intelligence and Security has more potential to make a difference, but again conditions and restrictions undermine the role. Overseas experience has shown that there is a high risk of individuals in these roles being 'captured' by the intelligence organisations for which they are supposed to act as a watchdog. Therefore an immediate and fundamental flaw in the legislation is that the Inspector-General is appointed by the Prime Minister (the leader of the Opposition only needs to be consulted). Governments tend to choose for these roles people who can be relied on not to rock the boat. The more a government needs an independent watchdog, the less likely it is to provide one.

The functions of the Inspector-General are limited strictly to whether the organisations are acting within the law. He or she also investigates complaints by New Zealand citizens, residents and organisations about the

The GCSB director Ray Parker looks on (from the rear) during a 1996 hearing on new intelligence oversight legislation. Weaker than any equivalent overseas legislation, the bill was packaged to look like openness while entrenching the secrecy of the agencies before the first MMP election.

intelligence organisations, but only about whether they have been 'adversely affected in a personal capacity'. Again there is clause after clause of secrecy provisions.

Checking that the GCSB and SIS act within the law sounds good, but it would be more pertinent to be checking the ethics, appropriateness and mandate for their actions. Many public submissions made this point, but the committee report on the bill concluded that 'a further extension of the Inspector-General's jurisdiction to include matters of "the public interest" is not desirable'. But merely checking that they act within the law contributes little. The GCSB has no statute defining its functions, powers and limitations on these — so there is no law against which to test it. Chapter 10 described how the GCSB successfully sidesteps telecommunications legislation anyway.

It will be years before the results of these legislative changes can be assessed, but experience in other UKUSA countries shows that the intelligence activities most needing investigation are the ones the politicians are least likely to find out about. There is a strong likelihood that the public will notice no change at all — and it appears that this was the purpose from the start.

The legislation was prepared by the same officials who have effectively kept intelligence activities outside government control in the past. The restrictions already described and the techniques by which the officials' recommendations became law are a good example of how their influence works.

A comparison of the New Zealand bill with parallel legislation in Australia and Canada shows that, in almost every respect, this one had been drafted with more limitations on its effectiveness.

The long review that led to the legislation was conducted entirely by officials, with no public involvement. A small, hand-picked group of bureaucrats, academics and past and present politicians was minimally consulted. Then the legislation arrived in Parliament without warning just two days before the Christmas break, with the carefully timed briefing for journalists to ensure the right spin on the news stories.

The advertisements calling for public submissions were published just before Christmas, the traditional time for announcements intended to be missed, with submissions due six weeks later when most New Zealanders were still concerned only with summer holidays. A special committee chaired by the Prime Minister and composed mainly of senior government ministers 'considered' the 100 submissions — virtually all of which opposed the bill — over three days of hearings early in 1996 and then the legislation, in most important respects unchanged, was hurried through Parliament.

This does not sound like legislation motivated by a desire for greater openness and accountability. The point of the exercise appears to have been not the token areas of greater transparency, but putting into legislation all the restrictions that went with these. When the legislation was introduced to Parliament there was less than a year to go before New Zealand had to hold its first general election under the MMP proportional representation system, with the likelihood of coalition government. The legislation to 'increase the level of oversight and review of intelligence and security agencies' could be seen as a clever bureaucratic manoeuvre to entrench secrecy and secure the alliance links before some unpredictable future multi-party Parliament could decide to introduce its own, possibly more effective, oversight structures and mechanisms.

This explanation of the legislation, and of *whose* legislation it really is, was reinforced by the comments from Sir Geoffrey Palmer, one of those consulted on the bill. He told National Radio:

> *I think what has happened here is that the intelligence community in New Zealand, which is a very thoughtful community, has thought: we've got to*

*make sure that these activities are secure in an MMP environment, we've
got to secure that there's parliamentary support across the board for them,
we've got to therefore secure that there is parliamentary involvement in
oversight.... I apprehend that there was some nervousness on the part of the
intelligence community as to what might occur if this problem was not
dealt with before the first MMP election.*[22]

Intelligence staff say that there was a mood of confidence and satisfac-
tion in the agencies after getting 'their' bill passed. Unless a majority can be
found in a future Parliament to amend it, this legislation prohibits politicians
from ever being able to investigate what goes on inside the intelligence organisations.

Effective government control of intelligence organisations requires the
politicians in charge to have sufficient time and information to do the job,
colleagues and officials with whom they can talk over issues and work out
policy, ways of ensuring that policy decisions are implemented and some
debate in wider fora (including Parliament) to review and challenge, provide
new and alternative ideas and ensure that the politicians involved are doing
their job.

None of this is currently happening, and the result is that Prime Ministers and Parliament tinker at the margins, if they have any influence at all.
They mostly leave the GCSB to be, as one Prime Minister put it, 'a ship
which runs itself'.

There is a final fundamental issue to consider about the limits of government
control over secret intelligence activities: can the Prime Minister of a junior
alliance partner make major decisions that clash with the interests of the
dominant allies and stay in the alliance? It seems doubtful.

Lange did know some of what the GCSB was doing while he was Prime
Minister. He knew, for example, that over half of the intelligence effort of
the GCSB during his term went to spying on Russia and China. Although
Lange would have chosen neither country as a prime target — he believed
that New Zealand's intelligence effort should be focused on the South Pacific — Russia and China remained priorities.

Why? The Labour government had already had a serious conflict with
the two nuclear-armed UKUSA allies over nuclear warships. The Australian
government had sided with the United States and Britain against New Zealand. Lange was being continually told by his advisers that antagonising the
allies further would be highly damaging.

What Lange did instead was to try to satisfy himself that the GCSB was at least not doing too much harm. Although he never discussed any of the detail, he did confide to close colleagues that it was 'harmlessly dated, antediluvian', but that it 'didn't imperil New Zealand'. 'As long as it doesn't hurt New Zealand's interests,' he is recalled as saying, 'I don't care if they study lunar craters.' He also accepted (questionable) reassurances that the Tangimoana station had no role in Cold War nuclear strategies. In other words, as an already embattled Prime Minister, trying to change the GCSB to fit New Zealand's, rather than the allies', needs did not seem sufficiently important to warrant all the trouble and effort involved.

The prevailing view in the intelligence agencies is that the alliance is highly beneficial to the country and that New Zealand is extraordinarily lucky to be involved. The intelligence officials are prepared to provide whatever the alliance wants of them in exchange for privileged access to intelligence from the massive global network. This is the main argument they use within organisations such as the GCSB and in their dealings with Prime Ministers. Its simplest version is that New Zealand acts as the alliance's source of intelligence on the South Pacific (and occasionally elsewhere) in exchange for intelligence about the rest of the world.

Prime Minister Jim Bolger. A senior public servant summed it up: 'Centralising control of intelligence on the Prime Minister suits officials very well, because the Prime Minister cannot control them but their status is enhanced by being able to say they are acting with his authority'.

Although, privately, Lange always questioned this 'reciprocity argument', since New Zealand was giving intelligence on the region it was most concerned about and in return receiving large amounts of intelligence on Russians, he did accept a wider argument, which was that to lose the alliance links would be 'totally destabilising'. This is the main force of the officials' argument. They regularly argue that New Zealand must conform to the international systems, procedures and regulations, provide whatever information is asked for and, in fact, please the allies in every other area of foreign and defence policy as the price of retaining privileged alliance status.

Overall, the only person in a position to control the intelligence organisations in New Zealand, the Prime Minister, is, in practice, not in control. If the officials can 'capture' the Prime Minister, as frequently occurs, political control becomes little more than a formality. Even if the Prime Minister wants to assert control, he is hindered by insufficient information, the ever-present constraints of time, wily and politicised officials and, underlying it all, the lack of manoeuvrability of a small country inside a big intelligence alliance.

The signals intelligence alliance is the strongest part of a much wider structure of American alliance links. There is a series of interlocking five-nation alliance agreements between Britain, Canada, Australia, New Zealand and, always in the dominant role, the United States, which, combined, are far more influential than any temporary government. These include agreements covering other types of intelligence, such as a security intelligence agreement (probably called CAZAB) which links the New Zealand SIS to allied organisations such as Britain's MI5.[23] Equally significant are 12 separate military agreements,[24] including ABCA (see Chapter 11) and the CCEB agreement (on standardisation of allied communications and electronic systems), under which GCSB and military staff are currently involved in planning a new communications link between the allies for the 21st century. These agreements, and many other agreements involving two, three or four of the allies, openly commit member countries to pursue 'the fullest co-operation and collaboration, as well as the highest possible degree of interoperability'[25].

The practical work of integrating the allies' equipment, training and doctrines occurs in some 130 working groups and committees formed around these agreements.[26] Irrespective of what Prime Ministers and other politicians do or say, this is where most decisions are really made.

There are no regular publications or annual reports to Parliament available about the GCSB and the other secret intelligence organisations. The only official ways to get information are requests under the Official Information Act and questioning by MPs at occasional select committee meetings or in parliamentary question time.

The Official Information Act was introduced in 1982, replacing the old British-style Official Secrets Act. Using the act, any person can write to a government organisation to ask questions and request documents. The purposes of the act are:

To increase progressively the availability of official information to the people of New Zealand in order —

(i) To enable their more effective participation in the making and administration of laws and policies; and

(ii) To promote the accountability of Ministers of... and officials —

and thereby promote respect for the law and promote the good government of New Zealand... [and]

To protect official information to the extent consistent with the public interest....

It sounds perfect, and overall the act is a powerful tool, but in the case of intelligence agencies it rarely works. Most MPs and members of the public who use it give up after one or two unsuccessful attempts. Even the tenacious Peter Wills eventually decided it was futile.

Well over 100 official information requests were made during the research for this book, constituting by far the majority of requests received by the intelligence organisations over a 10-year period. There were so many refusals that the information gained makes up only a tiny fraction of the material contained in these pages.

The GCSB proved to be the most secretive of the government agencies, withholding all files concerning the Second World War,[27] refusing to release old staff numbers (all of which are in open public service publications anyway), deleting almost everything from the staff circulars it did release and so on. Replies were usually dispatched on the very last day they could legally be sent and quite often contained terse comments.

The GCSB gets away with these refusals because the act is stacked against the public on intelligence and military subjects. One of the many places within the bureaucracy where Foreign Affairs made sure its influence was felt was the Danks Committee, which originally drafted the Official Information Act. Section 6, defining 'conclusive reasons for withholding official information', allows information to be withheld if making available that information would (among other things) 'be likely to prejudice the security or defence of New Zealand or the international relations of the New Zealand Government....' Section 10 goes further, allowing the organisation to 'neither confirm nor deny the existence or non-existence of that information'. Section 9 specifically excludes any consideration of the public interest in decisions made under sections 6 and 10, and section 31 allows the Prime Minister to issue a certificate preventing the Ombudsman from recommending information be released if it would be likely to prejudice the security and defence of New Zealand. (The restrictive section 6 wording — 'would be likely to prejudice the security or defence of New Zealand...' — is repeated word for word in the 1996 Intelligence and Security Committee Act as grounds for agencies withholding information from MPs. This wording has a proven record of blocking almost all important information, giving the committee little hope of playing a serious oversight role).

The effectiveness of the act also depends on the attitude of the officials concerned. One former Foreign Affairs officer described in detail taking a ministry-run course on the Official Information Act in which those involved had to prepare answers to information requests. He said the clear objective was to give as little information as possible and they were marked accordingly. As a result, it is easier for a researcher in New Zealand to get information about United States intelligence activities (using the American Freedom of Information Act) than it is to extract information about New Zealand's intelligence agencies.

Questions in Parliament and by select committees are also easily and routinely evaded. They always receive some variant of the following reply: 'Successive governments have had a well-established policy of not commenting on operational intelligence matters and I do not intend to depart from the policy'.[28] Whether the Intelligence and Security Committee can extract more information is yet to be seen, but it appears doubtful.

Intelligence officials believe they have good reasons for maintaining operational secrets. If the target individuals and organisations know that they are being intercepted, and how the interception occurs, they are likely to try to avoid it (known as 'counter-measures'). Releasing information about an operation can, therefore, render it less effective or even useless. But most information is not about precise targets and equipment; and in normal circumstances, even when some intelligence details are involved, there may be other more important considerations such as ensuring that the intelligence agencies are under democratic control.

Secrecy can be a cloak for such undesirable behaviour as New Zealand spying on its small, vulnerable South Pacific neighbours and giving the intelligence it gathers to large, often unsympathetic outside powers. Removing that cloak is, surely, both necessary and desirable.

A good comparison is the New Zealand Police. They conduct very secret operations — including many times more telephone taps each year than the SIS — yet manage to operate far more openly. For example, I arranged to be

233

shown, without any fuss, around a police covert operations centre.

Around the walls were cabinets of interception equipment — containing the filters and recording equipment used for bugging faraway rooms and telephones — and safes (to store evidence untampered), a microwave, a fridge and all the other things needed for maintaining 24-hour operations. The only time the room is strictly off-limits is when an interception operation is underway and the equipment is connected up to the inside of a suspect's home.

We may not always agree with what the police do, but police priorities and policy are regularly debated in public and in Parliament, all their activities are governed by legislation and there are formal channels for investigating and challenging what goes on. Information about the police is much more accessible to Parliament and under the Official Information Act than that about intelligence organisations. Police secret operations and secret capabilities are kept secret, but the whole system is more open and also more controlled. And that openness is, of course, the best defence against corruption and abuse of power.

How the Official Information Act can operate in practice is seen in a standard refusal letter I received from the Department of the Prime Minister and Cabinet. The Minister of Foreign Affairs, Don McKinnon, had said on radio in 1991 that the United States had lifted its ban on military intelligence to New Zealand while the New Zealand military was involved in the Gulf War. My official information request had sought elaboration on these comments.

The brief letter of refusal as usual cited section 6 as justification for providing no information, but this time the bureaucrat slipped up and posted off more than he intended. Neatly attached to the back of the letter was the memo he had sent to the Prime Minister discussing the request, which had been noted 'OK' and initialled 'JBB' by Jim Bolger and stamped 'Prime Minister SEEN'. It said:

> *A methodical researcher into NZ intelligence agencies and relationships, Nicky Hager, has written in terms of the Official Information Act seeking elaboration of the Deputy Prime Minister's disclosure during the Gulf War of the fact that we were receiving US intelligence material.*
>
> *The US embassy called very quickly at the time to express concern that these comments had been made. The fact disclosed by Mr McKinnon cannot now be denied. We would get no thanks from the US for going beyond those comments. Consequently I propose to reply to Mr Hager telling him that in terms of sections 6(a) and (b)....[29]*

One of the positive aspects of the Official Information Act is that anyone can refer a refused request to the Ombudsman for review, often resulting in more information being released. The Ombudsmen and their staff have given a lot of time to reviewing numerous requests relating to this book.

The GCSB has used two main arguments to justify its secrecy to the Ombudsman: the so-called 'mosaic argument' and, recently, the 'operational security argument'. The former is that although many items of information on their own may look innocuous, when combined carefully together they may threaten national security. It is an argument for releasing little or nothing. The operational security approach purports to assess each piece of information in terms of its usefulness to hostile overseas interests (in practice a repackaging of the mosaic argument).

Over several years the Chief Ombudsman, Sir John Robertson (who, years before, as Secretary of Defence, had established the GCSB) found that the wording of the act — for example, the 'would be likely to prejudice the security or defence on New Zealand' clause — repeatedly enabled the intelligence organisations to get away with withholding information. He finished his term in late 1994, aware of how little he had achieved in this area and used his final report to address the issue of obtaining information about intelligence organisations:

> *The public perception has been that such information is difficult to obtain. Given the low threshold required to satisfy the "would be likely" test of the Act and the absence of any requirement (as in s.9 of the Act) to take into account any countervailing public interest considerations favouring release of such information, most requests can be refused under the Act, often with very little explanation as to the grounds for refusal.*
>
> *This has tended to be the situation even where the information requested is of an historical nature and would seem to have little impact on current operations of the agency concerned. Such refusals do not do much to engender public confidence that the fundamental principle of the Official Information Act... is not being subverted by an unnecessary concern with secrecy justified by vague references to national security.[30]*

Sir John proposed two possible options to try to remedy this situation. The first was the creation of an independent intelligence review agency or a special parliamentary select committee. The second was to make the withholding of information by an intelligence agency subject to a countervailing public interest test. Sir John concluded by saying that an independent assessment of whether more information on intelligence agencies could be released was overdue.

An independent intelligence review agency, such as the Canadian Security Intelligence Review Committee, with its own research staff and access to the organisations' files, would have been a significant improvement in oversight, as would making the public interest a factor in decisions whether to release information. But Bolger referred the recommendations to his officials and neither suggestion was heard of again. Instead they seized on the parliamentary committee option and wrote the legislation to ensure it would make no difference.

Those attitudes to informing the public and the Official Information Act of course only force information to find some other exit point. Access to information is not a small issue; it is a foundation of democratic government. As in all situations of closed government, concerned people with access to information ensure that it still reaches the public.

For example, the GCSB fought the Ombudsman for over two years to stop fragments of information about its internal structures reaching the public under the Official Information Act. But already some years before this request, and again since, from most unlikely sources, I have been shown copies of the GCSB's complete organisational plan.

Very secret organisations have a tendency to undermine the democracy they are set up to protect. In this situation, and in the absence of any major external threats, reform of the agencies is more important than operational secrecy. The information must get out.

CHAPTER FOURTEEN

LEAVING THE INTELLIGENCE ALLIANCE

The swearing in of a new Prime Minister in Suva in May 1987 should have been the beginning of Fiji's first multi-racial government, a government committed to reforms supporting poorer indigenous Fijians and Indians and to a New Zealand-style nuclear-free policy. Instead of the ceremony, balaclava-clad troops entered and marched away Prime Minister Timoci Bavadra and his government at gunpoint. Multi-racial government ended before it had begun. A New Zealand diplomat rushed back to the embassy with the news of the coup but staff there could not contact Wellington. Colonel Sitiveni Rabuka had dispatched soldiers to the international exchange to disconnect the lines. The American embassy used its alternative communications system to send out news of the coup.

New Zealand's secret intelligence organisations were all soon busy. Tangimoana intercepted Fiji Defence Force radio communications, Navy EW operators on the frigate *Wellington* monitored short-range radio and the Navy ship was dispatched to Fiji with replacement Navy interception staff and Special Air Service (SAS) intelligence collectors. The lights stayed on late on the 14th floor of the Freyberg Building as GCSB analysts processed the raw intelligence being collected.

It all sounds quite high-powered. But it was not. A very senior public

Reuter

Fijian soldiers guard Parliament House after the May 1987 coup. The GCSB and military intelligence units were immediately active, but senior officials say they contributed next to nothing of use to decision-makers.

servant, with access to all the available intelligence at the time, summed it up plainly: 'Secret intelligence provided nothing useful before, during or after the coup'. The Fiji coup created New Zealand's most urgent need for foreign intelligence in recent decades, but signals intelligence and the huge UKUSA system proved of almost no use when they were needed most. Screeds of top secret NSA reports on faraway subjects such as Soviet troop movements in Afghanistan were hardly compensation.

New Zealand did have very good sources of information about Fiji, the public servant said, which it shared with the intelligence allies. But the GCSB, Navy and SAS were almost totally irrelevant. The same official noted that the New Zealand military had helped to create and train the Fiji Defence Force, including training Colonel Rabuka. He also noted that, although New Zealand military personnel were posted as instructors inside the Fijian military headquarters, the New Zealand military authorities knew nothing in advance about the coup and did not help to stop it. He believes they were embarrassed by this and that the Navy and SAS intelligence missions were partly an attempt to save face.

Rabuka had been trained too well not to know how to avoid electronic interception. He also knew how to stop news leaking out before the coup; his military studies had even included a research paper on conducting a coup. The SAS mission was short-lived. Soon after they went ashore the two soldiers were recognised and one was arrested by Fijian soldiers who had been trained by the New Zealand military.[1]

The more useful and relevant sources of intelligence were mostly the result of normal diplomatic work. The public servant explained that the New Zealand High Commission had built up personal links and friendships over many years with people throughout the Fijian public service and the Fijian military. These were the main source of information, and were regarded as highly reliable. Also, after the coup, the New Zealanders posted inside the Fiji military provided some news.

Most of the top secret intelligence reports circulating in Wellington (and sent from New Zealand to the overseas allies) were based on information of this type received in reports from the embassy staff in Suva. This was the main source and, according to the public servant, 'far more useful than technical intelligence'. They were also, he added, much better sources than Australia had.

With Fiji so much in the news, even the New Zealand SIS decided to participate. (Lindsay Smith, the SIS director at the time, was known to be keen to extend his organisation's work into external intelligence collection.) In late May, a week or two after the coup, an SIS agent flew to Nadi airport on a commercial flight and travelled to Suva. His instructions for the trip appear to have been vague, but included trying to meet with the SIS's usual contact in Fiji's internal security unit. The situation in Suva was so tense that he stayed in his hotel for a few days, achieving next to nothing, and then returned to New Zealand.

The most useful part played by the GCSB at the time of the coup had nothing directly to do with intelligence. It was assistance provided by staff from one of the non-intelligence sections, which provides secure communications systems for government communications.

Shortly after the coup New Zealand High Commission staff were tipped off that their phones were being monitored by a Fijian soldier sitting in the telephone exchange building. Prime Minister David Lange wanted to be able to communicate privately with the New Zealand embassy staff so a secure telephone system was requested. It is hard to believe, but no suitable equipment was available in any government or military organisations. After about two weeks of slow bureaucracy, an Inmarsat mobile satellite telephone unit was hired, including a small dish antenna.

Ian Worthington, a GCSB technician with many years' experience in government communications, flew to Fiji with the equipment. A helpful Fijian soldier helped him to unload it from the plane and Worthington travelled to Suva to install it. Unable to hide the dish on the commission building, he eventually set it up on the High Commissioner's home verandah, together with a 'black box' containing a scrambler.

That was it. That was all that years of secret development of a signals intelligence organisation had contributed. As for the New Zealand military, its main contribution had been to train the coup-makers. It still regularly exercises with and trains the Fiji military and the militaries of questionable regimes elsewhere.

Other emergencies such as the terrorist attack on the Greenpeace ship *Rainbow Warrior* tell the same story. This was another example of failure by the organisations when they were most needed. Secret intelligence neither gave any warning before the bombing nor helped to catch the French agents afterwards. And 40 years of New Zealand loyalty to the United States-British alliance were not enough to move Ronald Reagan or Margaret Thatcher to condemn France's actions, not even with a formal slap on the wrist. Yet at that time both leaders were publicly campaigning against terrorism.

In spite of examples like these, the public hears nothing but unqualified support for the secret intelligence organisations from the government. The citizens in all the UKUSA countries are repeatedly told by politicians about the value of the intelligence organisations and allied intelligence co-operation. There is a huge gap between this rhetoric and the reality.

In late 1993, a former head of the Australian Security Intelligence Organisation and former deputy secretary of the Department of Defence, Alan Wrigley, spoke to a security conference about the DSD: 'In my exposure, over ten years, to increasingly sensitive classified information, I can think of no major policy position or decision that was influenced significantly by secret intelligence'. He went on to say that changes in Australia's strategic environment made it difficult to justify the high cost of technical intelligence collection in the region: 'The most costly intelligence and processing programmes Australia conducted [i.e. by the DSD] were initiated because of our role as a minor partner in the Western Alliance'.[2]

Precisely the same can be said about the GCSB. During interviews with a wide range of senior government officials, none could think of a major policy position or decision that had been influenced significantly by secret intelligence coming from the UKUSA allies or from the GCSB. Having access to covert intelligence, like reading someone else's private mail, can be intriguing and interesting. How useful or crucial it is, is quite another matter.

Users of the intelligence in other New Zealand organisations (such as EAB analysts) appreciate having access to the widest possible range of information sources and also to the different perspectives that the UKUSA sources provide. But it does not make a significant difference to eventual government policy. Various people regularly handling intelligence have told me that, in practice, open sources and diplomatic reporting are much more important in the issues affecting New Zealand.

This is how one former Prime Minister described it:

> *We didn't get any significant information, from a government point of view, from signals intelligence. The information was little more than one would have gleaned from periodicals and publications....*
>
> *I never felt I was given a preview on history. More often, when something happened everyone in the intelligence community was surprised.*
>
> *If you're going into agreements like GATT you do need to know what positions other nations will take, what coalitions are forming.... But we've been much better provided with good intelligence by people on the spot than by secret intelligence.*

Another Prime Minister said (referring to encryption): 'There's a limitation to covert intelligence: the more useful a communication will be, the less likely you are to get it'.

In the 1990s the most frequently heard justification for secret intelligence organisations and their budgets is the 'increasing importance of economic intelligence'. This argument has become an article of faith in public discussions of intelligence and has been eagerly embraced by intelligence officials. Few details are ever given to substantiate the claim.

Former Prime Minister Geoffrey Palmer is on record commenting about the value of economic intelligence received from overseas. Asked in 1985 about whether such intelligence was vital to New Zealand, he said: 'Not, I think, a great deal. The finance ministers who have looked at this say that in the time they have been finance ministers they have not received anything of any significance.'[3] According to another former Prime Minister, New Zealand used to get useful economic intelligence, but he said that structural changes in the New Zealand economy have made economic intelligence 'all pretty irrelevant these days'. In the past, when New Zealand had various state organisations and regulated foreign exchange markets, economic intelligence was much more useable, but a process of privatisation and deregulation during the last decade has mostly changed this, 'taking away the intelligence organisations' second string' (the first string being the traditional military and political intelligence).

As he explained:

> *There are insurmountable difficulties involved in trying to channel useful economic intelligence to private companies. How do you choose which of rival companies to give intelligence to? Should you help a foreign-owned company operating in New Zealand or a New Zealand-owned company producing its products in China?*

A GCSB officer echoed this point, saying that the economic intelligence seen at the bureau was interesting, but that its usefulness was doubtful.

> *What can the Ministry of Foreign Affairs and Trade do [with economic intelligence] which obeys the rules? You can't give it to one company over another or you might tread on other agencies' toes [e.g. a New Zealand company getting advantage over an Australian or US company]. So it's hard to get it to a level where it is useful. It is debatable whether it has found any useful or strategic use.*

One is left with the impression that economic intelligence is primarily just a convenient argument used by intelligence organisations to justify their existence and budgets in the post-Cold War era. Thus, for example, the changes to the New Zealand SIS Act in 1996 to include 'economic well-being' in the definition of 'security'. In practice the economic intelligence obtained is of minor importance to a country such as New Zealand and even in the United States it is far from being the main focus.

In a farewell memo to his staff in 1992 NSA Director Vice-Admiral William O. Studeman, who may well have emphasised economic intelligence if he were speaking in public, urged: 'The military account is basic to NSA as a defense agency, and lack of utter faithfulness to this fact will court decline'.[4] There has been some increase in production of economic intelligence at the GCSB and elsewhere, but we should not be misled into believing that this is the main purpose of these organisations or that it in any way justifies their existence.

Aside from questions of relevance, senior officials interviewed also spoke of the unhelpful distorting effects of foreign secret intelligence. There are

Gulf War overkill: Iraqi soldiers killed as they retreated from Kuwait, 1991. 'Being in the intelligence circles is pretty heady wine for people.... It is hard to see beyond the United States position.'

two parts to this: the internal bias it inevitably carries and the barriers secrecy creates in the processes of government. They said that the greatest effect of signals intelligence is to reinforce the tendency for officials to see issues through their allies' eyes. If the most secret and valued intelligence sources are dominated by screeds of information about particular issues, there is a natural tendency for these issues and concerns to assume more importance.

A New Zealand intelligence officer during the Vietnam War explained that although New Zealand had joined the war for alliance reasons — 'the US wanted some tokens to hold up to the world to show that right-minded nations agreed with them' — the American intelligence invariably presented events in a light that justified continued involvement:

We believed Foster Dulles' view that Vietnam was a client of the Soviet Union, which was rubbish.... [Also] we were probably all influenced by the idea that China was large and dangerous, with territorial ambitions, and that it was in our interests to stop the domino effect. For much of this stuff, there was no other source of information.

Western intelligence about the Soviet Union throughout the Cold War, and about more recent crises in Panama, Iraq and North Korea, has performed a similar function. Intelligence about non-military issues has the same kind of internal bias, concerning which countries are targeted, which issues are reported on most frequently, which areas are ignored and so on.

The reason for this was explained by two very senior former government officials. The first was asked whether he agreed with the view, often repeated in intelligence circles, that intelligence is just neutral information, neither good not bad. He did not: 'Facts *don't* tell a story. It's what's included, what's not included and how they're ordered which matters. You have to wonder about the value of overseas intelligence. It just helps you to see situations through other countries' eyes.'

The other, a former Foreign Affairs official, was even more sceptical: 'When people provide intelligence they assume recipient countries will make decisions that will be favourable to the policies of the country providing it.... After a time, we were always very aware what the American or British position was: it was fortified by their intelligence reports.'

The high level of security required for secret intelligence can distort government decision-making in another way too. There is a strong tendency for politicians to put more weight on a report stamped 'TOP SECRET' and 'US/UK/CAN/AUST/NZ EYES ONLY', and carrying warnings about its sensitivity, than on ordinary sources of information and advice — even though 'ordinary' reports from diplomatic posts and open sources such as magazines may provide more relevant insights.

As one senior New Zealand diplomat put it: 'Being in the intelligence circles is pretty heady wine for people. It is difficult to rise above the excitement of being in the presence of high-powered analysts and getting all the information.... It is hard to see beyond the United States position.'

During the years since the supposed 1985 cut of United States intelligence to New Zealand, there have been many public statements about how valuable access to United States/Western intelligence is for New Zealand. The 'loss' of this intelligence has often been given as a reason for dropping New Zealand's nuclear-free legislation, to allow a resumption of 'full alliance relations'.

The description in Chapter 12 of the foreign signals intelligence received in New Zealand and the comments of the senior politicians and officials quoted in this chapter make it clear that the value of the overseas intelligence has been highly overrated. It has done little of value for New Zealand and its disadvantages are never mentioned. It is only its secrecy that has allowed the inflated claims of its worth to be made.

New Zealand intelligence organisations have not just 'co-operated with the traditional allies', or 'shared intelligence' or even 'worked closely' with them. The New Zealand organisations have *functioned as part of* the allied intelligence networks and almost entirely adopted their priorities.

The main targets throughout the Cold War period were, of course, Communists: the Soviet Union, China and independence movements ('Communist terrorists') in Vietnam and various other South East Asian countries. From the secret Singapore station, NR1 at Waiouru and the current Tangimoana station, New Zealand signals intelligence staff have spied on all things Russian and helped outside powers to meddle in the affairs of South East Asian countries. Inside the secret JTUM facility in Melbourne, New Zealanders took part in a high-tech spying operation against China over which New Zealand had no control at all.

Inside the GCSB headquarters, too, the priorities have come from outside New Zealand. The first analysis section established was to produce Russian intelligence, the next was to contribute to an NSA project targeting Japanese diplomatic communications and the third was focused on the French nuclear intelligence. Once these were underway, it moved into wholesale spying on the South Pacific countries. The GCSB spies on the South Pacific nations and territories and indiscriminately passes on their secrets to the outside powers.

Despite the end of the Cold War and claims that Waihopai provided an independent intelligence capability, the GCSB's entry into the ECHELON system meant a whole new level of integration into the Cold War-inspired alliance. The Waihopai station, operating as one component of a global interception system, combines 21st-century technology with 1950s thinking.

In the 1990s the GCSB stations function for the allies just as though they were openly NSA, GCHQ or DSD stations located on New Zealand soil. The other junior UKUSA allies fare little better.[5] Whenever control of these organisation is discussed, it is worth remembering that only when the secret details of intelligence operations are known is the lack of independence revealed. The alliance links have persisted and grown over these years because they have served the interests of the large partners and because almost the only New Zealanders who have known anything about them have been supporters of the alliance.

Membership of such a close alliance assumes an equivalence of interests. It assumes that the countries involved have the same friends and the same enemies. It assumes that they have the same world view and the same objectives for their foreign and defence policies. This is obviously not the case.

Michael Kopp

Vietnam 1969: 'After a time, we were always aware what the American or British position was: it was fortified by their intelligence reports'.

New Zealand's involvement in the UKUSA alliance grew out of a shared struggle for democracy and freedom in the Second World War and the 'defence' of these in the years that followed. But during the last 50 years the United States and Britain have had a poor record of being on the side of democracy and human rights. From Saddam Hussein in Iraq (pre-Gulf War) to Marcos in the Philippines and from the Contras in Nicaragua to Suharto in Indonesia, the United States and Britain have supported undemocratic and often violent regimes and groups around the world.

As New Zealand's nuclear-free policy showed, it is very difficult to pursue different foreign and defence policies within an alliance. Ten years of diplomatic strife between New Zealand and the United States over a piece of nuclear-free legislation, democratically decided and only ever covering New Zealand territory, is a poor advertisement for alliance membership.

Sadly, there are no easy options for reform. If New Zealand stays in the intelligence alliance, little can change. So many of the secrets, regulations and operating systems come from overseas that it is probably not within the power of a New Zealand government to change them and remain in the alliance. Given the established influence of the overseas allies (and of pro-alliance government officials within New Zealand), any minor reforms, such as forming a parliamentary intelligence committee, will have an insignificant impact. The only serious option for change is to leave the intelligence alliance.

The intelligence alliance is only one component of the wider alliance between the five UKUSA countries, but it is the deepest and most secret part, helping to perpetuate unequal alliance relations in many other areas of foreign and defence policy. Fear of losing the intelligence ties is also used by officials to bolster support for other components of the alliance. Reconsidering the intelligence alliance (and, in particular, UKUSA) is a necessary step in reconsidering the rest.

The most convincing argument for remaining in the intelligence alliance and retaining the GCSB in its current form was advanced by one of the senior people interviewed during the research for this book. He said that an organisation like the GCSB is like the defence forces: 'If you look at its use in peacetime it is not cost effective, like the police force on a Monday night. But you need it to be prepared for contingencies....' He was not, however, an enthusiastic supporter of the GCSB's work. There was a sense that this was merely the best argument he could adduce to justify why it seemed too difficult to leave the alliance.

The first reply to this argument was illustrated by the Fiji coup. In most circumstances, it is very questionable how vital or useful this kind of secret or 'technical' intelligence is; in other words, whether they are the right capabilities to be building up for New Zealand's needs anyway.

A more important reply, just as with a military alliance, is to question whose wars and what kind of wars the system is likely to be used for. Earlier chapters documented New Zealand signals intelligence involvement during the Vietnam War, various South East Asian conflicts, the Falklands War and against Russia and China during and after the Cold War nuclear confrontation. There were strong ethical arguments against New Zealand contributing practical and moral support to most aspects of these conflicts.

The Monday night police force argument is initially convincing, but it makes sense only if the country is preparing for another world war — a possibility that no one, either in the military or out of it, regards as serious. The most telling point against the intelligence alliance is that the small allies have no say in what the information collected is used for and who it is used against. The alliance is more like the Hells Angels gang on a quiet Monday night, with countries like New Zealand having almost no say in who will be beaten up on Friday night but still going along for the ride.

The strongest argument for leaving the intelligence alliance is that to do so is a pre-condition for achieving an independent foreign policy, one that fits with an increasing number of New Zealanders' sense of what is right and their views about this country's role in the world. Just over 50 years ago New Zealand's armed forces and intelligence operations were literally a component of British military and intelligence structures. In the decades since, much of the intelligence and military activity has been as a small New Zealand contribution to British and United States operations. Leaving the intelligence alliance is the next stage in the slow process of becoming an independent state.

Leaving the intelligence alliance would mean the end of the GCSB as we know it. It is so much a creature of the alliance that it is doubtful it could function outside it. What is the alternative? Fortunately, it is doubtful that signals intelligence is an effective way for a country such as New Zealand to collect foreign information. Other, less secret forms of intelligence gathering would serve the nation better.

GCSB signals intelligence currently uses up most of New Zealand's foreign intelligence budget. If this money was spent instead on an expanded External Assessments Bureau and extra diplomatic research staff posted in embassies around the world, one could expect far more useful and relevant information to be produced. Intelligent research and enhanced diplomatic contacts are a practical alternative to putting most of the resources into technical intelligence collection. If economic intelligence really is a priority, then some of the new overseas staff could be trade specialists.

Some types of information may be accessible only by electronic spying operations, but not having them should be more than compensated for by an increase in other important types of information that are available by non-covert means. The loss of some United States secret intelligence would be a major disappointment to intelligence staff but probably of no great significance elsewhere in the government system. New or renewed intelligence sharing relationships, including those with Australia, could evolve on a different basis.

Some signals intelligence operations could possibly still occur, but New Zealand would be accepting reduced capability without allied support in exchange for independence of operations. They could be funded from the military budget. A decision would have to be made, however, whether the information produced from signals intelligence was of sufficient value to New Zealand in the first place. It is doubtful that it would be.

One of the greatest obstacles to change will be the attitude of some New

Zealand government officials who are wedded to conducting foreign affairs and defence from within a traditional alliance framework. Restructuring the Ministry of Foreign Affairs and Trade would also be a necessary part of any new policies, to open the way for a generation of more independent-minded officials.

Leaving the intelligence alliance is also a pre-condition for bringing intelligence activities under democratic and government control. The secret intelligence world is not just a symptom, but a deep underlying cause of the lack of democracy and independence in the New Zealand Foreign Affairs and Defence bureaucracy. It was the allies' demands that New Zealand protect their intelligence secrets which led originally to the draconian New Zealand Official Secrets Act of 1951 and the formation of the Security Intelligence Service five years later. A culture of secrecy has entrenched the power of officials and undermined control by politicians and the public ever since.

Intelligence organisations *can* be more open. They should routinely provide information to the public on the types of work they are doing, how many staff they have and which foreign countries they co-operate with and assist. Most important of all, the public should be involved in deciding for them who their enemies are. Although it is impractical to allow the public to review the day-to-day operations of intelligence organisations, this should at least be done by elected representatives. The notion that only officials can be trusted with this role must be comprehensively and thoroughly rejected.

A cross-section of politicians from the parties making up Parliament should have access to information on intelligence operations. Reductions in 'operational security' would be outweighed by the enhanced political control over and increased relevance of the intelligence produced. Much more than at present, they would be New Zealand's secrets and New Zealand politicians would have the right to know about them.

Excessive secrecy is the key to what is wrong with the intelligence organisations. The central problem is not the influence of the alliance, although that alone determines most of what goes on. Nor is it this or that secret operation, although many of them are highly questionable. It is not even the misuse of power by officials, although this alone has been enough to subvert democratic processes. All these can change if the people whose right it is to direct these organisations know enough about what is going on to assert their control. In some cases the institutions themselves may even be shamed into changing spontaneously if the public knows what they are doing.

Secrecy remains at the heart of the problem. When organisations are so secret, and so impervious to democratic processes, it seems inevitable that their priorities will be those of the powerful, irrespective of what the public or elected representatives want. Ethics barely figure. Secrecy allows and encourages dishonesty and corrupt behaviour in government, in business and probably every other area of life. Secrecy, the maintenance of illegitimate power and wrongdoing seem to be inextricably linked. The reduction of secrecy in every area is the most effective route to better government.

Leaving the intelligence alliance is not a radical step to take. It is the natural outcome of the direction New Zealand has been moving in since the 1960s. It is part of a process that began with public disillusionment over the Vietnam War, and with Britain's decision to join the Common Market, thereby forcing New Zealand to redefine itself in relation to the Pacific and Asia. It is also part of the process that led to the nuclear-free policy in the 1980s, with which New Zealanders adopted a strikingly different view of their national interest in relation to nuclear weapons from their traditional allies — and found that the world did not end as a result. The republican movement in the 1990s is part of the same impetus.

For people primarily concerned about economic relations, it makes no sense for New Zealand to be seen by its Asian and Pacific neighbours as junior spies for the United States and Britain. In the 21st-century New Zealand cannot afford to be seen as willing to spy on the nations of its region on behalf of their Western economic competitors.

The partly foolish, partly irrelevant but also, often, highly sinister intelligence activities documented in this book could not have continued had they not been so secret. The bureaucrats judged, accurately, that the intelligence organisations needed to be protected from the public and Parliament. That is what a GCSB officer was talking about when he said, during our first interview, 'The secrecy is not for the Russians, it is for the general public. If they knew what the bureau does, it would not be allowed to continue.' The purpose of this book has been to lift the secrecy which has protected these organisations from change. Fifty years after the signature of a British officer took New Zealand into UKUSA, it is time to leave an outmoded and unnecessary alliance. What is needed now is a government with the courage to take that step.

Who's Who in New Zealand Foreign Intelligence Organisations

SENIOR GCSB STAFF IN 1996

Director	Ray Parker (F)
Director of Operations	Warren Tucker (A)
Director of Technology	Mike Spring (F)
Director of Information Systems Security	John Brandon (A)
Director of Corporate Services	Tony Fryer (F)
New Zealand Liaison Officer (Washington)	John Willson (A)
New Zealand Liaison Officer (Canberra)	Keith Smith (F)
Officer in Charge, Tangimoana	Barry Keane (F)
Officer in Charge, Waihopai	Colin Waite (F)

Unit Managers:		
	K Unit (SIGINT production)	Glen Singleton
	C Unit (SIGINT collection)	Bruce Miller (N)
	L Unit (customer support)	Leon Crosse (F)
	N Unit (network services)	Bob Ohlson (N)
	TS Unit (computer services)	Robert Walter
	D Unit (technical services)	Roy Anderson
	S Unit (technical security)	Brian Nokes (F)
	E Unit (COMSEC engineering)	Ian Howie (F)
	R Unit (computer security)	Malcolm Shore (F)
	M Unit (COMSEC)	Chris Farrow (N)
	P Unit (protective security)	Mike Loughran (F)
	A Unit (administration)	Heather McKenzie
	F Unit (finance)	Chris Carson
	L Unit (logistics)	Ian Juno (A)

Senior Executive Officers:		
	Information Security	Peter Ross (A)
	Information Systems	David Hilling
	Legal	Hugh Wolfensohn (N)
	Office of the Director	Brian Gore (A)

Nearly all of these staff were previously high-ranking New Zealand military officers (F stands for ex-Air Force, A for ex-Army and N for ex-Navy). One of the four information security units was disestablished and the staff moved into another unit in January 1996.

GCSB DIRECTOR- AND MANAGER-LEVEL STAFF 1977-96

Operations

Director of Operations (O)	Jim Blackford	1978-82
	Larry Lynch	1982-89
	Warren Tucker	1989-

Technology

Director of Engineering (E)	Keith Smith	1978-94
Deputy Director of Technical Support (later, of Information Processing)	Dave Hilling	1988-93
Director of Information Processing (Z)	Michael Spring	1993-94
Director of Technology (T)	Michael Spring	1994-

Information systems security

Deputy Director Communications Security (M)	Dave Hilling	1978-85
Deputy Director Communications and Technical Security	John Willson	1985-89
Director of Security (X)	Michael Spring	1990-93
Director of Information Systems Security (X)	John Brandon	1993-

Policy and plans

Director of Policy and Plans (P)	I.C. Alford	1977-
	Warren Tucker	1983-84
	Glen Singleton	1984-87
	John Brandon	1987-89
	John Willson	1989-95

Corporate services

| Director of Administration (A) | Brian Punnett | 1977-89 |
| Director of Support Services/Corporate Services (C) | Tony Fryer | 1989- |

Executive Director

| | Barry Keane | 1995-96 |

Liaison officers

New Zealand Liaison Officer (Washington)	Jim Blackford	1982-84
	Larry Lynch	1984-84
	Warren Tucker	1984-89
	John Brandon	1989-92
	Barry Keane	1992-95
	John Willson	1995-

New Zealand Liaison Officer (Canberra) and their predecessors

	Kelvin Brayshaw	1968-71
	Harold Stokell	1972-73
	I.C. Alford	1973-76
	Jim Campbell	1977-80
	John Orchard	1981-88
	Larry Lynch	1988-92
	Neil Catley	1992-94
	Keith Smith	1994-

Station officers in charge

Station Radio Officer, NR1 station, Waiouru	H.E. Stutton	1955-59
	Jim Timlin	1959-68
	Wally Brendon	1968-72
	Jim Timlin	1972-82
Officer in charge, Tangimoana	Harold Stokell	1982-87
	Tony Robinson	1987-88
	John Orchard	1988-94
	Neil Catley	1994-96
	Barry Keane	1996-
Officer in charge, Waihopai	Colin Waite	1989-
Manager SIGINT Production	John Brandon	1979-85
	Barry Keane	1985-89
	Brian Gore	1989-91
	Ian Brownlie	1991-94
	Glen Singleton	1994-
Manager SIGINT Collection	Wally Brendon	1984-89
	Barry Keane	1989-91
	Bruce Miller	1991-
Manager Cryptanalysis	Thomas Weiss	1988-90
	Mark Kininmonth	1990-94
	Susan Kelly	1994-
Manager Customer Support	Kevin Bonnici	1988-93
	Leon Crosse	1993-
Manager Network Services	John Parkes	1982-93
	Barry Dittmer	1993-94
	Bob Ohlson	1994-
Manager Computer Services	Graham Starkey	1988-94
	Robert Walter	1994-
Manager Technical Security	Peter March	1980-93
	Brian Nokes	1993-
Manager COMSEC Policy	Eric Morgon	1977-84
	Neil Catley	1984-92
	Chris Farrow	1992-
Manager Computer Security	Dave Hilling	1985-88
	Malcolm Shore	1991-
Assistant Director Policy and Plans	John Brandon	1985-87

January 1996 Organisation Plan
Each acronym indicates a position in the GCSB Headquarters

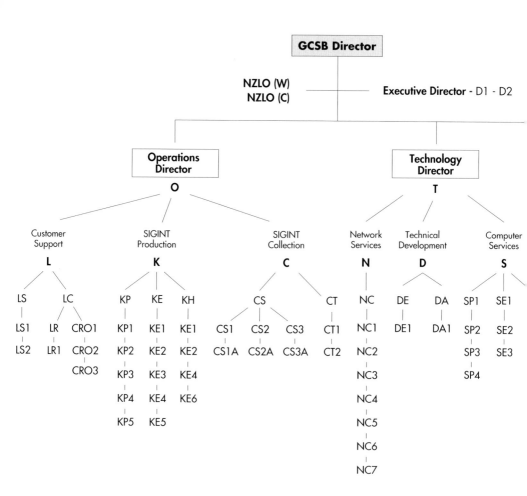

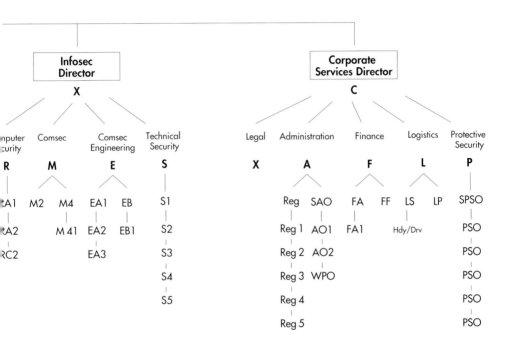

Assistant Director Operations	Tony Robinson	1988-?

(Note that some titles of director positions have changed over time, some positions have been amalgamated and some areas have both director and assistant director positions. Manager positions were assistant director positions until 1989.)[1]

Senior radio officer staff posted to GCHQ, Cheltenham	Jim Timlin	1957-59
	Wally Brendon	1963-65
	Jim Timlin	1968-72
Head New Zealand radio officer, Singapore station	unknown	1955-62
	D.F. Giddens	1962-65
	Brian Veale	1965-66
	I.C. Alford	1966-69
	D.F. Giddens	1970-72
	I.C. Alford	1972-74
Head New Zealand radio officer, DSD Perth station	P.T.M. Tahi	1978-
	Les Whitney	1984-87

NEW ZEALAND SIGNALS INTELLIGENCE LOCATIONS: PAST AND PRESENT

NZCSO Distribution Office Departmental Building 15-20 Stout Street, Wellington	1955-77
GCSB Headquarters Departmental Building, 1st floor 15-20 Stout Street, Wellington	1977-82
GCSB Headquarters Freyberg Building, floors 10-14 Aitken Street, Wellington; or GCSB, PO Box 12-209, Wellington Telephone 04-472 6881, Fax 04-499 3701	1982 - present
NR1 station, Waiouru Maukuku Road, Irirangi; or C/- NZCSO, Box 1 Army Training Group Registry, Waiouru	1949-82
New Zealand staff GCHQ/DSD Singapore station, Chai Keng station CK2 Kranji station KR2 Singapore	1955-71 1971-74

New Zealand staff
DSD Pearce station
Pearce Air Force Base,
Perth   1978-?

Tangimoana station
Tangimoana Road, Tangimoana; or
Defence Communications Unit (Tangimoana),
PO Box 45, Bulls
Telephone 06-324 8488 and fax 06-324 8029   1982 - present

Waihopai station
Waihopai Valley Road, Renwick; or
Defence Satellite Communications Unit (Blenheim)
PO Box 2, Renwick
Telephone 03-578 1069 and fax 03-578 1068
Officer in charge extension 812   1989 - present

Government Communications Liaison Office (Melbourne)
and Joint Telecommunications Unit Melbourne (JTUM)
Victoria Barracks
256-310 St Kilda Road
Melbourne, Australia   1970s - 1992
                                                               (JTUM 1982-91)

New Zealand Liaison Officer Canberra (NZLOC)
c/- Defence Signals Directorate Headquarters
Russell Hill complex
Canberra, Australia
NZLOC Keith Smith's direct line 61-6-265 0290   1992 - present

New Zealand Liaison Officer Washington (NZLOW)
National Security Agency Headquarters
Fort George G. Meade
Washington; or
C/- New Zealand Embassy,
19 Observation Circle, N.W.
Washington DC 20008
Telephone 1-202-265 1721   1978 - present

NEW ZEALAND'S EXTERNAL INTELLIGENCE ANALYSIS ORGANISATION

Name changes:
Joint Intelligence Office (JIO)   1949-53
Joint Intelligence Bureau (JIB)   1953-75
External Intelligence Bureau (EIB)   1975-88
External Assessments Bureau (EAB)   1988-

Directors

Vic Jaynes	Officer-in-Charge JIO	1949-52
	Director JIO	1952-53
	Director JIB	1953-75
Richard Atkins	Director EIB	1979-85
Bernard Hillier	Director EIB	1985-88
Nancy Mullins	Acting Director EIB	1988
Michael Green	Director EAB	1988-94
Hessel Baas	Acting Director EAB	1994
Christine Cassells	Acting Director EAB	1994-95
John McKinnon	Director EAB	1995-

(Since March 1993 Mr Baas and Ms Cassells have served as the the EAB's two Assessment Managers.)

JIO/JIB/EIB/EAB LOCATIONS IN WELLINGTON

Stout Street Defence Building, second floor (location of the wartime intelligence centre)	1949-51
Hutt County Council Building, cnr Bowen St and Lambton Quay, ground floor	1951-54
Government Life Insurance Building, Post Office Square, fifth floor	1954-62
Stout Street Defence Building, first floor (shared with DDI after 1964, then GCSB took JIB's office after 1977)	1962-75
North End Branch, Bank of New Zealand building, cnr Ballance and Stout Streets	1975-88
Ministry of Foreign Affairs and Trade building, Stafford House, The Terrace, 4th and 5th floors	1988 - present

CO-ORDINATORS OF DOMESTIC AND EXTERNAL SECURITY

Gerald Hensley	1987-89
David McDowell	1989-91
Simon Murdoch	1991-

DIRECTORS OF THE DOMESTIC AND EXTERNAL SECURITY SECRETARIAT

Tony Browne	1989-?
Adrian Simcock	1994?-

NEW ZEALAND DEFENCE FORCE POSITIONS

Directors of Defence Intelligence

Group Captain Colin Hanson	1975-77
Colonel R.I. Launder	1977
Colonel A.C. Hamilton	1978-79
Colonel O.E. Mann	1979-84
Colonel P.G. Hotop	1984-87
Captain K.R. Moen RNZN	1987
Captain J.G. Leonard RNZN	1988-89
Group Captain R.A. DeLorenzo	1990-92
Group Captain J.S. Barclay	1992-94
Group Captain W.J. Barnes	1994-

Staff Officer Electronic Warfare

Lieutenant Commander Ross Sanson	1987-88
Squadron Leader John Lawton	1988-89

Assistant Directors Electronic Warfare

Squadron Leader John Lawton	1988-90
Major Janet Castell	1990-
Major Scott Turner	1994-

Officer in Command, Defence Electronic Warfare Data Base

Squadron Leader John Lawton	1990-95
Flight Lieutenant Jeff Price	1995-

Commanders of the Special Air Service (SAS)

Major F. Rennie	1955-57
Major J. Mace	1960-62
Major M. Velvin	1962-64
Major W. Meldrum	1964-65
Major J. Mace	1965-66
Major I. Burrows	1966-67
Major D. Ogilvy	1967-69
Major N. Kidd	1969-72
Major D. Maloney	1972-73
Major A. Kiwi	1973
Major N. Kidd	1973-75
Major G. Shattky	1975-80
Major J. Maloney	1980-82
Lieutenant-Colonel A. Howell	1982-86
Lieutenant-Colonel N. Philp	1986-89
Lieutenant-Colonel B. Isherwood	1989-

A GUIDED TOUR OF
SECRET INTELLIGENCE FACILITIES

WAIHOPAI

The highway from Blenheim runs perfectly straight, between vineyards and orchards, out across the Wairau Plains before a few trees and a small cemetery mark the turn-off to the Waihopai Valley.[1] A few kilometres down the Waihopai Valley Road, at the edge of the river terrace, you suddenly see the Waihopai station, set in a wide, dry Marlborough valley between low brown hills. The view is dominated by the large white radome which covers the single satellite dish, and by high security gates and fences that look out of place in the quiet countryside. Inside Waihopai's buildings, in a room almost twice the size of an indoor basketball court, is the heart of the station — the secret operations centre. Here, in sharp contrast to the warmth of the Marlborough sun, the atmosphere is cool and still, regulated not for the people who work here but for the machines that run the station.

There are only about 35 staff at Waihopai. They include various kinds of technical staff, radio officers, administrative staff and security officers. Over half of the staff are shift workers supporting the 24-hour, seven-day-a-week operation of the station; the rest are day workers. Although the technical staff know which satellite is being targeted, they have very little idea what they are helping to intercept. All programming of targets and handling of the resulting intelligence occurs across Cook Strait in Wellington.

The main workers at the station are the technical staff who look after all the equipment. Of these, the largest group, 12 in number, are the collection technicians. They are electronics technicians, experienced in digital electronics and telecommunications, who work in shifts operating and maintaining the collection equipment in the large operations room. Much of the time they are just checking that it runs smoothly, but they have a workshop for testing and repairing equipment that goes wrong.

The two maintenance technicians look after the large dish antenna and the mechanical systems that move it around. Their functions are defined as 'maintenance of electro-mechanical plant and large antenna structures' and require electrical rather than electronic expertise. There is also a small two-person development section, located off the operations room and headed by Tony Aimers, which is involved in specialist projects for the station.

The staff in charge of the station, in descending order of seniority, are: Officer in Charge Colin Waite, Station Engineer Paul Bruckel, Assistant Engineering Officer Stephen Prentice and his assistant, Tony Aimers. The head of the administrative staff, Station Administration Officer Ken Newport, oversees about six staff, including clerks and a receptionist. There are also five security officers who work in shifts (one per shift) around the clock. They are based in a room in the main building which has video monitors connected to security cameras positioned around the perimeter fence. Their shifts, and those of the collection technicians, change over at 8 am, 4 pm and midnight.

The other type of staff are five radio officers, previously employed at the Tangimoana station as radio intercept officers. These staff in 1996 had an average of 17 years' experience each in signals intelligence: three of them started work at the old NR1 station (before the move to Tangimoana) and three had one or more postings to the secret JTUM operation in Melbourne. The radio officers work as day staff in the main operations room.

The Officer in Charge, Colin Waite, is an engineer by training who has worked for the GCSB since retiring from the Air Force as a wing commander in November 1983. He worked at the GCSB headquarters as a senior engineering officer (with also one period at Tangimoana) before being posted to the DSD in March 1987, for planning and training in preparation for his Waihopai position, which he took up in about March 1989.

The Station Engineer (also called the Senior Engineering Officer or SENGO) is Paul Bruckel, who was brought into this senior role directly from the British GCHQ. In the GCHQ he worked in a station like Waihopai, which means either the Morwenstow or the Hong Kong station. Bruckel's deputy, Assistant Engineering Officer Stephen Prentice, was previously a GCSB radio officer who worked at Tangimoana and at JTUM in Melbourne. When he joined the GCSB in 1979 from the Navy he was already experienced in electronic interception: he had been an electronic warfare officer.

When specialist outside technicians are brought in occasionally from the companies that have supplied particular pieces of equipment, the whole process occurs with strict security. The outside technicians are not allowed into the main operations area nor even to see the piece of equipment they are repairing. Instead the GCSB technicians strip all components off the faulty equipment except for those requiring testing and repair. The outside technician then does the work in a low-security room under the gaze of a minder.

Most of the staff at the Waihopai station are men, including all the technical staff and all but two or three of the other staff. In 1991 about half the staff were ex-military, generally from the Air Force. Most of the staff live in the nearby towns of Renwick and Blenheim. They travel to work in white vans provided by the GCSB.

The staff work in a long single-storey building in the centre of a compound protected by tall security fences, security lighting, video cameras and an additional 3-metre electrified fence inside the main fence.[2] There is also a services building and a small security building beside the gate. Everything is dwarfed by the huge white radome.

The services building houses a workshop, garages and a stand-by generator to ensure continuous power supply to the station. The long operations building has a lower security area (at the east end), containing the administrative staff, amenities and the station management, and a high security area with the technicians and the main operations room.[3] The GCSB has refused to reveal the cost of the station. It was about $20 million. (Even those responsible for the station have expressed doubts about its appearance. In 1988 GCSB Director Colin Hanson told local farmers, 'Aesthetically I think it's a disaster. But they tell me it blends with the surroundings.')

If you were allowed to visit Waihopai, a security guard would meet you at the large, steel gates and escort you up to the main entrance on the north side of the operations building. Inside the front doors is a reception area, with corridors leading off to the left and right along the building. To the left is the administration section and an area with toilets, showers and a locker room.

As you turn right down the corridor, first there are the senior staff's offices. Officer in Charge Colin Waite has the first office on the right and Assistant Engineering Officer Stephen Prentice is next door. Across the corridor from them is the Station Engineer

Paul Bruckel's office. This room contains books and manuals concerning the operation of the station and technical issues such as the reduction of 'white noise' in the intercepted transmissions. Next to Bruckel's office is a storeroom with heavy double doors.

Beyond these offices there is the entrance to the cafeteria on the right, a short corridor to a back entrance on the left and, in front, high-security double doors (requiring a punched in combination and magnetic swipe card to enter) separating off the more secret parts of the building. The cafeteria has a door out onto the front lawn, where the workers can sit during their breaks on fine days, and photographs on the wall show the various stages of the station's construction.

Over two-thirds of the operations building and all the real workings of the station lie beyond the double doors. Each door has a large, circular No Smoking sign stuck to it: not for the health of the workers, but to protect the delicate electronic and computer equipment located within.

Through the security doors the corridor runs on down the centre of the building, with rooms off to each side, before opening out into the large main operations room at the west end of the building. On the right of the corridor is the staff training room and then a large workshop for the technicians. The workshop has brightly lit benches positioned around the walls where the technicians test and repair equipment. At the west end of the workshop a large window looks out across the main operations room.

In the middle of the long workshop is a large British-made walk-in vault for storing top secret materials, including manuals, equipment and encryption programmes for sending the intercepted communications in code from the station to Wellington.

Six rooms come off the corridor to the left. First is the Uninterruptable Power Supply room, which contains a large bank of batteries, constantly being recharged to ensure that the interception equipment never loses power. It provides direct current (DC) power to the equipment in the main operations room, most likely 24 or 48 volt for this type of equipment. Next on the left is a general photocopying cum office room and then the maintenance workshop (with work benches, drill presses etc). The fourth room on this side is a library with shelves running high up the walls to hold many publications, manuals and folders used by the staff. The fifth room belongs to the two technicians (Tony Aimers and his assistant) who make up the special projects team. This room has three computer work stations connected to computer data bases, two printers and a high work bench for using specialised electronic equipment. Last on the left is the small room containing the security officers who monitor the main gate and perimeter fence through the video cameras and look out through glass walls across the main operations room.

The main operations room at the end of the corridor is the heart of the station. The normality of the rest of the building does not prepare you at all for this room. You imagine it will be very functional and ordinary, its significance hidden in the invisible workings of the machines. But the first time you see this room it can be a strange and unsettling experience. It is a huge room with a handful of workers during office hours but most of the time no people at all. Banks of very sophisticated equipment and spaceship-like control areas run themselves. The only movement comes from constellations of small blinking red, green, orange and white lights. The equipment is supplied by the UKUSA allies and wholly integrated into their system — you could just as well be in the United States.

The equipment consists of 50 tall blue electronics cabinets,[4] arranged into banks of seven or eight cabinets running lengthwise along the building. The computers, where the day staff work, are located in two separate control areas at opposite ends of the room. Looking like something out of *Star Trek*, the computers are arranged in half-circles, with nine computer monitors on one, seven on the other.

Once the instructions directing the interception have been programmed in, the equipment works automatically: receiving the satellite signals from the dish, processing them and sending on intercepted communications electronically to the Wellington communications staff for further distribution within the GCSB headquarters and overseas. The equipment comes from various manufacturers, including the United States Honeywell company. Most of the high-security end of the building has a false floor (of removable white 600-millimetre square tiles) with a space beneath for running ducts and cables. All the windows in the operations building are covered with steel bars and security curtains.

The dish antenna, which is located on the north side of the operations building, was manufactured in the United States and arrived in pieces from Houston in seven shipping containers. Two people from the US company came to New Zealand for a few weeks to oversee its on-site contruction.[5] Mounted on an 8-metre pedestal, the steel dish has a diameter of 18 metres, the standard size for antennae at all the Intelsat earth stations around the Pacific. Locating a large dish in an 'electronically quiet' area like the Waihopai Valley helps the station to pick up even very faint signals.

The whole antenna structure is contained within the 30-metre high radome, which is made of a very strong, non-flammable high-tech fabric (probably kevlar). When it was being installed it hung loose, like an empty balloon, as a crane lifted it over the completed dish (there is a photo of this on the wall in the station cafeteria). The radome (which was also built in the United States) is kept permanently inflated by large fans that pump air into it so that it maintains its rigid shape even in strong winds (and even if it had small punctures). For additional security, the radome is enclosed in a separate steel mesh and barbed wire security fence. (None of the satellite dishes at Morwenstow, Hong Kong or Yakima has ever been covered by radomes. The decision to cover the Waihopai and Geraldton dishes appears to indicate a sensitivity about the public discovering what satellites the stations are targeting.)

The radome is entered through two doors, with an air lock between, because the pressure inside is much greater than the atmospheric pressure outside. The inside of the radome is completely empty except for the dish. Visitors to the radome are often encouraged to stand on opposite sides of the radome with their heads up against the fabric and whisper to each other. Because of the perfect circular shape, even small sounds travel around the wall and can be heard clearly on the far side.

Although hidden by the radome, the satellite dish can at times clearly be heard changing its direction. Mechanical systems, controlled from inside the operations building, tip the dish up and down and move it sideways, automatically adjusting it to follow the position of the satellite. The original Intelsat 5 target satellite moved about 5-7 degrees each day in a figure of eight motion across the sky, requiring frequent adjustment of the dish. The new Intelsat 7 satellite is much more stable, moving only about 0.2 of a degree each day.

If anyone has any doubt about the station's target, a stroll around the perimeter fence at night confirms what is already known. After dark the dish can be clearly seen projected against the radome by the lights of the main operations room (which is located directly behind it). The shadow shows the dish facing directly north, consistent with the position of the Pacific Intelsats.[6]

Waihopai station is to eavesdropping what a huge pulp and paper mill is to paper-making, or McDonalds is to fast food. It is industrial-scale spying, using high-tech equipment and automation to handle the immense throughput of intercepted communications.

The dish antenna, aimed at the target satellite, collects all the signals being transmitted. These signals, which are very faint, are directed into the operations room to a low noise amplifier that amplifies them into stronger signals. These are then fed to racks of radio receivers in some of the blue cabinets (designed for the microwave frequencies on which satellites transmit). The satellite will be transmitting on various frequencies, each containing a number of bands that can carry large numbers of communications simultaneously. Each receiver is tuned to a different band, taking just this out of the mass of incoming signals.

Each of these bands of signals has had hundreds of individual telephone, fax, telex and data messages electronically combined together into it when it is sent (this is called multiplexing), and the communications equipment at Waihopai must unravel this combined signal back into the individual messages again (demultiplexing). (This same operation has to occur in a normal satellite telecommunications ground station.) Most of the banks of blue cabinets contain United States-built Statmux equipment ('mux' is the abbreviation for multiplexing) which does this work of converting the satellite signals back into individual messages.

The output from the Statmuxs may go through another computer at this stage to select certain channels from each band (each of the hundreds of channels in one band carry one telephone conversation or several data links). Either directly from the Statmuxs or through this computer, the intercepted communications are now fed to the powerful computer that is the basis of the ECHELON system.

The key element of this massive spying operation is the FLINTLOCK Dictionary computer. Using its huge processing capability, this computer 'reads' every word of every message gathered so far in the process, looking for the hundreds of keywords — names of individuals and organisations, embassy telex numbers and so on — on the station's search lists. The messages containing the pre-programmed keywords are automatically identified and extracted from the rest of the intercepted communications.

Before the computer can search for the keywords, special computer programmes convert the various types of messages into standard computer language so that they can be processed electronically. Even if a message is in code it will begin and end with uncoded electronic instructions (called 'headers' and 'footers') which the normal telecommunications equipment reads to know to which telex or fax machine that message is going. When a message is in code, the Dictionary computer can recognise these headers and footers and still select the messages to and from target people and organisations. The decoding occurs back at the agencies' headquarters.

The link between Waihopai and Wellington occurs computer to computer. All the intercepted messages are put into unbreakable codes by computer and sent by modem to the GCSB headquarters. They are transmitted along standard telephone lines (the same lines that the farmers in the valley use for their telephone calls), since most of the bulk of the satellite traffic has been eliminated at the station. The codes ensure that no one can eavesdrop on the eavesdroppers.

The main human work occurring in the main operations room is done by the station's radio officers. Three of them work in the computer area at the back of the operations room, at 'patch panels' and computer monitors, the other two at the computers in the control area at the front of the operations room. This is the location of the station's Dictionary computer and also the computer communications link with Wellington.

The radio officers provide instructions to the intercept equipment, according to the collection schedule, to direct its automatic operations and also control the station's external communications. For example, since some of the bands and channels are more likely than others to contain intelligence of interest to the GCSB or its allies and the Dictionary computers' capacity is limited, instructions must be given about which parts of the incoming traffic to feed into the Dictionary for intensive searching. They also work with the CS1 satellite traffic analysts in Wellington to search through the thousands of channels carried by the satellite, identifying what each channel carries, when and for whom. Some channels may be sent unprocessed to Wellington for analysis.

Some channels will have lots of Internet messages, some will have telex circuits, some telephone circuits carrying lots of fax messages, some leased commercial data circuits and others point-to-point circuits between or within countries of interest. Because of the high cost of satellite services, some countries have only a relatively small number of permanent satellite circuits handling all their overseas communications. Once these are identified, it is very easy to target that country. The circuits carrying the Bougainville communications, for example, were identified in this way.

As a result of traffic analysis work, the GCSB operations staff decide which frequencies and bands to monitor when. A lot of the information needed for these decisions will come from the NSA, which has been intercepting Waihopai's INTELSAT 701 and its predecessors for many years. As one staff member explained: 'the satellite channels have already been subjected to thorough traffic analysis...they know there is enough good stuff in what they are targeting. Still, they are constantly experimenting with what Waihopai can get...working on what can come out.'

The result of this work is the station's collection schedule, which specifies which bands and channels from the target satellite will be processed at the station on what days and times. From 8 am until 11 am on week days might be one selection of bands and channels, followed by a different selection for the next period.

GCSB staff say that the collection schedule is worked out in co-operation with the overseas agencies to achieve the best production of intelligence for the overall network. At Waihopai this regularly includes giving lower priority to targets that interest the GCSB analysts because another agency can use the Dictionary better by tapping other channels at that time.

When a new schedule is set up, a test period follows during which staff check everything coming through to see if it is providing the types of intelligence wanted. After the test period, the station staff can just flick back and forth to that combination of selected channels according to the collection schedule.

Waihopai maintains communication with the Wellington headquarters through the computer communications links, secure telephone and fax links and a regular safe hand bag, which comes down from Wellington once a week and back the same day.

Constant advances in telecommunications technology — in both new forms of messages and how the messages are sent — mean that GCSB staff must regularly update their systems for exploiting communications. During the early years of Waihopai operations, for example, the staff had great difficulty processing fax messages reliably, which caused significant problems for intercepting South Pacific government communications that rely heavily on faxes. The GCSB has also had some problems with e-mail. Communication of e-mail via the Pacific INTELSATs involves packet switching, in which messages are routinely broken up and sent in segments, with each segment going by a different route, according to what is most efficient. There have been times when the Waihopai Dictionary has churned out only fragments of e-mail messages, scrambled messages or a few words of one message in the midst of screeds of some other irrelevant message.

Mostly, though, the Waihopai station ransacks the Pacific's communications with cold efficiency.

TANGIMOANA

Very few members of the public can ever see a facility such as the Tangimoana station. Those who ignore the trespass signs are still able only to peer at the anonymous outsides of the buildings through security fences.[7] Next we go inside Tangimoana to find out what goes on there.

There are three main buildings at Tangimoana: a low-security administration/cafeteria building, the main high-security operations building (connected to the administration building by a glass walkway) and a small separate services building containing workshops and a stand-by generator in case the power supply to the station is interrupted.[8]

These buildings are inside a security compound surrounded by a 3-metre fence topped with coils of razor-sharp barbed tape, a no-man's-land with infra-red detectors and then a second, even heavier fence.[9] It looks like a concentration camp. Security inside the operations compound was increased in the early 1990s, out of fear of public protests, by the addition of security lighting, video surveillance (monitored from the shift supervisor's office) and bars on all the windows.

Only people with special security clearances are allowed into the operations building. The entrance, which is reached from the glass walkway, leads into a central corridor with high internal windows and doors opening into the various sections. UKUSA regulations would never allow it, but if you walked down the corridor this is what you would find.

The Operations Centre, where the actual spying work occurs, comes off the left of this corridor through double doors. Here are the intercept staff, wearing headphones, working at the various types of equipment. These officers work in shifts, 24 hours a day, seven days a week, changing over at 4 pm, midnight and 8-9 am. Originally there were rows of officers working here, about 10 per shift; now there are only two or three.

Most of the radio officers are former Navy communications officers, others came from civil aviation jobs. The GCSB trains them for interception operations and requires them to work towards the GCSB Radio Officers Examination.[10]

The station Operations Manager, Daryl McPhee, and the shift supervisors work in offices with windows looking out into the centre. On the Monday to Friday day shifts the manager is in change of operations; at other times the shift supervisors serve as the station's duty officers. (They have been promoted to this job after years of experience as radio officers.)

The equipment units at which the radio officers work are about 1.8 metres high and the staff move between them for different operations. Some contain very modern computer systems, other older types still use dials to search through the frequencies. The Tangimoana staff have also intercepted telephone messages sent by HF radio. In recent years new types of intercept equipment have been installed to keep up with developments in communications technology such as digital HF radio, which can send computer data, faxes and so on.

The next area of the operations building is the Technical Search Unit. Headed by a manager, this unit is made up of radio officers called technical search officers and analysts, who also work in shifts. Each shift includes one or two technical search officers working in the 'tech search' room next to the Operations Centre. The technical search officers look for interesting new transmissions, while the analysts across the corridor analyse and document the frequencies, transmission times and other characteristics of the new transmissions for possible future use. This is the same type of work as occurs in the C Unit at headquarters.

Further along the central corridor, off to the left after the Operations Centre, used to be the location of the station's training unit, headed by a Training Manager, ex-GCHQ Mike O'Regan. Although the area still has the training equipment, it was closed in 1993. This is where the radio officers were taught to use the various types of monitoring equipment. Any training now occurs in Wellington. Similarly, until 1995 the station had its own communications staff, who worked in the highest security room in the building, the Information Centre, reached through the first door to the right off the corridor. Here the communications officers received instructions for the radio officers from GCSB headquarters and from other UKUSA stations, sent out some of the information that had been intercepted and acted as the terminal through which the computer communications (notably for the Dictionary computer system) were routed. This room is no longer used.

The communications duties are now handled by the Operations Manager. Working only day shifts, he receives all reports produced by the operations staff, checks them for accuracy and sends them from his computer directly to the headquarters Infocen. In addition a safe hand bag is carried between Tangimoana and Wellington each Wednesday by GCSB courier. The manager of the communications centre until the changes was a former GCHQ headquarters officer, Alec Jarnell,[11] who was one of the foreign signals intelligence staff recruited to work at Tangimoana.

The station's technical staff occupy most of the front of the operations building, including a large electronics workshop and storerooms for equipment and parts. There are two technicians, down from five following the cuts, under the control of the Station Engineer (or 'Technical Manager'). These are electronics specialists responsible for maintaining all the sophisticated electronic equipment and project development at the station. Maintenance of the antennae has been contracted out to Telecom. The Station Engineer is currently Paul Ropata, who has many years of technical experience in the GCSB and, before that, in the military. Specifications for the technicians' jobs show the scope of the operation: installing and maintaining radio receivers, radio demodulators, telephone equipment, communications equipment, information processing equipment and antenna and signal distribution systems.[12]

The administration building contains the Officer in Charge of the station and the Administration Officer and his small staff. Unlike the headquarters and Waihopai station, there are no security staff. The Officer in Charge in 1996 is Barry Keane, who took over in July 1996. He and his immediate predecessor are the first OICs who have not risen up through the radio officer ranks doing interception work. There are few visitors to the station besides contractors, although the GCSB Director turns up occasionally to show NSA and GCHQ visitors around.

In 1996, there are only about 20 shift staff and 15 day staff at Tangimoana. Except for some low-paid support workers, all the staff are men. There have only been two woman radio officers; one now works in the headquarters and the other left. The staff live mostly in the nearby towns of Marton, Feilding, Palmerston North and Bulls and arrive at work in white GCSB vans.

The first two antennae you notice at the station are rotatable log periodic antennae, which are shaped like huge TV aerials on top of tall towers. Built commercially in the United States, they are designed to rotate on their towers to point towards targets, usually ships, of interest (the short end towards the target).[13] Except on very windy days, when they are pointed into the wind, anyone with a compass can calculate the direction in which they are aimed and guess at the target. For example, these antennae have been measured pointing towards Port Vila, Antarctica and, in 1987 after the coup, Fiji.

The elaborately shaped omni-gain antenna is located in the same field as the rotatables and has the same technical characteristics. The difference is that it is omni-directional, that is, it picks up signals from all directions. It is also used continuously by the radio officers. With a height of 36 metres, it is said by its United States manufacturers to be 'ideal for roll call, shore-to-ship and ground-to-air communications involving transmission paths greater than 1000km'.

Next there are three rhombic antennae situated 500 metres along the access road beyond the operations building, connected to it by overhead lines that look very much like ordinary power lines on their wooden poles. Each rhombic consists of wires in a large diamond shape (200 by 75 metres), all suspended 24 metres in the air by towers in each corner. This type of antenna can receive even very faint signals with a high degree of accuracy from radio receivers located in the two directions of the diamond's points. The radio officers often use these for intercepting weak signals. The central rhombic points roughly north-south and the other two point about 45 degrees east and west of this out into the Pacific. The rhombic antennae have been designed to allow good reception in either direction, so they can also listen down towards Antarctica and beyond into the southern Atlantic and Indian Oceans. They were erected in late 1985.[14] No major new antennae have been installed at the station since then.

Finally, the 'circularly disposed antenna array' (CDAA),[15] used for direction finding, stands alone on the right of the road to the west of the operations building. It consists of three large concentric circles of poles, in total 150 metres across. In the centre is a small building — the 'aerial hut' — full of complex electronic processing equipment for making the direction-finding calculations. It includes mechanical goniometers, modern versions of the ones used in the Second World War direction-finding stations. This building is connected to the control panels in the operations room, where the radio officers use the system to search for and fix the directions of target radio transmitters (usually ships).

The system provides the frequency and time of the radio transmission and the bearing (i.e. compass direction) of the radio transmitter or transmitters. Two or more radios in communication with each other will be using the same frequency so that the circular array will get a bearing for each of them. Throughout the world the presence of a circular antenna array is almost certain proof of a signals intelligence station. Arrays like the one at Tangimoana, and in some cases identical to it, are found in many different countries operating as part of a UKUSA network.

OVERSEAS STATIONS

MORWENSTOW, CORNWALL, ENGLAND

Morwenstow is reached by travelling 100 kilometres east of Exeter to the coastal town of Bude, and then taking the winding roads that run 15 kilometres up the coast from Bude to Morwenstow. The station, which today has nine or 10 satellite dishes and extensive operations buildings, can be viewed from the road at Morwenstow or by walking along the top of the cliffs on the South West Peninsula walkway.

YAKIMA, WASHINGTON, USA

Yakima is 200 kilometres south-east of Seattle. It can be visited by taking the Interstate 90 highway through the Cascade Range to Ellensberg and then turning south down Interstate 82 towards the city of Yakima. Interstate 82 cuts through the army range that hides the station and passes within 5 kilometres of the station itself. The entrance is about halfway between Ellensburg and Yakima; turn left into the firing range land. If you avoid military police at the entrance gate, it is possible to drive through desert country and approach the station.

SUGAR GROVE, WEST VIRGINIA, USA

To find Sugar Grove, about 250 kilometres south-west of Washington DC, you need a very detailed map. The station can be visited by taking Interstate 66 from Washington DC and then Interstate 81 along the Shenandoah Valley to Harrisonburg. From there, Highway 33 crosses through the mountains to Brandywine, where a side road on the left winds the last 15 kilometres to Sugar Grove. A restricted and guarded 2-kilometre access road leads to the station.

WHERE THE INTELLIGENCE ENDS UP

EXTERNAL ASSESSMENTS BUREAU

The External Assessments Bureau is New Zealand's external intelligence analysis organisation, producing reports that keep the government informed on international issues. It has no role in intelligence collection or internal security matters. It is deliberately intended not to give policy recommendations; in practice, the reports are neutral, although often from a conservative perspective.

The EAB is the main New Zealand organisation using the intelligence produced by the GCSB and its UKUSA allies. Most GCSB and overseas reports go to the EAB, where they are combined with other types of information (mostly open sources) into intelligence reports for the New Zealand government and the intelligence allies.

The EAB's mission statement describes its role as:

Identification, collection, evaluation and analysis of information on topics likely to affect New Zealand's interests and preparation of intelligence reports on political, economic, social, biographic, strategic, infrastructural, scientific and technological subjects as required to assist the Government in the formulation of its policies.[1]

The EAB has had this broad scope since 1975 when its predecessor, the Joint Intelligence Bureau (JIB), became the External Intelligence Bureau (EIB). It was renamed the External Assessments Bureau in 1988. The bureau has an annual budget of about $2.5 million (1994-95) and in 1995 had 30 staff (18 research and 12 support) overseen by a director and two assessment managers. The EAB is located on the fourth and fifth floors of the Ministry of Foreign Affairs and Trade's main building, Stafford House, in central Wellington.

Until the early 1990s the research staff were divided into four sections with four to six members in each: Northern, Southern, Pacific and Scientific and Strategic. In the mid-1990s there are two groups of 10 research staff headed by the two assessment managers. The first group has long-time EAB analysts Des Rowe, who covers the European Union countries, and Michael Munro, covering the Middle East; two analysts working together on China, Hong Kong and Taiwan; an analyst covering North and South Korea and Japan; Ian Brownlie, who came from the GCSB, covering the former Soviet Union states; and an analyst covering South East Asian countries including Indonesia and Malaysia.

The other group has two or three South Pacific analysts, one or two covering environmental issues, one specialising in economic intelligence concerning international finance and trade, and analysts covering scientific and strategic intelligence. One of the staff is on secondment from Australia; for example, Paula Freeman had a two-year posting to the EAB from Canberra in early 1989 and worked as the specialist on Papua New Guinea during the first two years of the Bougainville conflict.

The Scientific and Strategic staff have produced reports on a wide range of military and scientific issues: missile developments in Russia and China, aspects of New Zealand defence policy (including regular strategic assessments provided to Defence as part of its planning process), Antarctica, controversial nuclear weapon and nuclear power issues and scientific developments that may be of interest to other government agencies.

Their main long-term project has been collating intelligence about the French nuclear weapon testing programme at Moruroa. They have used signals intelligence collected by the GCSB about the movements of French military aircraft to and from Moruroa in preparation for a test, together with other sources of information, to predict and monitor the numbers, times and sizes of the French tests.

Pat Helm, then head of this section, was posted to Washington in 1984-87 at the height of the New Zealand-United States conflict over nuclear warship visits. While there, he contributed to two important EIB reports concerning nuclear weapons on western warships. It was these reports which were given to Labour Cabinet ministers to read over a weekend before a crucial Cabinet meeting in late January 1985, where it would be decided whether to accept a United States request for the nuclear weapon-capable frigate USS *Buchanan* to visit. The reports, one of which concluded that 'experienced service personnel... would be able to reach a reasoned judgement on the probability that a particular nuclear-capable surface vessel or group of such vessels was in fact carrying nuclear weapons',[2] were accompanied by a recommendation from senior Defence staff that the government accept the visit. The government rejected the advice and New Zealand's nuclear-free policy was established.

Despite its comparatively small size, the EAB has a large output of reports every year. In 1988, for example, one of the senior staff estimated that up to 300 intelligence reports are produced each year plus another 300 biographical reports on prominent people in countries of interest, giving a total of up to 600 reports a year.[3] The EAB analysts draw on a wide range of sources to produce their reports. On average, about 70-80 percent of the information comes from unclassified sources:[4] regular cables from New Zealand diplomatic posts reporting on issues of interest to New Zealand (all cables go to the EAB as they come in), newspapers, journals and so on. There are two Reuters terminals in the library providing continuous international news reports. The rest comes from secret sources. But these proportions vary a lot, depending on the subject and the country being studied.

Although on many subjects secret sources such as signals intelligence tend to confirm information and interpretations available from open sources, for subjects such as missile and nuclear warhead testing, arms developments and defence spending levels in other countries, secret intelligence is often the main source of information. This was certainly the case throughout the Cold War when JIB/EIB reports on Soviet military developments relied primarily on United States intelligence information.

Various types of secret intelligence are available to EAB analysts, including the signals intelligence reports, gists and summaries from the UKUSA agencies and reports received from overseas counterparts of the EAB, such as MI6 in Britain and the CIA in the United States.

The establishment of New Zealand's formal intelligence links with the CIA occurred in the early 1950s, against the background of the Korean War and the signing of the ANZUS Treaty in 1951. The links were arranged in discussions between the CIA and Brigadier Walter McKinnon, New Zealand's Defence representative in Washington and father of the National government Minister of Foreign Affairs, Don McKinnon. The arrangements included liaison visits to New Zealand by the CIA representative based in Australia and a New Zealand liaison officer with the CIA in Washington.[5]

One CIA source highly valued by EAB analysts is information from the Foreign Broadcast Information Service (FBIS), located within the CIA's Directorate of Science and

Technology, which is responsible for technical intelligence collection. It is not actually secret intelligence: the FBIS's job is to monitor the public radio and television broadcasts of foreign nations, transcribe/translate them and (occasionally) prepare summaries. The EAB receives all reports from the FBIS.

The EAB produces most of its reports according to a schedule set by the Intelligence Requirements and Assessments Committee (IRAC), which includes representatives from the EAB, GCSB, the Ministry of Foreign Affairs and Trade, the Directorate of Defence Intelligence and occasionally the Ministries of Commerce and of Agriculture and Fisheries, the Treasury, the Security Intelligence Service and other departments. There are two types of IRAC reports, intelligence assessments and intelligence reports, delivered to ministers and to the departments concerned by weekly safe hand courier. A third category of reports, outside the regular weekly cycle of reporting, is 'current assessments'. These are situation reports produced quickly, probably in a few hours, as required on rapidly developing situations.

Other EAB reports include large numbers of biographical reports about prominent overseas people, usually individuals coming to New Zealand or with whom New Zealand representatives will be dealing in other countries. There is also 'provision on an ad hoc basis of data and information required by departments concerned with New Zealand's foreign relations'.[6]

Another specific EAB publication is the top secret *South Pacific Intelligence Notes*, known as SPINs, produced by the South Pacific analysts. These are regular updates of all significant intelligence about the South Pacific, including summaries of GCSB and other intelligence that has already been included in EAB intelligence assessments and reports with South Pacific themes or topics. They are about 6-8 pages in length made up of lots of short items. Each item has brackets indicating the security level of the source: top secret, secret or confidential.

A quite different type of report is the *New Zealand Intelligence Briefing Memoranda* (NZIBM), which have been produced and updated jointly with the DDI. Up to 100 pages in length, these provide 'a short summary of basic intelligence likely to be of use to Government departments and service staffs in outline planning and briefing'[7] about each of the countries within the New Zealand Intelligence Area. They are shared with the four intelligence allies, which share their equivalent publications with New Zealand. They are 'New Zealand' Intelligence Briefing Memoranda to distinguish them from the allied ones.

The segment of the South Pacific which the NZIBM cover, known as the New Zealand Intelligence Area, dates from British Empire days. The original lines were drawn by Britain as part of the division of the world's oceans into administrative regions called stations. The New Zealand station, previously part of the China station and formed in 1920, covered over a sixth of the area of the globe (larger than the Australia station): extending from a line between New Zealand and Australia across beyond French Polynesia to 120 degrees longitude, and from Antarctica to the Equator plus a large extension north of the Equator to include Hawaii and Midway Island. This area, with a few adjustments such as tactfully moving the northern line to just south of Pearl Harbor, became New Zealand's ongoing area of intelligence responsibilities in the late 1940s conferences which established the post-war intelligence structures.

In 1988, the Secretary of Foreign Affairs told a parliamentary committee that the (then) EIB had a 'good co-operative relationship with its opposite numbers in Australia, Canada and the United Kingdom' and also, although not on such good terms at that time, with the United States. He confirmed that the EAB exchanges intelligence assessments with these countries.[8] In addition, intelligence liaison and exchange occurs with some intelligence agencies of other countries on a more distant basis, including, according to one intelligence officer, 'some regional countries one wouldn't expect'. These include the Indonesian intelligence organisation, Bakin, although not on such an open and close basis as the Australian intelligence agencies have with Bakin.[9]

The EAB is a quite different organisation from the GCSB. Even though they both handle secret intelligence, the EAB is much more open. EAB staff are listed openly in the Foreign Affairs phone directory, while GCSB staff are not even supposed to tell their friends where they work. EAB's mission statement, staff numbers, structures, overseas postings and so on are public information while in the GCSB these are all secret. The EAB is not dominated by ex-military staff.

And, being less secretive, the EAB is more open to New Zealand government influence. It is consequently much more New Zealand-oriented in its day-to-day output.

DIRECTORATE OF DEFENCE INTELLIGENCE

The Directorate of Defence Intelligence (DDI) is regarded, within intelligence circles, as being a 'low powered' organisation compared with the External Assessments Bureau. It is a section within the New Zealand Defence Force headquarters.

The DDI's primary role is to provide military intelligence to the Defence chiefs rather than into the wider New Zealand intelligence system. It produces only about 5 percent of the intelligence reports and assessments requested by the inter-departmental Intelligence Requirements and Assessments Committee (IRAC) and provides some information to other government organisations such as the EAB.

Unlike the EAB, it also has an intelligence collection role: directing and co-ordinating some intelligence collection by Defence personnel (including Defence attachés) about countries of interest.

The DDI's official (but not necessarily actual) functions include: arranging collection of intelligence, collation of intelligence into intelligence briefs, summaries, reports and assessments and dissemination of this intelligence.

The DDI was formed in 1964 out of the previously separate Army, Navy and Air Force intelligence organisations, at the same time as the unified Ministry of Defence was established. A single Director of Defence Intelligence replaced the three separate service intelligence directors in 1975. The DDI directors since 1975 are listed in Appendix A.

Only about 15 staff in the DDI are involved in defence intelligence work. The intelligence staff include the director, a deputy director of defence intelligence, five assistant directors covering different areas, about nine intelligence officers and four administrative support staff (another seven DDI staff cover physical security, personnel security and security relating to defence industries).

The intelligence staff are divided into five sections, each headed by an assistant director. There are three two-person current intelligence sections — covering Pacific, South East Asia and Rest of World; a three-person operational intelligence section; and a five-person section concerned with producing the *New Zealand Intelligence Briefing Memoranda* (NZIBM). The DDI is located in a secure area on the sixth floor of the Defence Headquarters in Stout Street in central Wellington

The DDI intelligence analysts collate military intelligence mainly about the countries of the South Pacific and South East Asia. They are supposed to be experts on the armed forces in these countries and they collate geographical and infrastructural information on South Pacific countries (published in the NZIBM)[10] for New Zealand and allied military units which might have to go there. They also prepare political and military updates on current events of interest. In addition to these regional concerns, at least until recently the DDI has had a major preoccupation with all things Russian. The DDI had two staff assigned to monitoring Soviet ship movements in the Pacific (which for Soviet naval vessels entirely meant the North Pacific) and the Soviet fleet at Vladivostok.

The DDI is the second largest recipient of signals intelligence after the EAB — including both GCSB intelligence and that received from the overseas agencies. The same GCSB courier who used to deliver reports regularly to the EAB went on a round trip via the DDI as well (and the SIS). Since 1993 there has been a GCSB L liaison officer permanently based in the DDI with the reports on-line to be viewed by the DDI staff. From the GCSB this includes reports on Russian fishing and research vessels and Russian bases in Antarctica and a wide range of intelligence about the South Pacific.

But the most highly valued reports at the DDI were, at least until recently, those from the overseas agencies on Soviet forces. DDI received weekly reports giving position reports for all Soviet, Communist bloc and Chinese merchant and naval vessels in the Pacific and reports on other aspects of Soviet military forces and operations. The DDI receives a similar wide range and very large quantity of overseas (especially United States) signals intelligence as the EAB. This intelligence covers all the areas of the world where events concern one of the UKUSA allies and also includes information on international terrorist threats.

A confidential 1986 report about the break in New Zealand-United States military ties said: 'While the United States actions have had relatively little effect on the amount of general information that is available to New Zealand about our immediate strategic environment, the cutback has been most significant in the military area. The most serious result is that the Maritime Defence Commander now has an incomplete picture of the presence and movements of ships within New Zealand's strategic environment and our area of direct strategic concern.... This referred to a loss of intelligence from US ocean surveillance satellites 'particularly in the northern portion of New Zealand's area of maritime interest....'[11]

'New Zealand no longer receives the publications which were the prime source of technical data on Soviet ships, submarines, weapons and sensor systems.... Many of the Soviet systems described in these publications are also fitted in their research ships, and are of direct relevance to our Navy's operations....'[12]

Although 80 percent of United States military intelligence to New Zealand was cut in 1985, New Zealand continued to supply all its DDI reports to the four intelligence allies. The same 1986 report had recommended that New Zealand 'continue to supply comprehensive intelligence reports focusing on the South Pacific' to the allies. For example, the distribution list for the DDI's South Pacific Intelligence Summaries, produced sporadically in the late 1980s, included two sections in the United States Defence Intelligence Agency in Washington and an intelligence unit in the Hawaii military command, two Australian intelligence organisations and the Australian Navy, three defence intelligence sections in the British Ministry of Defence and section within the Canadian military headquarters. All the reports also went to the United States and British military attaché staff in Wellington.[13]

Much of the defence intelligence liaison occurs through defence attachés. The New Zealand High Commission in Canberra, for example, includes an Assistant Defence Attaché (Intelligence), whose functions include maintaining close contact with Australian defence intelligence organisations and informing them about New Zealand operational intelligence activities, reporting to DDI all items of intelligence interest and monitoring intelligence training opportunities.[14]

The DDI has close contacts with six countries that have foreign defence attachés in Wellington: the United States, Australia, Britain, France, Indonesia, Malaysia and, at one time, Papua New Guinea (each has a personal listing in the Defence Headquarters' internal telephone directory). The DDI regularly briefs them, supplies them with intelligence and receives foreign intelligence in return. Many New Zealanders would be surprised to know that the French embassy's military attaché is a frequent visitor to the DDI. Throughout the turbulent *Rainbow Warrior* affair and periods of controversy over nuclear testing, he has visited the DDI staff in their 6th floor offices every one or two weeks to discuss issues and exchange intelligence. The same applies to the Indonesian military attaché during controversy over East Timor.

Overall, the DDI does not have the EAB's experienced analysts and generally lacks a strong sense of purpose. Within intelligence circles the view is that the DDI staff feel that they are not doing very important work but that they do not know what to do about it. The changes in the Soviet Union, removing their allies' main intelligence target, has probably contributed to this lack of direction. The official functions of the DDI listed above are, in practice, often not fulfilled.

COURIER LINKS WITH THE OTHER UKUSA NATIONS

Most secret intelligence is sent electronically between the UKUSA countries in unbreakable codes, but another continuous movement of intelligence around the world involves special high-security couriers carrying intelligence materials in safe hand bags. Safe hand couriers, as the name suggests, must carry by hand or escort the classified materials at all times. New Zealand receives overseas intelligence and intelligence-related materials from the NSA, GCHQ and DSD in this way.

Signals intelligence bags from the NSA are delivered to the GCSB via the American embassy in Wellington about once a month, carried by staff of the United States Defense Courier Service (DCS), based at Fort George C. Meade, Maryland 20755, the NSA heaquarters. The special DCS couriers use defence courier stations in different countries as their bases while moving materials around the world.[15] There is such a station in Australia and the DCS couriers are also used to deliver NSA materials to the Australian DSD.

Twice a week a huge United States Air Force Starlifter aircraft lands at Christchurch International Airport as part of a regular flight around the Pacific. The flights go from California to American Samoa, then the crew stay overnight in Christchurch before going on to Australia. These flights arrive in New Zealand every Sunday and Friday, stopping outside the United States Air Force compound located to the north of the public terminals.

The flights through Christchurch regularly have a pair of American safe hand couriers on board, travelling in civilian clothing. These couriers can be seen accompanying classified cargo, standing nearby while special grey mail bags (with a red stripe around the middle) and large palleted boxes are being loaded and unloaded from the aircraft.[16] One of the couriers even sleeps with the cargo overnight in a room at the end of the main United States Air Force hangar. Some of the large boxes passing through Christchurch are marked 'CREDIBLE DOVE' and 'From Ft George C. Meade to Alice Springs'. They contain computer tapes being moved between the NSA headquarters at Fort Meade and the United States signals intelligence facility at Pine Gap, Alice Springs.[17]

This movement of classified intelligence materials is the job of the United States Air Force's Air Mobility Command, which flies the Starlifters. Its Special Activities Division conducts '1A3 secure airlift missions' within the continental United States, codenamed CREDIBLE CAT. These flights have 'mission couriers' escorting hundreds of classified cargo shipments each year, shipments described as their 'top priority peacetime mission'.[18] The CREDIBLE codeword obviously refers to the transporting of intelligence materials to different parts of the world.

Intelligence provided to New Zealand by the Central Intelligence Agency (CIA) is also brought into the country by couriers, or is sent via the New Zealand CIA liaison officer in Washington and returned to New Zealand in the diplomatic pouch. Safe hand bags containing signals intelligence materials from the British GCHQ are brought to New Zealand by British couriers and are delivered to the GCSB via the British High Commission in Wellington. The British safe hand couriers are called the Queen's Messengers. Australia also delivers to the GCSB using its safe hand service.

A co-operative system of safe hand couriers exists between the four Commonwealth UKUSA countries. For example, New Zealand handles safe hand deliveries in the South Pacific for Britain and Canada and they reciprocate in other parts of the world.[19] The safe hand couriers fly business class, using the spare seats next to them for their bags if they have a number to escort at once.

According to safe hand procedures, an outer envelope or package has 'safe hand' stamped on the front and back and the addressee's name or position. An inner envelope has the name of the person authorised to receive it, the security classification stamped on (e.g. 'Top Secret') and seals (e.g. New Zealand ones are red and black and say 'New Zealand Government'). The more people an envelope is passed between before it gets to its destination, the more envelopes (one within the other) addressed to successive 'safe hand addressees' are used.

Outgoing bags from the GCSB are handled by the M4 section in the headquarters building. The white canvas bags they use contain carefully closed boxes and are closed with special lead seals and tags. Receipts must be returned by the receiver acknowledging their arrival. M4 staff have been seen picking up and dropping off these bags at the Ministry of Foreign Affairs and Trade. New Zealand safe hand couriers based at Foreign Affairs transport the GCSB bags to the DSD headquarters in Canberra, and they are sent on to the other agencies from there. For example, GCSB materials being sent to the NSA are presumably transferred to the US Defence Courier Station in Australia. The safe hand bag to Canberra closes at Foreign Affairs at 2 pm each Thursday.

SECOND WORLD WAR
SIGNALS INTELLIGENCE OPERATIONS

The earliest New Zealand signals intelligence operations occurred in the First World War, but this type of intelligence became much more important in the Second World War. By 1939 radio had developed to a stage where, for the first time, it played a central role in the war. This meant that intercepting radio messages from the enemy forces and their allies could be very important, and at times crucial. It allowed Allied intelligence staff to estimate the strength, positions and plans of the Axis military forces.

Few New Zealanders would have doubted the necessity for signals intelligence operations and the alliance they were part of during the frightening events of the Pacific war — had they known about them. But, except for the few people directly involved, most of the history of these activities has been kept completely secret.[1] Nearly all official archives relating to signals intelligence have never been made public or were accidentally destroyed after 1945. Even 50 years later the government refuses to release some information about the period. It was possible to investigate this history only because some of the people working in intelligence during the war were still alive and prepared to tell their stories.

The first signals intelligence operations in New Zealand began on the outbreak of the First World War. Two days after Britain declared war on Germany on 3 August 1914, the first intercepted German message arrived in Wellington from a New Zealand radio station (and was delivered to the Governor-General by a local intelligence officer). This implies pre-war planning of which frequencies and call signs should be targeted for intelligence. There are records from October 1914 of German radio messages being intercepted by New Zealand wireless stations in Suva and Wellington — and also probably by the Post and Telegraph station at Awanui in New Zealand's Far North — and sent to an Australian centre (which began operating that month) for analysis.[2]

There are no known records of New Zealand signals intelligence activities between the wars, but the Second World War intelligence organisation was built on the foundations of a small district intelligence office established in New Zealand by the British Royal Navy after 1918 as one link in a chain of 'stations' across the empire.[3]

The intelligence of interest in the New Zealand station — the section of the Pacific Ocean allocated to New Zealand by the British government — was mainly naval. The main aim was to protect shipping from enemy attack: detecting and plotting the positions of Japanese and German submarines and ships, keeping track of New Zealand's own ships so they could be diverted away from possible attack and building up an overall picture of the positions, capabilities and, if possible, intentions of the enemy units.

There were other parts to this intelligence system besides signals intelligence. Early in the war a network of coastwatching stations was established around the New Zealand coast (62 stations by March 1940) and on dozens of inhabited and uninhabited islands in the South Pacific. Staffed largely by civilians, these stations kept a 24-hour watch, reporting by radio or telephone to Naval Intelligence any sightings of ships or planes.[4]

There were also port war signal stations watching the entrance to each port, coastal gun batteries and, by 1943, a network of radar stations collecting similar information to the coastwatchers.

A naval 'examination service' in each port boarded visiting ships and, together with a network of naval intelligence 'reporting officers' (made up of local consuls, high commissioners and so on) on Pacific islands, helped to keep a record of the movements of all commercial shipping in the region. If a report of a suspected enemy vessel came in from, say, a coastwatch station, a reconnaissance aircraft could be sent to do a 'square search' of an area of ocean, the Merchant Shipping Office could reroute commercial shipping and Australian and American authorities operating in adjacent regions could be alerted.

This intelligence network, although mostly staffed by New Zealanders and reporting to the New Zealand government, was part of a British system. New Zealand's Director of Naval Intelligence, Lieutenant Commander F.M. Beasley, like most other senior naval staff in New Zealand at that time, was a British officer. His job was to oversee the New Zealand link in the worldwide British intelligence network and expand it as the Pacific war got closer. The standard British intelligence procedures were tailored to fit local requirements, but all the elements of the New Zealand intelligence system, secret and not secret, plus all the procedures, terminology and regulations used there were British.

By far the most secret element of this system was signals intelligence. Codenamed Y intelligence, this system comprised a network of top secret radio stations intercepting enemy messages and teams of codebreakers and analysts in New Zealand, Australia and elsewhere trying to make sense of the intelligence gathered. Most (but not all) of this intelligence work concerned naval targets.[5] The network of New Zealand Y stations was part of a worldwide system of over 50 stations built up by the British Admiralty to cover all the oceans of the world. New Zealand had one Army and six Navy stations.

The first two wartime signals intelligence units were established in existing government radio stations, at Awarua in the south of the South Island and at Musick Point in Auckland. Just before the war both stations had been fitted with new radio direction-finding equipment, for civil aviation purposes.[6] After war was declared some of the Post and Telegraph staff at these stations were given special security clearances and began top secret signals intelligence work. (As was the case in 1914, some preparation must have occurred before 1939, at least at Awarua.) At this stage they mostly targeted Germany; later the focus shifted to Japan.

The Y-operators' work, like that of their modern equivalents at the GCSB's Tangimoana station, was aimed at two kinds of intelligence collection: intercepting and transcribing enemy radio Morse code messages, most of this work going to joint United States-Australia analysis centres in Australia (from 1942); and using radio direction-finding equipment to determine where signals from a particular submarine, ship or Army unit had come from and sending the results into the Allied direction-finding network.

One of the people involved during the early years of the war described the work as follows:

The dark side of the world picks up radio signals better, and so when darkness was across this side of the world we'd get the signals from German U-boats in the Atlantic. We'd pick them up from Awarua down south and Musick Point and we would immediately signal those to Intelligence Headquarters in London and they would [presumably instruct other stations to] take a cross bearing and work out where the submarine was.

Direction-finding bearings from New Zealand and other parts of the worldwide network were sent by signal to the War Registry in London, and from there were taken by hand to the underground Operational Intelligence Centre.[7] Intelligence staff at the Awarua station, sending intelligence to London in this way, believed that, together with a Commonwealth station in Bombay, they helped track the German warship *Admiral Graf Spee* in the South Atlantic in late 1939, leading to its defeat in the Battle of the River Plate.

As the Pacific war intensified, a decision was made to set up two more Y-stations, spaced as far apart as possible to allow the direction-finding network to triangulate on target transmitters. One would be in Fiji and one in Northland in New Zealand.

The Northland station was sited on mudflats beside the mouth of the Awanui River, a few kilometres east of Waipapakauri. At the same time Post and Telegraph staff in Fiji selected a site in scrubland at Tamavua in the hills just north of Suva. The new stations were ready in early 1942. All four stations were fitted with Marconi radio receiving equipment, shipped from Britain for the purpose.

By 1942 the Navy Y-stations were targeted predominantly on Japanese naval communications. At each of the four stations banks of intercept operators, trained in the Japanese Katakana 'alphabet', worked in shifts around the clock intercepting Japanese Morse code transmissions.

A fifth interception operation, run by the Navy and based at Wellington Radio, acted as a major facility throughout the war and, briefly during 1942, included an outlier — a small wooden hut on Mount Crawford in Wellington — when Wellington Radio got too crowded.

The sixth signals intelligence unit was the Naval Wireless Station Rapaura. Its long wire aerial disguised by being strung between two high trees, the station was based in a remote farmhouse, behind barbed wire fences, at the end of a dusty Wratts Road by the Wairau River near Blenheim. It operated until May 1944.[8] Staffed by eight members of the Women's Royal New Zealand Naval Service (Wrens), the station had three functions: call-sign monitoring, radio fingerprinting (studying the distinctive characteristics of particular target radio transmitters so a ship or submarine could be identified even when it changed its Morse operator, call sign or frequency) and classifying of the results. Four of the staff worked as operators, four as classifiers.

The station used sophisticated equipment provided by the British signals intelligence organisation and the information it gathered was used to build a picture (together with the Y-station direction-finding results) of the positions and movements of each Japanese and German unit around the Pacific. Of these, the most urgent intelligence targets were the large Japanese I-class submarines that attacked merchant shipping in the South Pacific during 1942 and 1943.

The Army had its own signals intelligence unit targeted on Japanese operations affecting Army personnel fighting in the Pacific. The Special Section of Army Signals, under the command of Captain Ken McKenzie, was based at the Army's large signals centre at Nairnville Park, in Ngaio/Khandallah, Wellington. This extremely secret unit intercepted Japanese Army and Navy messages from Japanese-occupied areas in the Pacific.[9]

The Army intercept officers worked first in a railway hut at Nairnville Park and then in isolated huts set among blackberry and gorse on a hilltop between Johnsonville and Newlands.[10] The intelligence was sent to American intelligence authorities for decoding and translation before being passed to Pearl Harbor for action.[11]

The hub of New Zealand's intelligence activities during the war, the Combined Operational Intelligence Centre (COIC), was established in October 1941 and worked out of the newly constructed Defence headquarters in Wellington's Stout Street Departmental

Building (now Defence House). The intelligence organisation was situated on the second floor in the rooms surrounding the Central War Room, where the Chiefs of Staff came each morning at 10 o'clock to be briefed on the latest developments in the war and where four Navy officers, acting as watchkeepers, received all the latest reports of attacks or sightings by coastwatchers and attempted to collate them with other sources into an accurate picture.[12]

Also on this second floor of the Defence building was the Merchant Shipping Office, where four Wrens and four Royal New Zealand Navy officers plotted the movements of the 100 or more merchant ships present in New Zealand's area of the Pacific at any one time. A US Navy liaison officer was also based in this office, and a Coding Room next door, staffed mainly by US Navy technicians, was off-limits to other staff. There was also the office of the Staff Officer (Operations), a British officer on loan to New Zealand, whose job it was to decide on the rerouting of any shipping in danger of attack when enemy submarines and raiders had been detected. On the other side of his office, giving him the other half of the information he needed, was the Direction-Finding (D/F) Plotting Room.

Further back into the building, the office next to the Central War Room belonged to the Director of Naval Intelligence and COIC Director, Lieutenant Commander Beasley, Royal Navy. Next to Beasley was the head New Zealand naval intelligence officer, Lieutenant Wally Brackenridge. In January 1943 he was sent to Noumea to act as New Zealand liaison officer on the staff of the United States Commander South Pacific, part of the increasingly close intelligence co-operation with the American military that developed as the war went on.[13]

The next office, known simply as 'Room 236', was the naval intelligence room. In June 1943 the officers here began to produce a Daily Summary of Submarine Intelligence — a chart that drew together information from all sections of the intelligence headquarters giving the estimated positions of all enemy submarines in the South Pacific area.

Also on the second floor was the rarely mentioned SO(Y)'s department, which covered signals intelligence. The Y organisation was headed by the Staff Officer (Y), Lieutenant H. Philpott, who controlled the six New Zealand Navy-run stations (no one could enter them without a pass signed personally by him)[14] and all naval signals intelligence arriving from other countries. He controlled who saw overseas-sourced signals intelligence and ensured that the secrecy, and indeed even knowledge of the existence of this type of intelligence, was protected.

All intelligence collected at New Zealand naval stations was received by Philpott's department and then sent, via the signals department located on the roof of the building, into the British and American intelligence systems. In addition, D/F and radio fingerprinting information (from New Zealand and overseas) went to the Plotting Room, messages in code probably went straight to the allied codebreaking organisations in Australia, and some information was passed on to a small special codebreaking unit near Philpott's office.

Most analysis of the signals intelligence collected in New Zealand occurred in Australia. There were two main allied codebreaking organisations: the Central Bureau in Brisbane and the Fleet Radio Unit in Melbourne (FRUMEL). The job of the Central Bureau, which existed from 15 April 1942 until late 1945, was analysis, including codebreaking, of the messages gathered by radio interception operations. After the war it was transformed into the Defence Signals Bureau (DSB), predecessor of the current Australian signals intelligence organisation, the Defence Signals Directorate (DSD). Headed by an American, the staff of the Central Bureau came from Australia, the United States,

Britain, Canada and New Zealand. FRUMEL, a large organisation run by the United States Navy, was also responsible for signals intelligence analysis. It acted as a subsidiary head-quarters to the main US Navy cryptanalysis organisation in Hawaii.

All Second World War New Zealand intelligence activities were an integral part of and entirely reliant upon the allied intelligence network. In the early years of the war this meant a British/Commonwealth system, but the structures all changed after the United States entered the Pacific War. From then on, the British-run intelligence network increasingly became an American-run network, and all New Zealand sources of intelligence — from coastwatching to signals intelligence — now went into the United States intelligence system.

By 1943 British-American intelligence co-operation — which meant Commonwealth-American co-operation — was highly developed. Following a long process of negotiation, Britain and the United States signed an agreement in May 1943 formalising links between the two countries' signals intelligence agencies: the BRUSA agreement (forerunner of the post-war UKUSA agreement).

James Bamford describes the BRUSA agreement as establishing 'for the first time intimate co-operation on COMINT [communications intelligence] at the highest level'. It established close technical co-operation, procedures for intelligence exchange and joint security regulations which 'even today... form the fundamental basis for all SIGINT activities of both the NSA and GCHQ'.[15]

BRUSA effectively covered those countries that were part of the British network. From that time on Australian and Canadian representatives were part of a series of signals intelligence conferences held under BRUSA auspices. There is no record of New Zealand personnel being at these conferences; if they were not, New Zealand would have been represented by Australia.

The effects of BRUSA were soon apparent. Shortly after the second of these Joint Allied Conferences, New Zealand received a letter from the British Admiralty concerning 'the measures necessary for effecting uniformity in British and American treatment of official documents'. Detailed instructions on how to apply the new regulations, 'adapting British practice as closely as possible to the terms of this Agreement', followed soon after.[16]

Other regulations stated that all authorised recipients of special intelligence must be carefully briefed and sign a document stating that they had read and understood the regulations and would observe them[17] — the same as the current practice of indoctrination. Still other regulations stated that messages and reports based on signals intelligence must be written so that their source was not identified and others specified how to store signals intelligence materials. All these rules still apply today.

ENDNOTES
_____

Chapter 1: 1984
1. The meeting was during the second half of 1984, or possibly the start of 1985.
2. Ewan Jamieson, *Friend or Ally: New Zealand at odds with its past*, Brassey's Australia, Sydney, 1990, p.3.

Chapter 2: Hooked Up to the Network: The UKUSA System
1. The generally accepted definition of communications intelligence is 'technical and intelligence information derived from foreign communications by someone other than the intended recipient. It does not include foreign press, propaganda or public broadcasts.' It generally refers to external intelligence and so does not usually include governments spying on their own people.
2. Duncan Campbell, *The Unsinkable Aircraft Carrier*, Michael Joseph Ltd, London, 1984, p.167.
3. Rick Anderson, *Seattle Times*, 19 September 1982, p.1.
4. M. Long, *World Satellite Almanac*, second edition, Howard W. Sams & Company, Indianapolis, 1987, pp. 206-208, 457-460.
5. James Bamford, *The Puzzle Palace*, Sidgwick & Guildford, London, 1983, pp.167-171.
6. The station may not have been initially targeted on Intelsat. Some photos of the station taken by Des Ball in June 1983 show the two interception dishes facing directly skywards, meaning either that they were temporarily not being used or that they were targeted at that time on satellites above East Asia (in the early 1980s there were no Intelsats there).
7. A US$29 million project codenamed LADYLOVE at the station, for completion in mid-1982, involved an 'interim deployment' construction of one dish and a 'new operational electronic system' housed initially in equipment vans. A US$21 million 'major new collection and processing complex with associated antenna systems' followed in 1987.
8. Ascension Island is a 20-square kilometre British territory, situated halfway between Brazil and Angola in the middle of the South Atlantic. It has a major radio interception station with joint GCHQ/NSA staffing, a base for US anti-submarine Orion aircraft, six separate radar and optical tracking stations for US strategic missile tests and its large US-built airfield was the main support base for the Falklands War (Richelson and Ball, *The Ties that Bind*, Allen & Unwin, Boston, 1985, pp. 194, 201 and 220; Duncan Campbell, *New Statesman*, 'Report reveals island base, 21 May 1985).
9. Mary Louise O'Callaghan, *Melbourne Age*, 'PNG to investigate Australian spy claim', 26 November 1991, p.1.
10. For a full description of these 'overhead' systems, see Jeffrey T. Richelson, *The US Intelligence Community*, Ballinger, Cambridge, 1989.
11. Information from Jeffrey Richelson.
12. Mike Frost and Michel Gratton, *Spyworld*, 1994, Doubleday, Toronto. The book describes in detail how and where these operations occurred.
13. Mike Frost helped to arrange a series of these operations, including investigating the microwave routes through some cities while assessing the suitability of the local Canadian embassy.
14. Brian Toohey and Marion Wilkinson, *The Book of Leaks*, Angus & Robertson, Sydney, 1987, p.139.
15. Archie Hamilton, Minister of State for the Armed Forces, Written Answers to Questions, British Parliament record for 9 June 1992, p.97.
16. Duncan Campbell, *op. cit.*, p.168.
17. James Bamford, *op. cit.*, p.102. Internal Menwith Hill station papers from the early 1990s still referred to a computer-based communications system called Platform.
18. Duncan Campbell, *New Statesman*, 'They've got it taped', 12 August 1988, pp.10-12.

Chapter 3: The Power of the Dictionary: Inside ECHELON
1. Unless specifically targeted, a hand-written fax is probably not yet able to be processed automatically in this way.
2. This system also means that an analyst can see whether any other agencies have been sent the same intercepted message, since that agencies' number will also be listed at the bottom of the text.
3. As each data base is filled — probably corresponding to a full computer tape — a new one is started. These data bases are ordered 'Raw A', 'Raw B' and so on, to allow reference back to them if necessary; and to distinguish them from the similar data bases of 'finished' GCSB and overseas intelligence reports also maintained at the GCSB.
4. Wiseman left the GCSB in about 1990-91.
5. The instructions to make these sorts of amendments come from GCSB Operations staff, and also from the overseas agencies whenever they want to alter their lists in the GCSB station Dictionaries. The GCSB Dictionary Manager also liaises with the equivalent officers in the other UKUSA agencies, requesting amendments to the

GCSB keywords in the overseas stations' Dictionaries.

6. Nick Davies, reporter, on *World in Action*, Granada TV, shown in an abridged form on TVNZ's *Foreign Correspondent*, 29 August 1991.

7. Campbell, 1988, *op. cit.*, p.11.

8. *Ibid.*

9. John Merritt, *Observer*, 28 June 1992.

10. Duncan Campbell, 'Spies boost arms sales profits', *New Statesman*, 18 June 1984.

11. Hugh O'Shaughnessy, 'Thatcher ordered Lonrho phone-tap over Harrods affair', *Observer*, 28 June 1992.

12. Frost and Gratton, *op. cit.*, pp. 234-238.

13. *Ibid.*, pp. 93-94.

Chapter 4: Fighting the Cold War: The Role of UKUSA

1. A more detailed description of New Zealand Second World War intelligence is contained in N. Hager, *Origins of signals intelligence in New Zealand*, Centre for Peace Studies Working Paper No. 5, University of Auckland, 1995.

2. 'Joint' refers to military arrangements that serve all three services: Army, Navy and Air Force.

3. Christopher Andrew, 'The Growth of the Australian Intelligence Community', *Intelligence and National Security*, Vol. 4 (April 1989) p.224. It is also worth noting that, although general geographic responsibilities were agreed to, signals intelligence collaboration never has strict boundaries. A New Zealand station may be well suited for providing signals intelligence coverage of a distant area of the world.

4. Australian archive source, provided by Des Ball.

5. Christopher Andrew, *op. cit.*

6. Interview source.

7. Although there are no records of who Travis met in New Zealand in January 1947, there is no doubt that he would have dealt mainly with the deputy head of the Prime Minister's and External Affairs Department, Foss Shanahan. Shanahan, who was seen by his contemporaries as the architect of all the New Zealand intelligence arrangements made at that time, was the main channel to the Prime Minister on intelligence and defence matters. He had responsibility for all defence and intelligence in the Prime Minister's Department during and after the war and had accompanied Nash to London the year before. Shanahan is said to have worked very hard to retain all intelligence business within the orbit of his department. He is probably responsible for initiating what has become a New Zealand prime ministerial convention of maintaining exclusive control of intelligence matters (especially signals intelligence and internal security).

8. Australian Cabinet Paper, 23 Febrary 1973, bearing the signals intelligence classification 'Secret Spoke'.

9. JIC (48) 19 (0) (2nd revised draft), 'Sigint Intelligence Requirements — 1948', reproduced in full in Richard Aldridge and Michael Coleman, 'The Cold War, the JIC and British Signals Intelligence, 1948', *Intelligence and National Security*, Vol. 3 (July 1989).

10. The two dates may be explained by the United States and Britain having signed the agreement in 1947 but it not covering all five countries until 1948 when, after negotiation, the three junior allies signed the protocols.

11. It is said to be the British government that insists on keeping even the existence of the agreement a secret.

12. Geoffrey Palmer, Prime Minister, letter to writer, 29 March 1990.

13. Information about the UKUSA signing from Des Ball. Poulden had arrived to set up the DSB with a 20-strong GCHQ team. He returned to Britain in about 1952.

14. According to someone who has read it, the UKUSA document itself, which runs to many pages, is made up of page after page of rather mundane agreed arrangements. But the practical effect of the agreement was immense, integrating Commonwealth and United States signals intelligence in a highly organised structure of common code words, procedures and technical systems.

15. Jeffrey Richelson and Des Ball, *The Ties That Bind*, 1985, Allen & Unwin, Sydney, p.40.

16. There is no evidence that the radio stations at Waiouru had a significant role in intelligence during the war. This is not surprising since they did not become operational until August 1943 when the main fighting in the Pacific War was moving far away from New Zealand's area.

17. It is not clear whether any signals intelligence operations occurred between the end of the war and early 1949 when NR1 opened. If something did continue (obviously on a much smaller scale), it would have been a small Navy operation probably based at the Waiouru naval radio station NR2. It may be relevant that some of the Navy aerials at NR2 were 'refocused' to the north in 1946. The purpose of this may have been to allow signals intelligence work.

18. By the 1970s the station had six rhombic antennae, designed to listen in a particular direction, a quadrant antenna, a long wire antenna and a tall 'directional multiple inclined Vee' antenna, which acts like a circle of 11 half rhombic antennae giving 360-degree coverage. The last of these aerials, with its tall tower and veil of wires, can still be seen there, next to the modern HMNZS *Irirangi* Navy receiving station recently constructed on the site of the 30- by 10-metre NR1 building.

19. The employment of women in signals intelligence work did not continue at the end of the Second World War.

20. Navy Department, *The Navy List*, October 1956.

21. Ray Parker, GCSB Director, wrote: 'For the years 1955-77 (as far as can be ascertained from existing records)

no foreign personnel worked in the NZCSO', letter to writer, 6 May 1991. The naval part of the British signals intelligence field station organisation, called the Admiralty Civilian Shore Wireless Service (ACSWS), was reviewed in 1956. In the course of the review ACSWS staff were identified at Bletchley, Ceylon, Malta, Melbourne and New Zealand. The one ACSWS officer in New Zealand was the Station Radio Officer: obviously H.E.Stutton. (Source: *Report of the Working Party on the Partial Navalisation of the Admiralty Civilian Shore Wireless Service*, undated (1956), Public Records Office file: ADM 1/26478, London. Provided by Andy Thomas.)

22. Chief Ombudsman, letter to the writer, 6 May 1991.

23. Navy Department, *The Navy List*, 1963-65. Lists for the three years show Brendon as 'On Course in the United Kingdom'.

24. Colin Hanson, letter to the writer, 16 January 1985.

25. His status was as 'functional head' of the NZCSO while not being a member of it.

26. The eight people holding this position between 1955 and 1977 included Squadron Leader Harold Hammond, Lieutenant Commander C.W. Holland Goodwin (1965-68) and Squadron Leader T.R. Mahoney (1968-71). The first Distribution Officer, in 1955-56, was a foreigner, most likely from the GCHQ or DSB. The small office of the Distribution Officer was located on the top floor of the Stout Street Defence building in Wellington (now the location of the SIS). It probably later moved next to the Directorate of Defence Intelligence on the first floor.

27. Secretary of Defence, memos to the Secretary, State Services Commission, 12 December 1968 and 10 February 1971, Services Commission files, AAFH, W3654, 24/2/50/24, National Archives, Wellington.

28. Director of Defence Communications terms of reference, Defence Manual 44, undated.

29. Jack Hunn, Secretary of Defence, submission to the Minister of Defence, 17 April 1965, NZCSO Overseas Postings', held in State Services Commission files, AAFH, W3654, 24/2/50/24, National Archives, Wellington.

30. A. Stripp, *Codebreaker in the Far East*, 1989, Frank Cass, London, p.60.

31. Secret Australian Cabinet Paper, 'SIGINT presence in Singapore and new station at Darwin', 22 February 1973.

32. *List of persons employed on the permanent staff of the public service*, annual lists 1955-73.

33. B.F. Veale, Radio Supervisor NZCSO Singapore, 'Conditions of service for NZCSO at Tropical Posts', report, 16 October 1966, New Zealand National Archives, AAFH, W3654, Acc 24/2/50/24.

34. In 1973, these staff comprised an Assistant Station Radio Officer, Supervising Radio Officer and eight Radio Officers.

35. C.S. McCann, report entitled 'Case of Regrading - NZCSO', 24 October 1966, State Services Commission files, AAFH, W3654, Acc 24/2/50/24, National Archives, Wellington.

36. Hand-written notes by indoctrinated States Services Commission staff member concerning conditions for NZCSO staff in Singapore, undated (1966 or 1967), State Services Commission files, AAFH, W3654, Acc 24/2/50/24, National Archives, Wellington.

37. Australian Cabinet Paper, 23 February 1973. This paper referred to there being 140 Australian personnel at the station in 1973.

38. Australian Department of Defence, *ZKJ2, No.3 Telecommunication Unit 1946-1991*, unit history, supplied by Des Ball.

39. Bruce E. Jones, *War without Windows: A true account of a young army officer trapped in an intelligence coverup in Vietnam*, Vanguard Press, New York, p.163.

40. The Singapore government made no response at all to publicity of the station and Singapore's *Straits Times* merely reproduced two stories, written by foreign papers, on its back page and then let the story drop.

41. Alan Barnes, 'We'll withdraw Singapore "spy base", Whitlam tells Sneddon', *Melbourne Age*, 16 February 1973. The publicity at this time included revelations about how few Australian Cabinet ministers, past and present, had been aware even of the existence of the station.

42. Secretary of Defence, memo to State Services Commission, 'Communications Personnel: Postings to Melbourne', 18 December 1973, State Services Commission files, AAFH, W3654, Acc 24/2/50/24, National Archives, Wellington.

43. Changes of government and political leadership appear to have had no influence on what went on. To the extent that politicians were involved, there seems to have been concensus about NZCSO activities.

Chapter 5: The GCSB, ANZUS and a Nuclear-Free New Zealand

1. Ministry of Defence, Defence Manual: DM44, restricted, undated (but from 1970s), paragraph 521b.

2. Roger Foley, 'Eavesdropping was Kiwi spy's speciality', *Evening Post*, 5 February 1988.

3. John Robertson, letter to the State Services Commission, 5 April 1977, State Services Commission files, AAFH, W3654, accession number 24/2/50/24, National Archives, Wellington.

4. Morgon became a civilian employee when he joined the GCSB, as did all the other former military officers who joined the organisation. When he returned from the NSA in mid-1985, following the New Zealand-United States nuclear policy dispute, he was very angry about what had happened. He resigned from the GCSB after giving a bitter speech to the staff.

5. State Services Commission, *Public Service Official Circular*, various issues 1978 and 1979.

6. M.T. Christy, itinerary of B.R. Inman, 19 September 1980. Released to Peter Wills by the NSA under the Freedom of Information Act, NSA letter, 19 July 1988.

7.   B.R. Inman, interviewed in Bob Woodward, *Veils: The Secret Wars of the CIA 1981-87*, Simon & Schuster, London, 1987.

8.   Richelson and Ball, *op. cit*, p.77.

9.   Defence news release, 'Defence denies intelligence claims', 5 March 1986. Jamieson was taking advantage of the fact that Richelson and Ball were unaware of the difference between the NR1 and NR2 stations.

10.   Joint Intelligence Organisation, *Fourth Annual Report, 1974*, Part 2, Canberra, November 1974, p.7.

11.   Ministry of Defence memo to Secretary, State Services Commission, 21 April 1966, 'NZCSO postings: overseas establishments', State Services Commission file, AAFH, W3654, Acc 24/2/50/24, National Archives, Wellington.

12.   J. Robertson, Secretary of Defence, letter to Chairman, State Services Commission, 5 April 1977, 'Staff ceilings: Ministry of Defence', State Services Commission file, AAFH, W3654, 24/2/50/24 Vol. 2, National Archives, Wellington.

13.   *RAAF News*, 'Communications unit given fond farewell', April 1991, p.16; quoted in Ball, *Signals Intelligence in the Post-Cold War Era*, 1993, p.68.

14.   Minister of Defence, Australian Senate Question No. 1313, 11 April 1994.

15.   *Defence Electronics*, 'Hong Kong's spy radio moves south', March 1982, p.30.

16.   Richelson and Ball, *op. cit.*, p.40. In May 1980 18 Army communications technicians, who would be involved in running the new Watsonia facility, went on a preparatory training course at the satellite communications facility which serves Fort Meade, the NSA headquarters (P. Joel, 'Satcom training in the USA - 1980/81', *Signalman*, No. 8, 1981, p.41).

17.   The JTUM operation is probably the Kittiwake project referred to in Toohey and Wilkinson, *op. cit.*, p.137.

18.   Joint Intelligence Organisation, *op. cit*, p.5. This report was, of course, prior to the station being operated remotely from Melbourne.

19.   Des Ball, *Pacific Defence Reporter*, 'The US naval ocean surveillance information system (NOSIS) - Australia's role', June 1982, p.42.

20.   *RAAF News, op. cit.*

21.   Toohey and Wilkinson, *op.cit.*, p.137.

Chapter 6: Behind Closed Doors: What Happens Inside the GCSB

1.   Richelson and Ball, *op. cit.*, pp. 170, 171.

2.   These ciphers are called OTPs, one time pads, although in the computer age they are actually one time disks: the message is electronically combined with a series of symbols (on the disk) and is unreadable until the same series is used to decipher it. Since each series is used only once, no amount of studying the encrypted messages will help to break the code. In the mid-1970s news publicity alerted the Japanese government to the fact that its coded diplomatic messages were being readily intercepted and deciphered by Australian intelligence authorities. After years of having its top level communications read, Japan changed to a computer-generated one-time cipher system. (Source: Brian Toohey, *Australian Financial Review*, 'Australia loses its Japan bug', 30 July 1976, p.1.)

3.   The first codebreaking computer arrived in 1982. Its main function was production decryption runs of overseas supplied intercept. The intercept was printed out on a long tape when it arrived in the GCSB communications centre and passed from there to a computer specialist. The codebreaking computer had a tape-reader attached through which were fed all the tapes of encrypted intercepts brought from the Commcen. The computer then provided printouts of the decoded Japanese telexes.

4.   *Sydney Morning Herald*, 'Japanese secrets tapped in Canberra', 29 May 1995, p.1.

5.   The three K cells initially had two staff each and this later grew to about four each.

6.   The New Zealander in charge of this intelligence work from 1971 to 1981, the period when the first wave of public protests against the testing occurred, was Graeme Beere, head of scientific and strategic intelligence at the JIB/EIB. After his retirement he let his attitude to nuclear issues be known publicly. Speaking strongly against New Zealand's nuclear-free law at a public hearing in 1992, he said that in his job in the EIB he had had a lot to do with following up French testing and that he had 'come to the conclusion that New Zealand's worst enemy is Greenpeace'.

7.   'Major sticks by France on nuclear testing', *Evening Post*, 9 November 1995, p.1.

8.   Throughout the existence of the K cells the staff have occasionally been supplied with audio tapes of messages to help translate and identify their origins, in part to support the C Unit in planning future interception.

9.   The DSD has since been shifted to Canberra, but at that time they went to the Melbourne headquarters, located in a five-storey mirror glass building at 256-310 St Kilda Road. The first floor was mostly computers, the second floor training and the top floor the DSD directors.

The New Zealand analysts mostly got to see the second to top floor where the DSD analysts and cryptanalysts worked. This was a large open plan area, with the cell leaders in glass box offices and walk-in vaults in the centre of the floor.

10.   The DSD's Shoal Bay station near Darwin, which is the closest station to Indonesia, is run by the Navy.

11.   Contract W2213-3-3593. Information from Bill Robinson.

12.   For example, an officer from the Australian Security Intelligence Service (ASIO) was working at the SIS headquarters in Wellington in 1994-95 on a staff exchange. Similarly, there is an exchange posting inside the Directorate of Defence Intelligence from British military intelligence, in 1995 an officer called Lewis Rowland.

13. GCSB memo to cryptanalysis trainees.
14. Of the known KH staff, of about six who did training in Melbourne in 1984-88, only one is still at the GCSB in 1994; out of two who arrived back at the end of 1990, neither is still there. Another two were trained in 1990-93 (arriving back in early and late 1993 respectively); only one remains.
15. The KH section is the equivalent (albeit smaller) of the DSD's PHR section and the CSE's O1 section.
16. DSD and CSE cryptanalyst trainees receive training at the NSA in Washington. The first CSE O1 staff member was sent to the NSA for training in March 1984 (within months of Thomas Weiss being the first GCSB trainee sent to the DSD). She was followed by others on one- to three-year training courses. New members of O1 undergo three years of classroom and in-work training before they become fully trained cryptanalysts (Bill Robinson, 'The fall and rise of cryptanalysis in Canada', *Cryptologia*, XVI, 1 January 1992, pp. 31-36).
17. 'Spymasters pull plug on snoop-proof telephones', *Times*, 29 May 1993.
18. Information from Brian Toohey, 1991.
19. Previously in the Navy, Miller joined the GCSB in January 1978 and trained as a radio officer at the old Waiouru intercept station before moving to Tangimoana in 1982. He moved to the GCSB headquarters in Wellington in 1988-89, at a time when a lot of Tangimoana radio officers began to be deployed elsewhere in the organisation. The first head of C was Wally Brendon. Later Barry Keane headed the section in 1989-91, after he shifted out of K.
20. Bamford, *op. cit.*, p.164. Seymour Hersh described the same system in 1986 (Seymour Hersh, *The Target is Destroyed*, Faber & Faber, London, 1986, pp. 256 and 257).
    Each target is given a TEXTA designator, made up of three letters and several numbers, which closely resembles the station designators described in Chapter 9. Two letters show the target country and one letter the type of target. The JAD intelligence produced by the KE section, for instance, has designators such as JAD07003. For many of Waihopai's targets, the third letter is C, indicating that a commercial telecommunications user is being targeted.
21. A small number of people are indoctrinated in these organisations. Before its privatisation in 1990, some staff in Telecom also received reports.
22. Called the Reading Service, these officers are regularly given access to New Zealand and overseas intelligence reports either at the GCSB headquarters or delivered to them by safe hand courier. The Australian and Canadian intelligence officers in Wellington are first secretaries and can be identified in the diplomatic lists because they do not have a specified role like 'commercial' or 'information'.
23. GCSB Personnel Information Bulletin 23/94, 20 December 1994.
24. The W position was at first a section of its own. In 1992-93 it was taken into the L section.

Chapter 7: The Organisation: Secret Structures of the GCSB

1. Ray Parker, letter to the writer, 13 January 1992.
2. The numbers of foreign staff in the GCSB since 1977 are: 1977-80 none; 1981-83 one; 1984-87 two; 1987-89 one; July 1991 two; August 1991 three; July 1992 two; July 1993 three; April 1994 five; July 1994 three; October 1994 three; April 1995 two; November 1995 two (letters from GCSB to writer, 24 October 1990, 30 August 1991, 8 October 1993, 27 April 1994 and 6 November 1995).
3. Jacobs joined the GCSB on 24 August 1977, the day after leaving his job at the Army's Waiouru Signals School. His first four years were spent training and working at the NR1 station near Waiouru. Then he was chosen for a three-year posting (1982-84) to the JTUM unit in Melbourne, shortly after it began operations eavesdropping on Chinese and Russian communications in 1981. For 10 years after that he went up through the hierarchy at the Tangimoana station, increasingly involved in a supervisor capacity overseeing interception operations.
4. Michael Spring was previously the Director of Information Processing (called Z), responsible for the communications and computing at the GCSB. He took over this role in 1993 from Dave Hilling, whose appointment in 1988 was part of a rapid growth of this division in 1988-89 in preparation for a new communications system, the opening of Waihopai and the introduction of the ECHELON Dictionary system. Hilling had entered the GCSB in 1978 as the Deputy Director of Communications Security. In 1993 he shifted to a position called P2, as Senior Executive Officer (Information Processing) — see the following note.
5. The GCSB is connected into the Automatic Digital Network used by United States' military and intelligence agencies through New Zealand's Second Generation Defence Communications Network, which was established in 1989. Together with Australia's identical Defence Integrated Secure Communications Network (DISCON), it is linked into the United States system, under the 1990 Simpson agreement, via a satellite terminal beside the DISCON switching centre on the outskirts of Melbourne. A new, more sophisticated link between the UKUSA allies, to be introduced in the late 1990s or early next century, is being planning under the auspices of the five-nation Combined Communications Electronic Board. It will be a 'X.400-based messaging system', primarily for electronic mail and data-interchange. The GCSB's Senior Executive Officer (Information Systems), Dave Hilling, is responsible for planning and introducing the GCSB's part of the new system. He has attended six-monthly UKUSA-nation meetings in Washington DC as part of allied planning for the new network (the first was in June 1991, the most recent in April 1996).
6. These officers are nearly all ex-military, from the Air Force Defence Communications Unit (DCU) in the Defence Headquarters or from Navy communications. They work two to a shift (one operator and one senior operator together). The officers on night shift in theory act as duty officers for the GCSB, contacting senior bureau staff for

any traffic that warrants immediate attention. Their boss is the network services manager, N, who for many years was John Parkes. The current manager is Bob Ohlson. Like many GCSB staff, N officers have been sent on courses at the other agencies including the NSA at Fort Meade.

7.   The current manager is Robert Walter, who joined the GCSB in January 1986 as the GCSB's first computer specialist (a systems analyst).

8.   The equipment looked after by the station engineers includes, at Tangimoana, the high frequency radio antennae and receivers, direction-finding and signal recording systems, radio demodulators, the secure telephone system and signal distribution systems; and, at Waihopai, the satellite dish, microwave receivers, signal demultiplexing equipment, data communication equipment and the secure telephone system.

9.   GCSB, *Personnel Information Bulletin*, Issue 15/93, 16 August 1993.

10.   In 1986 this area included a Director (COMSEC/TECSEC), a Deputy Director (Computer Security), an Assistant Director (COMSEC), an Assistant Director (TECSEC), and an Assistant Director (EMSEC). They directed three M sections (M2, M3 and M4), two TECSEC teams (S2 and S3), two EMSEC teams (E2 and E3) and a small R section. By 1989 the director was called the Director of Security (X). On 1 July 1991 the Security Division became the Information Systems Security Division, with a director called the Director of INFOSEC, still known as X.

11.   In 1987-88, for example, there were 'technical inspection visits by GCSB teams' to London, Vienna, Rome, Geneva, Moscow, Noumea, Suva (three months after the Fiji coup), Harare, New York with the Prime Minister in September 1987, Washington, Mexico, Bonn and, twice, Paris (Ministry of Foreign Affairs, Foreign Affairs and Defence Committee, Answers to Set Questions: Vote Ministry of Foreign Affairs 1988-89 Estimates, Annex C: Specialist visits to Posts 1987-88). The GCSB refused to release equivalent information for other years.

12.   The S unit was headed by Peter March, as Assistant Director (TECSEC) ADS and later as manager (called S), from mid-1980 until 1993; and has been located since the early 1980s on the 13th floor of the headquarters building. Peter March left the bureau in 1993 after 16 years, unhappy at the way that the ex-Air Force officers had a stranglehold on the senior positions. He was replaced by Nokes, who joined the GCSB in 1980.

13.   In 1988 this radar was used, on loan from the GCSB, to survey an old military site on Auckland's North Head. Also, according to a GCSB worker in the late 1980s, TECSEC staff were sent on three-month postings to New Zealand's Moscow embassy; while Australian TECSEC staff from the DSD had two-year postings in the embassies in Moscow and some other countries (e.g. Burma). Ministers' and officials' offices in the government's Beehive building are also regularly swept for bugs ('Beehive offices regularly swept for listening devices', *Evening Post*, 5 November 1991, p.12).

14.   An Official Information request asking which agency previously 'swept' New Zealand embassies was refused under Section 6(b). As this section relates entirely to information belonging to foreign governments, it was in effect an answer saying that, before 1977-78, TECSEC work was done for New Zealand by another government. In fact it was the GCHQ's TECSEC organisation, called the Diplomatic Telecommunications Maintenance Service, which has done this work for New Zealand since the 1950s (ever since a secret tip-off from Britain that New Zealand was being spied on 'by its friends'.)

15.   The GCSB's M2 and R sections, through the Interdepartmental Committee on Security, have produced three small security guides for government organisations: *Security in Government Departments and Organisations* (1983), *The Security of Communications* (1984) and *The Security of Computer Applications* (1986).

16.   The unit also provides secretarial support for two committees with representatives from various government departments: the Interdepartmental Committee on Security and the New Zealand Communications Security Committee (the NZCSC is referred to in Defence Council Order No.2/1981, New Zealand Defence Force, Wellington, 1981).

17.   A set of national INFOSEC standards and procedures has been developed in M2. These standards require each government department that uses secure communications to appoint a Departmental COMSEC Custodian (DCC), responsible to a Departmental COMSEC Officer (DCO). The DCC is responsible for the receipt, storage, issue, destruction and general accounting (i.e. keeping records) of COMSEC materials (the one-time keys used for encrypting machines). This means receiving COMSEC material from the National Distributing Authority at the GCSB, storing it in a safe and distributing it to the people using secure communications (i.e. encrypting) equipment. The standards also require departments to maintain a master COMSEC register showing the location and 'disposition' of each copy of COMSEC material issued to the department, regular 'routine and handover musters' of COMSEC materials to check against the master register, destruction of such materials after their specified date and reporting of security breaches.

18.   The M4 staff include the National Distribution Officer, an ex-Air Force officer, Mike Clark, and his assistant. They are also responsible for bringing secure communications equipment into the country for the GCSB. The section includes a computer facility, probably for generating one-time keys for New Zealand government secure communications. Each day's codes are distributed to the departmental INFOSEC officers of all government organisations using secure communications equipment. The MFAT INFOSEC custodian will distribute materials to the head office communications centre, the communications staff in the diplomatic posts overseas and the Prime Minister's communications unit (staffed by a Foreign Affairs communications officer) on the 10th floor of the Beehive Building. Special secure communications are also arranged for when the Prime Minister is travelling overseas.

19. A system of 'safe hand' procedures — set by the UKUSA countries and in use for decades — governs all the movements of materials by the NZNDA. See Appendix C.

20. He is a former Air Force squadron leader who was previously Assistant Director (Information Systems) Policy in the New Zealand Defence Force headquarters.

21. Jeffrey Richelson, *Foreign Intelligence Organisations*, Ballinger, Cambridge, 1988, pp.79-80.

22. The EMSEC technicians have a workshop on the 13th floor for their work. Their equipment includes a large metal box, known as a Faraday cage, which completely shields its interior from electromagnetic radiation. This is used for very sensitive testing of equipment, which even the emissions of nearby computer screens would be enough to interfere with. Official concern about emission security increased through the 1980s as the use of computers and computer-based communications systems grew and the potential for interception became understood.

23. There appears to have been a Policy and Plans section in the GCSB since 1977 when I.C. Alford, a senior NZCSO radio officer, was transferred to Wellington. Alford had joined the NZCSO in September 1954 and during his career had been the head of the New Zealand radio officers in Singapore and Melbourne. His role as Assistant Director of Policy and Plans presumably related to planning, recruitment and training in preparation for moving the GCSB station from Waiouru to Tangimoana in 1982 (the work relating to radio interception was taken over by another senior radio officer, Jim Bryer, in 1984, called P2: Planning Radio Officer (Policy and Plans)). In 1995, staff under Director of Policy and Plans, John Willson, were: Hugh Wolfensohn, the GCSB's Senior Executive Officer for legal matters; Dave Hilling, called P2, who, from September 1993, was the Senior Executive Officer (Information Processing) overseeing planning of the GCSB's future communications system; and Brian Gore, who joined the GCSB in about 1989 as Assistant Director of SIGINT, K. In June 1991 he was moved into P to conduct a major review of the Operations Division structures and later did other policy work in P.

24. The Director of Corporate Services is Tony Fryer, called C. Previously a wing commander (most recently commanding officer at the Wigram Air Force base), he is said to have brought with him some strict Air Force attitudes. This position, then called Director of Administration, was previously held by Brian Punnett, who moved into the role in late 1977 as the GCSB was established. Punnett joined the NZCSO as a radio officer in 1968 and had spent time at the Singapore station and several years in the Distribution Office in Wellington.

Under Fryer is an Administration Manager, Heather McKenzie. She has done this job for over a decade and is the only woman in a senior position in the organisation. Her Administration Unit includes typists, records staff, salary clerks, a telephone receptionist and tea attendants. There has also been a GCSB librarian since 1990 who looks after a small library on the 11th floor. The Finance Unit is headed by the Finance Manager, an accountant who is responsible for all the GCSB's accounting functions (financial management reporting, budgeting and cashflow management) and his small staff. The Logistics Unit (until 1992 called the Equipment Unit) orders and purchases the stores and equipment used throughout the GCSB. This is a four-person unit including the Logistics Manager, who, until March 1994, was John Allen, an ex-Air Force Squadron Leader (he appears to have since moved to Tangimoana). He was replaced by Ian Juno.

25. Appointed directly from the Army in March 1985, Don Allan was the first security officer at the GCSB.

26. In the 1980s, before these changes, the top (14th) floor contained the GCSB Director's office with a conference room connected to it, offices of other directors and managers (including Policy and Plans, Operations and SIGINT), the analysis K cells, C Unit, the liaison L unit and the communications centre. The 13th floor was, as now, the technical floor, containing the communications and technical security sections, the Computer Security Section, the Engineering Division, the National Distributing Authority, an electronics workshop and relevant directors and managers. The 12th floor had the H Section codebreakers, the J computing staff, security section and administration staff. There was also a secure storage area in the basement of the building.

27. The meetings occur on the second Wednesday of every month at 11 am and were mentioned in the GCSB *Personnel Information Bulletin* No. 22, 9 November 1990.

28. The Daily Security Checklist includes: 'Safes locked and Security records completed; Classified Waste bag put in safe; Workstations logged off or locked and Pizza boxes locked; Printers cleared; Open surfaces clear of classified materials; In/Out trays emptied and inverted; Waste bins cleared of classified material; and Appliances and lights switched off'.

29. The British indoctrination papers are reproduced in Richelson and Ball, 1985, *op. cit.*, pp.148-149.

30. Director of Central Intelligence Directive 1/14, effective 14 April 1986, Annex C, 'Minimum standards for [Sensitive Compartmented Information] security awareness programmes in the US intelligence community'; provided by Jeffrey Richelson.

31. There are indoctrinated military people in electronic warfare positions, at ANZMIS, and in some senior officer positions.

32. Foreign Affairs staff are indoctrinated by the Defence Liaison Officer, for many years and currently Murray Watkins.

33. Politicians, including the Prime Minister, are indoctrinated by the Co-ordinator of the Domestic and External Security Secretariat, Gerald Hensley until 1989 and currently Simon Murdoch.

Chapter 8: Secret Squirrels: Who Runs the GCSB?

1. Roger Foley, 'Eavesdropping was Kiwi spy's speciality', *Evening Post*, 5 February 1988.

2.   Even before he was GCSB Director, Hanson travelled extensively in his defence intelligence role. For example, as Director of Defence Intelligence he visited the Intelligence Division of the Commander-in-Chief, US Pacific Forces (CINCPAC) Headquarters in Hawaii in 1975 (Command History, CINCPAC Fleet, 1975).
3.   Parker's salary is between $100,000 and $110,000 a year (Ray Parker, letter to the writer, 25 July 1995).
4.   This includes a two-week trip to the NSA in Washington each year, usually in November.
5.   The other agencies' special liaison officers are called SUKLO, CANSLO and AUSLO.
6.   The International Regulations on SIGINT set the standards and guidelines that enable the UKUSA allies to work together as a co-ordinated system. There are many volumes of them at the GCSB. They include regulations about the security classifications that must be used on signals intelligence materials, the methods that must be used for communicating such material (e.g. safe hand techniques), indoctrination and the other security procedures that signals intelligence personnel must obey. They even specify such things as the thickness to which all paper must be shredded before being thrown away. The most sensitive papers shredded at the GCSB must be shredded into tiny slivers of paper 1mm wide by 10mm long; over 6000 pieces from one sheet of paper.
7.   There are dozens of volumes of the United States Signals Intelligence Directives in the GCSB vaults. Some are only about two pages, some up to 8 centimetres thick. They include directives on SIGINT operating policy, security, SIGINT reporting and targeting lists. GCSB analysts in the K Unit use one of these (presumably that on SIGINT reporting) to check that their work is compatible with the NSA. For example, it sets out the rules governing 'sanitising' of finished intelligence reports (as discussed in Chapter 12). A number of security manuals are also often used. Another directive, concerning the NSA and its structures, has apparently been very influential as it has been used to model the GCSB on its large alliance partner. Jeffrey Richelson, 1989, *op. cit.*, p.399; and information from Jeffrey Richelson.
8.   There are also about five volumes of New Zealand manuals based on the NSA directives, which provide the rules and guidelines that all New Zealanders involved in signals intelligence are expected to follow. They are described as 'how to do it' manuals by people who use them. In addition there are numerous other types of UKUSA-supplied manuals, including those covering operation and maintenance of individual pieces of equipment or larger systems supplied by the overseas agencies. These 'New Zealand' manuals are used by all the New Zealand organisations involved with signals intelligence. Copies will be held in the External Assessments Bureau, Directorate of Defence Intelligence, Foreign Affairs, the Department of the Prime Minister and Cabinet and military intelligence units such as ANZMIS in Singapore, as well as by all the GCSB directors, various unit managers and at Tangimoana and Waihopai.
9.   In 1994 Bruce Miller, the manager of C Unit, attended the course.
10. The complex is located along Russell Drive, 2 kilometres from Parliament House, at the opposite end of Kings Avenue just after it crosses Lake Burley Griffin.

Chapter 9: Station NZC-332: Electronic Eavesdropping from Tangimoana
1.   Most often searching for and monitoring particular ships for them.
2.   The UKUSA station designators are made up of country and staffing codes. The country codes are AU (Australia), CA (Canada), NZ (New Zealand), UK (United Kingdom) and US (United States). The staffing codes are N (Navy), A (Airforce), M (Army), F (joint service — mainly civilian), J (joint service — mainly military), C (Civilian) and D (Detachment).
3.   Tangimoana was singled out for all the GCSB staff reductions in the 1990s, when the director was under pressure to cut costs. The first positions went in 1992, still more in 1993 and the biggest cuts occurred in July 1995, 'because of reduced activity at the base' ('Listening post jobs go in reshuffle', *New Zealand Herald*, 22 July 1995).
4.   This comment refers to shipping. There is no interception of aircraft communications nor of transmissions from satellites passing over the region. The station is described as mostly a 'Morse code, shipping station'.
5.   Military communications instructions for PIC warnings contained in the New Zealand Defence Force manual DM44, Addressee Indicator Group (AIG): 3-6348.
6.   In a 30 October 1992 letter to the writer, the Ombudsman upheld a decision by the New Zealand Defence Force to refuse to reveal the meaning of PIC.
7.   One example is the Russian satellite tracking ship *Cosmonaut Gyorgy Dobrovolsky*, which was turned away from Wellington Harbour in October 1988 because 'Defence experts' said they believed it was carrying communications intercept equipment. The ship later visited the port of Bluff where it was opened up to investigation by a TV team. Another ship, the biological oceanography ship *Akademik Oparin*, was banned from Auckland a year later, as the Berlin Wall was coming down. The off-the-record story given to one journalist was that it had intended to make a visit near to a Defence underwater sonar research range. The ship had American scientists on board and was allowed to visit Wellington, where it had visited twice before and been opened up to the public and journalists (Owen Wilkes, *Wellington Pacific Report*, October 1988 and August 1989, Wellington).
8.   Commander-in-Chief US Pacific Fleet (CINCPAC) Instruction 3130.6F, 'Pacific Area Ocean Surveillance Report Services', 8 November 1982, on FOSIC and the Fleet Command Centre.
9.   This section includes information from Richelson and Ball, *op. cit.*, pp.198-199; and personal communication from Jeffrey Richelson.
10. The manual was called *Government Communications Headquarters Handbook No. 131 for Antenna System*

Type AX - 19.

11. R.D. Muldoon, press statement, 18 August 1982.

12. Des Ball, *Dominion,* 5 April 1984.

13. Legal right of way across the land is granted to forestry blocks further along the road but access to the Department of Conservation (DOC) administered Pukepuke Lagoon wildlife sanctuary is only by permit from DOC.

14. David Lange, 'Tangimoana dish claims rejected', *Dominion,* 12 January 1985.

Chapter 10: Under the Radome: What Happens at Waihopai

1. David Lange, press statement, 'Defence Satellite Communications Station', 2 December 1989.

2. There are three other Intelsat satellites above the Pacific: the satellite at 177 degrees is also used for telecommunications (and is intercepted from Australia), one at 180 degrees is mainly for leased television and one at 183 degrees is mainly kept in reserve to cover for faults in the others.

3. Geostationary satellites are spaced about 1 or 2 degrees apart (amounting to several hundred kilometres apart) to avoid interference between their signals, around the full 360 degrees of the globe. The other type of (non-geostationary) satellites, for example photographic satellites, are those in orbits which take them in regular passes above the surface of the earth so that they pass above different areas of interest at different times.

4. The Pacific Ocean Area Inmarsat satellite's global beam covers a third of the earth including all of the Pacific Ocean from Singapore in the west to Mexico in the east. Anyone wanting to phone a ship with an Inmarsat system in the Pacific, for example, simply dials 872 instead of a country code, then the number of that ship, and the call goes straight to the ship via the Inmarsat satellite above the Pacific. There are Inmarsat earth stations around the world that link the Inmarsat system into the commercial telecommunications network. The South Pacific earth station for Inmarsat is in Perth, West Australia.

Inmarsat also provides a worldwide mobile telephone system, as used by CNN News from Baghdad during the 1990-91 Gulf War and also used by New Zealand Defence Force units operating in other countries. An Inmarsat A system provides direct dial telephone, telex, fax, electronic mail and computer data communications. A cheaper data-only system, Inmarsat C, was introduced in 1989 and its use has grown very rapidly since. With Inmarsat C the operator on a ship or elsewhere types a message into a unit like a standard personal computer and the message is transmitted through a small cone-shaped antenna.

The growth of Inmarsat use is significant for the UKUSA alliance because of its activities monitoring Communist and other shipping around the world. Ships in the Pacific mostly did not begin using Inmarsat until the second half of the 1980s. The main limitation on its use is that it is expensive for ships to install and use. For this reason very few Russian ships and fishing trawlers had installed Inmarsat systems by 1994. Despite the cost, however, international regulations are increasingly making it obligatory. This type of target will therefore become more important.

By the early 1990s international regulations made Inmarsat obligatory for large ocean-going ships and on 1 April 1994 it became obligatory for most fishing vessels in the New Zealand 200-mile exclusive economic zone. These regulations require regular position reports (which the Inmarsat computers on the ships do automatically) and, for the fishing boats, daily catch reports to the New Zealand fisheries authorities. By 1999 international emergency and safety regulations will require all the ships in the world to have Inmarsat.

5. CIT Research Ltd, *Satellite Communications in Asia and the Pacific 1994,* London, 1994, p.65.

6. Although a 5 percent angle in the sky is said to be the minimum for operating an earth station, telecommunications technicians have found that bases in Antarctica can also use Intelsat (and Inmarsat) as long as they are not shadowed by high points such as Mount Erebus.

7. See, for example, Bamford's *The Puzzle Palace,* Frost and Gratton's *Spyword* and material later in this chapter.

8. Owen Wilkes, 'Backgrounder on the Waihopai Satellite spy base', *Peace Researcher,* No. 17, February 1988, Christchurch, p.6.

9. Intelsat Corporation, 'Intelsat 701 satellite begins commercial operations', news release 94/01, 14 January 1994.

10. Duncan Campbell, 'They've got it taped', *New Statesman,* 12 August 1988, p.12.

11. 'US data loss impact "small"', *Evening Post,* 17 August 1988, p.13.

12. The document read:

Attachment E GENERAL PRINCIPLES FOR WARRANTS

1. Each warrant should be in respect of a particular line or a particular subscriber — not for each individual message.

2. DSD will need to sample a large number of messages in order to select those authorised for interception. This contingency should be allowed for but provision should be made for expunging and/or destruction and non-dissemination of traffic not within the terms of this warrant.

(Reproduced in *The Eye,* Brian Toohey, Glebe, September 1987, p.9.)

13. Information from Jeffrey Richelson. Under this rule, the NSA is authorised to intercept these communications, but not to compile a file on the American making or receiving the call.

14. This report would be consistent with the 'don't spy on UKUSA citizens' rule as long as the information about Ken Douglas came from interception of others (e.g. his Russian contacts), rather than Douglas himself.

15. Article 22, entitled 'Secrecy of Communications', states:
1. Members agree to take all possible measures, compatible with the system of telecommunication used, with a view to ensuring the secrecy of international correspondence.
2. Nevertheless, they reserve the right to communicate such correspondence to the competent authorities in order to ensure the application of their internal laws or the execution of international conventions to which they are treaties.
16. Kevin Hackwell, Letter to Auditor-General, 17 April 1988.
17. I. R. Hutchings, Ministry of Commerce, memo to General Manager (Communications), 7 March 1989.
18. Radio Frequency Service, Licence No. A102716, 6 April 1989.
19. Defence Review Officials' Committee, *ibid.*, p.48.
20. P. Dibb, *Review of Australia's Defence Capabilities*, Commonwealth of Australia, March 1986, p.116.
21. Information from Des Ball.
22. Defence Review Officials' Committee, pp.65-66.
23. Information from Des Ball.
24. Bronwen Reid, 'Chatters of State', *Listener*, 21 May 1988, p.27; and see Lange's press conference comments from March 1987 below.
25. Reid, *ibid.*
26. Foreign Affairs and Defence Committee, Supplementary Question 13 on Vote Defence, 27 October 1989.
27. Reid, *op. cit.*, p.27.
28. *Marlborough Express*, 7 April 1989, 18 May 1989 and 9 June 1989.
29. Information from Jeffrey Richelson.
30. *Marlborough Express*, 20 October 1989.
31. Ray Parker, letter to the writer, 18 July 1991.
32. Ray Parker, letter to the writer, 13 June 1994.
33. *The Defence of Australia 1987*, Australian Government Publishing Service, Canberra, 1987, paragraph 4.4, p.35.
34. *Geraldton Guardian*, 27 April 1988, quoting Tim James, Director DSD.
35. The DSD, far from hiding behind the need for 'security', distributed a booklet on the planned station to people living in Geraldton, including details of staff numbers and layout of the station. It even displayed a scale model of the station in the shopping centre for the locals to come and look at. The station is located 30 kilometres north-east of the coastal town of Geraldton. It has about 125 staff, half on day work and the other half on around the clock shift work. The workers include specialist technical operators; radio, electronic, computer, engineering and technical staff; and security and support staff.
    Ten GCHQ personnel are doing a three-year posting at the Geraldton station. According to the DSD Director, Tim James, the British staff are to help get the ADSCS off the ground, as well as teaching their Australian counterparts (*Geraldton Guardian*, 27 April 1988). The station consists of 11 buildings and four dish antennae, covered with radomes, with room for a fifth dish (Senator Ray, Minister of Defence, answer to Senate Question No. 1313, April 1994). The four dish antennae were built by AWA Defence Industries and Baulderstone Hornibrook Engineering for $30 million. Each dish is 26 metres in diameter, weighs about 250 tonnes and is covered by a 40-metre diameter radome (*Asia-Pacific Defence Reporter*, July 1990, pp.25-26).
36. It was scheduled to be replaced by Intelsat 709 in December 1995.
37. When asked officially if any GCSB staff had been present, Director Ray Parker would 'neither confirm nor deny the existence or non-existence of the information'. Letter to the writer, 13 June 1994.
38. David Lange, post-Cabinet press conference, 2 March 1987.
39. Quoted in Reid, *op. cit.*, p.28.
40. Reid, *ibid.*
41. It is a 3-metre dish antenna, Type SP.601.20T, manufactured by Mark Products in the United States (Ray Parker, letter to writer, 13 June 1995).
42. Ray Parker, letter to the writer, 25 July 1995.
43. Frank Nelson, *Marlborough Express*, 27 February 1988, pp.1,3.

Chapter 11: The Facts in the Filofax: Military Signals Intelligence Missions
1. Ray Parker, letter to the writer, 27 April 1994. By chance I had written to the GCSB only a month before the filofax hit the headlines asking: 'What are the formal channels through which the GCSB requests and gains access to support from the New Zealand Defence Force (e.g. the name of the relevant committee, or director to director contacts, or via the DESC committee etc)?' Shortly after Parker's denial of NZDF support I wrote again asking detailed questions about NZDF support for the GCSB based on revelations in the filofax. This time Parker declined to answer the questions at all, claiming that providing information would be likely to prejudice the security or defence of New Zealand (13 June 1994 letter).
2. John Seward, quoted in the *Dominion*, 'Defence man did not report missing diary to his superiors', 13 April 1994.
3. Memo for Bill Hayden, Minister of Foreign Affairs, 5 December 1983, Secret Spoke; reprinted in *The Eye*, Sydney, September 1988.

4. Warren Cooper, Minister of Defence, Question for Written Answer, 2 October 1991.
5. Report of the Defence Review Officials' Committee, 18 November 1986, p.65, leaked.
6. Commander Anson was the Director of Naval Warfare.
7. *Monowai* ship log, 1987, New Zealand Defence Force file, W3595, National Archives, Wellington. *Monowai's* usual complement is 125 crew.
8. *Wellington* in October-November 1988 and October-November 1989; *Southland* in May-June 1990; *Canterbury* in July-August 1991 and July-August 1992; *Wellington* in March-April 1994. In addition to the annual trips, during 1989 two frigates visited Papua New Guinea during a period of intense internal troubles. The 1990 *Southland* and 1991 *Canterbury* trips included the first New Zealand naval visits to Papeete, Tahiti in French Polynesia since 1979. Although the GCSB only began training and tasking of EW operators in 1986, signals intelligence has apparently been collected using New Zealand Navy ships since the 1950s or 1960s and passed on into the UKUSA network through the Navy Office in Wellington. These operations may explain why Navy officer Tony Lewis (later Commodore of the New Zealand Navy base in Auckland) was sent on a one-year Japanese language course in Australia in the early 1970s (*Reveille*, 'Commodore takes new post', April 1991).
9. These aerials are a vertical dipole manufactured by Tait, a small horizontal log periodic pointing north-west at about 340 degrees (non-commercial design), a Supreme Disconemaster 360-degree antenna and a two and a half metre AVW-2/D whip antenna. In early 1990 the GCSB Director, Ray Parker, wrote to the Ministry of Commerce to extend the station's radio licence to cover these aerials: 'we have recently identified an operational requirement to extend our coverage at Tangimoana beyond the presently-authorised HF frequency range into the Very High Frequency band. The frequency range now required is 9kHz to 300MHz' and is still 'reception only' (Radio Frequency Service, Radio Apparatus Licence A103513, 5 February 1990 to 30 June 1990. Released by the Ministry of Commerce under the Official Information Act).
10. 'Navy scandal: new claims of harassment', *Melbourne Age*, 14 September 1993.
11. M.J. McNamara, NZDF, letter to the writer, 4 October 1995.
12. Ministry of Defence and New Zealand Defence Force, Annual Report for the year ended 30 June 1990, p.26.
13. Warren Cooper, Minister of Defence, Question for Written Answer, 2 October 1991.
14. The 'Electronic Warfare Systems (Army)' item first appeared in expenditure forecasts, under 'projects not yet approved', for the 1986/87 year.
15. 'Work out your pay rate', *Army News*, 17 April 1991, Issue 11, New Zealand Defence Force, Wellington, p.6.
16. These were Exercise Ravens Review, Exercise New Raven and Exercise ANZAC Exchange. Australian Senate Hansard, 11 April 1994, Answer to Questions No. 1312 by Senator Ray.
17. Australian Senate Hansard, 7 October 1992, Answers to Questions, Question No. 2154, Page 1355.
18. Warren Cooper, Minister of Defence, Question for Written Answer, 6 August 1991.
19. Scott Turner is based on the first floor of Defence House in Stout Street, Wellington, location of the NZDF Directorate of Joint Command, Control, Communications and Information Systems (JCIS) and the Defence Communications Unit.
20. New Zealand Defence Force letters to the writer, 25 May 1994 and 12 May 1995. As an associate member of ABCA, the New Zealand representatives are formally described as observers. Information about the subjects of the meetings is secret.
21. Memorandum of Understanding between the Government of Australia and the Government of New Zealand concerning Defence Communications-Electronic Cooperation, signed 3 April 1985 by the Secretaries of Defence of the two countries, 5pp.

Chapter 12: What Are the Secrets? The Intelligence Product

1. Australia is said to restrict quite a lot of reports on South Pacific matters to ANZEO (Australian and New Zealand Eyes Only). But only in rare cases, for example where a report includes criticism of the country concerned (particularly the United States), might a decision be taken not to pass on intelligence.
2. *Naval Intelligence Bulletin*, Office of Naval Intelligence, ONI 2400-002-90, Fall/Winter 1990, p.27, released under the Freedom of Information Act, noted that the NSA 'controls all SIGINT product dissemination, including that of Field Reporting Sites and Second Party Producers (UK, Canada, Australia, New Zealand)'.
3. Toohey and Wilkinson, *op. cit.*, p.139.
4. Walter R. Agee, Acting Director of Intelligence, 'Memorandum for the Coordinator of Joint Operations. Subject: Proposed U.S.-Canadian Agreement', Enclosure 1 'Amendments to Paragraphs 5, 6(a) and 17 to Proposed Canadian Letter as Amended', 7 June 1948. Supplied by Jeffrey Richelson. It notes that 'translation and gists will be exchanged' and that 'the same definition should be used as in the BRUSA' (the British-US communications intelligence agreement, predecessor of UKUSA) so that the word 'gist' should be used instead of 'any published summaries of translations' since 'summaries of translations are not produced'.
5. All signals intelligence reports, messages, planning documents and administrative papers must be stamped with the special UKUSA codewords and caveats. Caveats include categories like CONFIDENTIAL, SECRET, TOP SECRET and NEW ZEALAND EYES ONLY. Codewords include the special signals intelligence words UMBRA, SPOKE AND MORAY. The NZSIS vets all people before being granted a clearance for any of these levels of secrecy; involving, for SECRET clearances and above, interviews with four referees and a declaration whether he or she has 'ever been associated in any way with a communist or fascist movement'.

6. Two of these documents, PACCAT and WECAT, appear to focus on the Pacific and Western Europe. The third is titled HOCCAT.

7. David Lange, Sir Keith Hancock Memorial Lecture, Southern Cross Hotel, Melbourne, 13 May 1990. The South Pacific was, after all, New Zealand's area of responsibility within the UKUSA alliance.

8. Each line of the readout gives the time, the frequency of the radar signal detected, its estimated location and what type of radar they believe it to be. The location is given with an accuracy of within a few kilometers, 'accurate enough to be useful'.

9. Lange, *Nuclear Free - The New Zealand Way*, Penguin, Auckland, 1990, p.72.

10. Mary-Louise O'Callaghan, 'PNG to investigate Australian spy claim', *Melbourne Age*, 26 November 1991, p.1.

Chapter 13: Who Watches the Watchers? Overseeing the Intelligence Agencies

1. United States House of Representatives, Hearings before a subcommittee of the Committee on Appropriations, 'Military Appropriations for 1985', Part 6, 1985, p.136, listed the following waivers:

Australia	1981	HGX-83 Discom Equipment	US$308,312 waiver
New Zealand	1982	HGX-83 (COMSEC)	US $29,942 waiver
Australia	1983	HGX-83 (COMSEC)	US $36,272 waiver

2. Ministry of Defence, letter to the writer, 2 November 1987.

3. Over the preceding three years the number of GCSB communications officers had been built up from about five to 16, to staff the two new communications centres. Communications before 1982 were on a smaller scale and handled by New Zealand Combined Signals Organisation staff located within the Defence headquarters communications centre in Wellington.

4. David Lange, letter to Peter Wills, 7 May 1985.

5. David Lange, address to the annual conference of the New Zealand Labour Party, 3 September 1988, p.3.

6. Hensley's diplomatic career appears to have included a period in 1969-73 as New Zealand's liaison officer to the CIA (the current head of the Prime Minister's department, Simon Murdoch, appears also to have had this position in the 1980s). After he finished as intelligence co-ordinator in 1989, Hensley lived in the United States on a Harvard scholarship. He returned to New Zealand to become Secretary of Defence under a National government. McLean later became New Zealand ambassador to Washington under the National government. After his term there he decided to remain in the United States. (The New Zealand CIA liaison officer in Washington and the equivalent intelligence liaison officer in London are identifiable in the diplomatic lists as they are counsellors and are listed without specific duties such as 'commercial'.)

7. These positions, in 1996, include Secretary of Defence, Director of the External Assessments Bureau (EAB), Chief Executive of the Department of Prime Minister and Cabinet and the Director of the Domestic and External Security Secretariat.

8. The Officials' DESC oversees security policy in New Zealand and also, in theory, supervises the budgets and tasking of the GCSB and EAB. The committee was created in April 1987 (replacing the New Zealand Intelligence Council) and consists of the head of the Prime Minister's Department (chair), the Secretary of Foreign Affairs and Trade, the Chief of Defence Force, the Secretary of Defence and the Director of the SIS. Heads of other departments (e.g. Treasury and Police) attend as required. It meets once or twice a month. Sub-committees include the Intelligence Requirements and Assessments Committee (meeting weekly) and the Working Committee on Terrorism (meeting about six times a year). It is supported by a small permanent staff located within the Department of the Prime Minister and Cabinet, called the Domestic and External Security Secretariat.

9. Ray Parker refused to provide a copy of the Corporate Plan to Parliament's Finance and Expenditure Committee in July 1991, saying it was a 'classified document'.

10. Simon Murdoch, Chief Executive of the Department of the Prime Minister and Cabinet, letter to the writer, 14 June 1994. Recently the Leader of the Opposition began to be shown some GCSB budget information too.

11. Including some or all of the GCSB's '5 Year Strategic Overview and Plan' and the Divisional and Station Goals and Objectives.

12. 'NZ spies come under new watchdog', *Dominion*, 20 December 1995, p.1.

13. *Dominion*, 17 August 1988, reporting on consideration of the Domestic and External Security Secretariat's vote.

14. 1988 Report of the Foreign Affairs and Defence Committee: VOTE DEFENCE 1988/89, 1988, Wellington, p.12.

15. Peter Hilt, chair of the Government Administration Committee, 1993/94 Financial Review of the Government Communications Security Bureau, 28 February 1995.

16. Ray Parker, letter to John Blincoe, MP, 8 March 1994. In an 8 March 1995 letter to the writer, Parker said he did not refer this request to the Prime Minister, but subsequently sent a letter to the Prime Minister notifying him of his actions.

17. Intelligence and Security Committee Act, 1996, section 7.

18. ISC Act, 1996, section 6(2)(b).

19. ISC Act, 1996, 1995, section 17.

20. ISC Act, 1996, 1995, section 3.

21. United States Senate Select Committee to Study Government Operations with respect to Intelligence Activi-

ties, *Final Report: Intelligence Activities and the Rights of Americans*, US Government Printing Office, Washington DC, 1976, Book II, p.ix.

22. Sir Geoffrey Palmer speaking on *Good Morning New Zealand*, National Radio, 20 December 1995.

23. The exception is exchange of finished intelligence, like that from the External Assessments Bureau. Exchange does occur between the five allies, but apparently not under a formal agreement.

24. Standardisation and interoperability agreements, and the subjects they cover, include:

ABCA	Interoperability of allied armies
ABCANZ	Exchange of information on the following:
ABCANZ-2	Anti-submarine and anti-mine warfare
ABCANZ-3	Navy torpedoes
ANCANZ-5	Naval communications
ABCANZ-6	Naval research
ASCC	Interoperability of allied Air Forces
AUSCANNZUKUS	Interoperability of allied Navy communications and electronic systems
CCEB	Interoperability of allied communications and military electronic systems
COMBEXAG	Combined exercise agreement
TTCP	Military research co-operation.

(NZDF letters to the writer, 18 June 1991, 4 October 1995 and 6 November 1995.)

25. John Flux, New Zealand Defence Force, letter to the writer, 18 June 1991. This wording is from the ABCA agreement.

26. New Zealand Defence Force, *Corporate Plan 1992-93*, 1992, p.53.

27. There is nothing like a 30-year rule for releasing files in New Zealand.

28. Jim Bolger, Question for Written Answer No. 3907, 18 July 1995.

29. Tony Browne, note to the Prime Minister, undated.

30. Sir John Robertson, Report of the Chief Ombudsman on leaving office, 1994, Wellington, p.17.

Chapter 14: Leaving the Intelligence Alliance

1. The two SAS soldiers were supposed to collect intelligence by mixing with the local military personnel, but the mission did more harm than good and, as a result, the *Monowai* was ordered out of Suva. The government, which had not known about the SAS mission, was furious. A counter-terrorist SAS team was also put on alert after the attempted hijack of an Air New Zealand jet at Nadi airport, but was not needed. This was a sad attempt by a Fijian Indian man to attract international support for the deposed government. He was dealt with not by any security or intelligence organisations, but by an airline steward giving him a swift blow on the head with a whisky bottle.

2. Alan Wrigley, speaking to a national security conference in Canberra, quoted in the *Press*, 27 November 1993.

3. Geoffrey Palmer, Acting Prime Minister, transcript of post-caucus press conference, 28 February 1985, p.8.

4. The memo was among official documents obtained by opponents of the NSA's Menwith Hill station.

5. For example, an Australian television exposé in May 1995 described how Australian intelligence staff installed a network of sophisticated fibre-optic bugs, supplied by the United States, throughout the Chinese embassy building in Canberra. The bugs were linked via the British High Commission next door directly to the NSA in Washington. The leak came from disgruntled Australian spies who said that the United States not only controlled the operation but also strictly limited the intelligence supplied to Australia from it (Wallace Brown, 'Embassy spy row deepens', *Queensland Courier-Mail*, 27 May 1995, pp. 1-2).

Appendix A: Who's Who in New Zealand Foreign Intelligence Organisations

1. Sources include: *The Navy List*, Navy Department, Wellington, 1956-65; *List of persons on the permanent staff of the public service*, Supplement to the Public Service Official Circular, State Services Commission, Wellington 1955-88; Michael Green, EAB Director, letter to writer, 30 January 1992; and New Zealand Defence Force, letter to writer, 5 February 1992.

Appendix B: A Guided Tour of Secret Intelligence Facilities
Waihopai

1. To find the station, turn off the Blenheim-Nelson highway at Renwick onto the West Coast Road. The Waihopai Valley Road turns left shortly afterwards.

2. The electric fence is a standard Gallagher cattle fence. Overall security at the station was contracted to Harding Signals (as at Tangimoana).

3. The operations building is 83 metres long and 19 metres wide. The services building is 42 metres long and 7.5 metres wide.

4. The cabinets are 2 x 0.6 x 0.6 metres.

5. Ray Parker, letter to the writer, 18 July 1991.

6. Leaving aside satellite television transmissions and American and Australian satellites, which would not be targets, Intelsat (and Inmarsat at 177 degrees) happen to be the only possible targets in the area of sky north of Waihopai between 170 degrees east and 170 degrees west.

Tangimoana

7.   You are not actually trespassing until personally asked to leave by the owner. Unless that happens, the signs should not deter sightseers, who are usually left to themselves.

8.   The operations building is 33.3 metres long and 28.2 metres wide, the administration building is 16.3 metres by 16.3 metres and the services building is 13.9 metres by 15.9 metres. According to the GCSB, the cost of the station buildings and associated works was $1.39 million. A further $1.2 million was spent on the equipment, giving a total figure of $2.59 million (Colin Hanson, letter to Dr John Campbell-Macdonald, 18 September 1984).

9.   These fences replaced a single, low-security fence in 1995.

10. The radio officers are also encouraged to do language training to assist their interception work. For example, in 1984 one of the workers was known to be learning Russian. Also, in 1988 an internal staff notice invited staff at Tangimoana and the headquarters to take language training to 'expand the Bureau's language capability'.

11. Jarnell was transferred to work in the headquarters.

12. *Evening Post*, 30 July 1988, GCSB advertisement for Tangimoana technicians.

13. The antennae were built by California-based Technology for Communications International (TCI), model 521-3-02.

14. The rhombic antennae were used for signals intelligence work at the old NR1 station from the early 1960s until they were moved, with the staff, to Tangimoana in late 1982. There they were stored in parts at Tangimoana until being erected.

15. The circular array is made up of three concentric circles of vertical poles, with an inner circle of 24 6-metre poles and two outer rings of 24 12-metre poles. The double outer ring of poles indicates that the CDAA is a Mark II version compared with the more usual single outer ring.

Appendix C: Where the Intelligence Ends Up
External Assessments Bureau

1.   External Assessments Bureau, Mission Statement, released under the Official Information Act, 16 October 1990.

2.   External Intelligence Bureau, Intelligence Report 108/84, 'Factors affecting the deployment of nuclear weapons in the South Pacific', Prime Minister's Department, 24 December 1984. The other report was 'Nuclear Capabilities of Ships, Submarines and Aircraft', 16 November 1984.

3.   Des Rowe, speaking to Parliament's Foreign Affairs and Defence Committee on the EIB Budget estimates, 20 August 1988.

4.   According to a classified internal funding document.

5.   McKinnon had wanted the contact to be through military channels, but the External Affairs Department took over this job.

6.   Ministry of Foreign Affairs, 'Answers to set questions' for the Foreign Affairs and Defence Committee on Vote Foreign Affairs 1988-89 Estimates, Part III — Programme II External Assessments Bureau, Question 2, 1988.

7.   External Assessments Bureau, *New Zealand Intelligence Briefing Memorandum: New Caledonia*, Ministry of Foreign Affairs, Wellington, December 1988, inside page.

8.   M. Norrish, Secretary of Foreign Affairs, speaking to Parliament's Foreign Affairs and Defence Committee on the EIB Budget estimates, 20 August 1988.

9.   'The Timor papers' in Toohey and Wilkinson, *op. cit.*, pp.191-195, contain secret minutes of friendly meetings between Australia's Office of National Assessments and Bakin in 1976 and 1978, shortly after the invasion of East Timor.

Directorate of Defence Intelligence

10. Fourteen NZIBM have been produced about island groups in the New Zealand Intelligence Area: Fiji, Vanuatu, Kiribati, Tonga, Cook Islands, Solomon Islands, Western Samoa, Niue, Tokelau, Tuvalu, French Polynesia, American Samoa, Pitcairn Group and New Caledonia. Until sometime in the 1980s these publications were produced together with the Australian sister organisation, the JIO, and were called ANZIBMs. For example, NZIBM No.16 on New Caledonia, produced in December 1988, replaced the JIO's ANZIBM No.16, produced in June 1982.

11. Cabinet External Relations and Security Committee paper, ER (85) 4, '1985 Preliminary Defence Review', 24 March 1985, designated Confidential, New Zealand Eyes Only, p.7.

12. Report of the Defence Review Officials Committee, 1986, leaked sections, pp.27-28.

13. New Zealand Defence Force manual 44, Addressee Indicator Group 6394.

14. Minister of Defence, question for written answer no. 97, New Zealand House of Representatives, 6 August 1991.

Courier Links with the Other UKUSA Agencies

15. US Joint Chiefs of Staff, *Dictionary of Military and Associated Terms, 1984*, Washington.

16. Labels on the bags say 'US Government, AFC/SS. If found, call 202 - 6922288 (collect)'. Personal observation, August 1992.

17. The Sunday flight goes to Alice Springs and the Friday flight to the United States bases at Nurrungar and North

West Cape, both via the Richmond RAAF base near Sydney. Information from *Peace Researcher*, No. 30, December 1991, Christchurch, pp. 19-20.

18. Information from US Air Force annual staff assessment forms for MAC personnel, 1989-92, which include job descriptions. Information from Jeffrey Richelson.

19. Australian safe hand couriers cover some of Asia, Canada covers Latin America and so on.

Appendix D: New Zealand's Second World War Signals Intellgence History

1. For example, the volume of the *Official History of New Zealand in the Second World War* about the Royal New Zealand Navy, which was responsible for Navy signals intelligence, contains no reference at all to this work.

2. I.C. McGibbon, *Blue Water Rationale*, Government Printer, Wellington, 1981, p.26, footnote 44.

3. The district intelligence office was run by two Royal Navy officers. In 1927 the New Zealand government agreed to pay for the running of the office provided that Britain still provided the two officers.

4. D.O.W. Hall, *Coastwatchers*, War History Branch, Department of Internal Affairs, Wellington, 1951.

5. All the information on Second World War signals intelligence operations, unless otherwise stated, is based on interviews.

6. The stations were used by the Post and Telegraph Department to take direction bearings on radio signals from the first commercial Auckland-to-Sydney passenger aircraft as they crossed the Tasman Sea, allowing estimates of the aircrafts' positions to be radioed to the pilots to assist their navigation.

7. D. McLauchlan, *Room 39*, Weidenfeld & Nicolson, London, 1968, p.57.

8. Details of the station are contained in the WRNZNS history: Grant Howard, *Happy in the Service*, produced by Word Publishers for the Ex-Wren Association, Auckland, 1985.

9. Later, when McKenzie served in Indonesia, he visited a recently captured Japanese radio station and discovered by looking at the radio crystal frequencies that it was one of the stations which the Nairnville Park unit had been intercepting.

10. At one stage the two separate stations were both being used while the volume of work required it. The unit had about 40 intercept operators, including some from the Women's Army Auxiliary Corps (WAAC). The first WAACs began work in the Special Section in October 1943.

11. Denys Bevan, *United States Forces in New Zealand 1942-1945*, Kakanui, 1992, p.148.

12. The description of the different sections of COIC is based on unattributable interviews combined with information from various letters, reports and minutes concerning the Second World War naval intelligence organisation, including a 19/5/42 list of all people authorised to enter the COIC and Central War Room: Navy Department Series 2 08/1/18, 'Intelligence centres — combined operations intelligence centre', Part 1, March 1938-October 1944, National Archives, Wellington.

13. S.D. Waters, *Official History of New Zealand in the Second World War 1939-45: The Royal New Zealand Navy*, Department of Internal Affairs, Wellington, 1956, p.442.

14. Howard, *op. cit.*, p.49.

15. Bamford, *op. cit.*, p.314.

16. Admiralty letter, 14 March 1944; Navy Department Series 1 17/8/1 'Combined Security Classification Agreement 1944-52', National Archives, Wellington. Instructions contained in this document, for example defining the terms 'Top Secret' and 'Secret', are identical to those for handling classified materials in the New Zealand Cabinet Directive on Security Classifications issued 38 years later.

17. SRH-196 'Regulations for Maintaining the Security of Special Intelligence in Pacific and Asia Theatres of Operations', 1944; quoted in Alan Stripp, *Codebreaker in the Far East*, Frank Cass & Co., London, 1989, p.119.